COLORS FOR MODERN FASHION

DRAWING FASHION WITH COLORED MARKERS

NANCY RIEGELMAN

NINE HEADS MEDIA

Colors for Modern Fashion—Drawing fashion with colored markers

by Nancy Riegelman

Published by 9 Heads Media
Mailing address: 9 Heads Media, PO Box 27457, Los Angeles CA 90027–0457, USA
Website: www.9headsmedia.com
Copyright © 2006 9 Heads Media

Printed in China

Publisher's Cataloging-in-Publication Data

Riegelman, Nancy

Colors for Modern Fashion—Drawing fashion with colored markers/Nancy Riegelman
1st edition

560pp 33 x 23 cm
LCCN: 2005923611
ISBN: 0-9702463-2-3

1. Fashion Drawing 2. Drawing—technique I Title

Lib. Cong. Class. No. TT509 DDC 741.672

The paintings by James Whistler and Sir Joshua Reynolds are reproduced courtesy of the Tate Gallery,
London and Art Resource, New York; the painting by Jean-Honoré Fragonard is reproduced courtesy of
the Hermitage Museum, St. Petersburg, Russia and Art Resource New York; the painting by Francisco de
Goya is reproduced courtesy of the Hispanic Society of America in New York. Vik Muniz's work appears
courtesy of Brent Sikkema Gallery in New York, Xippas Gallery in Paris and Fortes Vilaça, São Paulo. The
drawings by Ruben Alterio and Demetrios Psillos appear courtesy of the artists. Inquiries regarding
these artists should be directed to the publisher.

colors for modern fashion

contents

colors for modern fashion

nancy riegelman

colors for modern fashion

drawing modern fashion with colored markers/learning to draw

COLORS FOR MODERN FASHION

Colors for Modern Fashion is written for all those with an interest in modern fashion, fashion design and drawing who want to learn how to make realistic drawings of modern fashion garments in color, either because of a wish to design fashion or simply a desire to draw beautiful fashion garments. It teaches how to do this using colored markers—a medium with many advantages of speed, ease-of-use and cost over the more traditional artistic media.

Drawing is a language that enables visual ideas to be expressed and communicated to others. In fashion drawing ideas are expressed about garments that do not yet exist outside the mind of the designer, either to inform others or as a way of developing one's own thinking about a garment design.

Colors for Modern Fashion shows how ideas for fashion designs that exist in the imagination can be expressed in clear, tasteful and elegant drawings that will be attractive both to those who make them and those who view them. It does this by showing and explaining in detail how to draw a wide variety of modern fashion garments. The large number of original fashion drawings it contains are also intended to serve as inspiration, guidance and reference for all those interested in fashion design and drawing.

Drawing is a wonderful activity that can bring great pleasure and satisfaction, as well as being a valuable tool of self-expression and communication. Anyone can learn to draw, quite often up to and beyond the standards of the drawings included here, and *Colors for Modern Fashion* provides all the information on materials and techniques as well as the detailed explanation of how drawings are made, coaching, practice and exercises to lead a student through from a beginner's to an advanced level of fashion drawing.

DRAWING MODERN FASHION WITH COLORED MARKERS

Colors for Modern Fashion is a full course in fashion drawing in color, designed to be accessible to those who are relative beginners to fashion drawing through to those already at an advanced level who might wish to improve certain skills or learn specific techniques for drawing with colored markers.

Colors for Modern Fashion teaches how to make attractive and persuasive fashion drawings in color. It teaches how to draw to a level where virtually every type of fabric and garment can be drawn accurately and realistically so that the drawing by itself conveys all the information about garments necessary to understand their design and construction. Not only does the book teach how to make realistic, complex drawings, it shows how to make much quicker, less elaborate, but still professional sketches, so important where more than one figure is being drawn. It teaches these types of drawing using the medium of colored markers, supplement-

ed only by colored and graphite pencils and gel pen. Compared with traditional artistic media—watercolors, oils, gouache and so on—that have been mainly what have been used to produce detailed fashion drawings in color to date, markers have some enormous advantages of speed, ease-of-use, convenience and cost, and relatively few disadvantages, as is discussed in depth in Chapter One Materials and Technique.

Colored markers have been used in fashion drawing for a number of years, but, despite their advantages, have not fully supplanted the traditional artistic media for making detailed fashion drawings in color. There are a number of reasons for this, but probably the main reason is that the techniques for using markers to their full potential are not well known, in large part because there are practically no texts available that explain and illustrate in detail how they are used.

This book addresses this need for a full set of detailed explanations of the techniques for using markers effectively, along with illustrations of how they are applied in drawing a large variety of garments made of all kinds of fabrics. It does so in the context of a full, advanced course in modern fashion drawing that shows how the levels of realism and accuracy that were the hallmark of the great masters can be reproduced, while also providing a treatment of the subject of composition and design of the fashion drawing itself.

The overall intention of *Colors for Modern Fashion* is that if the techniques and methods it teaches are mastered, the student will be able to draw at a level such that drawing can be used as a sophisticated visual language for expressing complex ideas about fashion precisely, and more quickly and easily than was possible using traditional media.

LEARNING TO DRAW

Can drawing be learnt and if so, what does it take? Yes, anyone can learn to draw. Not only can anyone learn to draw, but, almost anyone can learn to draw well.

Being able to draw is not a matter of having an "eye" or "gift" for drawing. Some discover an aptitude for drawing and are soon able to draw well and others make take longer, but with application and practice almost everyone can achieve their goals.

Learning to draw can often take much less time than is commonly expected, and many who have had no prior experience learning to make attractive and realistic drawings within only a few weeks of begining to study.

Drawing is a visual language that allows visual ideas to be developed and communicated to others. The actual process of learning to draw also has many similarities to learning a language: first the basic skills and techniques are learned and then every opportunity is taken to practice so that these basic skills are developed and refined. A large portion of

colors for modern fashion

demetrios psillos

Demetrios Psillos
Ball-Gown

colors for modern fashion

learning to draw/colored markers

the skills required for drawing in fact are based on simple arithmetic–calculating proportions and measurements and are acquired with relative ease.

An important part of the process of learning to draw is also the process of learning to see objects in such a way that they can be easily represented on paper: learning to perceive and understand the interaction of objects and light and translating that three-dimensional appearance onto a two-dimensional surface. In learning to draw fashion, particularly if it is one's first introduction to drawing, two learning processes in fact take place at the same time: one, learning to perceive objects–the figure, garments and accessories– in such a way that they can be effectively represented on paper, and two, learning about fashion itself—the appearance and construction of garments and fabrics—and then incorporating that knowledge into one's own drawings and designs. Although this book does not *focus* on the teaching of the technical elements of fashion design as such, it does contain extensive technical information about fashion: the content of the drawings in this book—and indeed all fashion drawing—is technical fashion information, and that information has to be clear and accurate. Learning to draw fashion is in itself an excellent way to learn about fashion and to reinforce the knowledge of fashion learned elsewhere.

As with learning a foreign language, practice is the key to success: practice helps develop speed and accuracy and the hand/eye/ mind coordination that allows for objects to be clearly perceived, quickly analysed and then correctly drawn. Once the initial effort has been made to master the basic techniques of fashion drawing progress becomes more rapid: the process becomes more intuitive and one's drawing becomes quicker and more fluid.

COLORED MARKERS

To me, as a member of the faculty of a major US design school, the increased use of markers over the last twenty years and more in the major fields of design— graphics, product, automobile and architecture—has been conspicuous. To me also as a member of the faculty of a major US fashion school, the adoption of the use of colored markers in the fashion industry and fashion education has been conspicuously non-existent—or almost non-existent—over most of that same period. In most fashion schools it is only over the last three to four years that markers have supplanted the traditional artistic media of watercolors, colored pencils, gouache and oils as the preferred medium for fashion drawing in color.

Part of the reason for the late adoption of markers in the fashion industry and education—other than in some specialized areas such as sports shoe design—has to do with the nature of the subject matter—fabric and fashion garments—and markers' perceived significant shortcomings as an artistic medium for representing them: fashion embraces a huge variety of inputs—fabrics and other materials—and end products–garments and accessories for

garments—presenting a huge variety of different appearances. Many fabrics and garments—especially in women's fashion—are extremely delicate, subtle, nuanced, often with great intrinsic beauty, and drape in flowing, sinuous curves and folds. In this sense they are very different from the end results of other types of design, which tend to be big, hard objects often with straight, sharp edges such as buildings, cars or tables. Fashion garments in fact often more closely resemble fine art than other man-made products. If fashion garments are to be faithfully—or even close to faithfully—represented in a drawing, the medium for doing so has to be such that it can capture that delicacy, subtlety and intrinsic beauty. For a long time it was considered that markers, with the flat, saturated two-dimensional effect that came when they were applied "straight from the tube" were not well-suited to create the types of effects required for successful fashion drawing, and that fashion drawing in color should be made in the domain of watercolors and oils.

What has changed over the recent few years to cause markers to rise to prominence as an artistic medium in fashion drawing? In short, both the markers themselves have changed and also the general approach to using them has also shifted markedly: Markers are now available in, literally, hundreds of different colors, including many variations of single hues, whites, greys, delicate pastels, metalics and fluorescents. This improved range of colors means that a wide range of effects *can* now be easily achieved using markers "straight from the tube", including the subtle tonal gradations of color seen in draped fabric. The approach to using markers in fashion drawing is now also one of greater willingness to experiment and explore the full potential of the medium, not simply to accept the flat results of application of colors straight from the tube but to mix and blend markers with each other and with colorless blender to open up a wealth of new effects.

A key tool in enabling this extension in the variety of effects that can be achieved with markers is the colorless blender. Colorless blender is the raw solvent that holds the marker pigment in suspension—the equivalent, for markers, of water for watercolors or oils and thinners for oil paints. Unlike solvents for watercolors or oils or other media, however, colorless blender is conveniently available in the same tube as markers come in, and is as easy and clean to use as the markers themselves.

Although colorless blender has been available for a number of years, its range of potential uses has not been widely understood and it is still not widely used (it is telling, for example, that the latest edition of a popular practical handbook for artists contains 31 pages on oil paints and one short paragraph on markers with no mention of colorless blender at all). A large portion of the use of markers to create the effects needed for in the representation of fabric and garments involve the use of colored blender and it is hoped that the examples of the results that can be obtained with it in this book open up its potential to a wider audience.

colors for modern fashion

christian lacroix

Christian Lacroix
Spring Collection 1998

colors for modern fashion

techniques of the masters/fashion drawing and design

COLORS FOR MODERN FASHION: COPYING AND REPRODUCING THE TECHNIQUES FOR DRAWING FASHION USED BY THE MASTERS

Coming to fashion drawing, as I did, with an education and background in fine art has the advantage of enabling one to approach problems in fashion drawing from the perspective of a fine artist, and to introduce to the subject the wisdom, lessons and solutions of a much longer-established but closely-related discipline. Fine artists spend long periods studying and analysing the work of the great masters of art. They also have an innate fascination with materials and a disposition to constant experimentation—mixing colors, combining different media, adapting tools to make marks on the surfaces they work with or materials they shape, and so on.

Years before starting to draw fashion in color with markers, when learning for the first time to draw fashion using watercolors and oils, I had spent long periods studying the work of the great masters of fashion drawing—Singer Sargeant, Whistler, Joshua Reynolds, Fragonard, Goya and others—trying to determine how these artists were able to draw and paint garments to appear almost life-like. My conclusions were that the sometimes-acute realism of their paintings and drawings, their three-dimensional accuracy which created the impression that one was almost in the presence of the subjects and could reach out and touch their garments resulted from a number of key factors. These were: one, a painstakingly accurate observation and representation of the effect of reflected light on the surface of fabric as it bends towards and away from the light source, involving subtle shifts and gradations of colors between dark and light, use of extremes of value—almost luminescent white highlights, and profoundly deep black shadows; two, an understanding of the richness and intricacy of color and the use of layering and underpainting to achieve saturation and complex coloring; three, great attention to detail and four, a deep understanding of the structure and configuration of the human figure and face in its various poses.

Upon starting to work with colored markers I revisited some of the works of the great masters to refresh myself on the effects that were key to good fashion drawing. I began experimenting with markers to work out the techniques that could achieve those same effects, in some cases—a standard exercise for all art students—copying as closely as possible the original oils and watercolors but using markers. Many of the effects, I found, involved the realistic representation of subtle gradations of color, and the techniques for creating them called for, as mentioned, the use of colorless blender.

The techniques I worked out for creating those and all the other effects used throughout the book are explained in the chapter on materials and technique, and whenever called for in the descriptions of how to draw different garments or fabrics (I hesitate to claim to have *invented* these techniques as I suspect that others may have worked out some of them for themselves, but, having searched extensively, I have not been able to find them anywhere in print). The impor-

tance of mastering these techniques cannot be stressed enough. Markers are a surprisingly easy-to-use medium and, if used correctly, allow for a wide range of effects to be achieved that are invaluable for drawing fashion with far less effort than required with traditional media.

FASHION DRAWING AND FASHION DESIGN

Fashion drawing and fashion design are closely related: to make drawings is to make designs, and in order to design something, we draw it. In French the same word—*dessiner*—is used for both drawing and design.

As already stated, drawing is a language that permits visual ideas about garments existing in the imagination to be expressed and communicated. As with a spoken and written language, the greater the degree of fluency and command of the elements of the language, the better the level of communication and the better the quality of the end result—the drawing of a new garment.

The end result in fashion drawing is a design for a new fashion garment or accessory. Inside the fashion industry the purpose of the fashion drawing (the concept drawing, as opposed to the technical flats and patterns used in the fabrication stages) is to present a design for consideration for possible fabrication. A drawing can be considered successful, from the point of view of the *designer*, if it presents the design concept as clearly and positively as is possible, showing the garment in its best light. Such a drawing is likely to stand the best chance of succeeding in convincing the audience of the merits of the design and receiving the go-ahead for production.

From the point of view of the *audience*—those who view the drawing and make decisions whether or not to fabricate a garment—a successful drawing will be one where the garment is presented not only in its most positive and attractive light but also where it is presented realistically, so that an accurate impression is gained of the look, feel and overall effect of the final garment. To be able to obtain an accurate impression of the garment *before* fabrication of a prototype or preliminary samples is very appealing as it will potentially save considerable time and resources.

As already mentioned, the aim of *Colors for Modern Fashion* is to teach the techniques for drawing in color with the degree of precision required for an accurate and realistic impression of the final garment to be communicated. The fact that markers are so much quicker and easier to use also means that the output of drawings, as well as being high quality, can be far greater in number than can be achieved with other media. This in turn means that more design iterations can be made, each with more clarity and precision, and the overall design process becomes better informed and takes place at a lesser remove from what will be visual reality of the final design of the garment. If they were to come about, such developments would be to the advantage of everyone involved in the fashion design and production process, and particularly to that of the designer.

colors for modern fashion

goya

Francisco Jose de Goya y Lucientes
Duchess of Alba
Hispanic Society of America

colors for modern fashion

fashion drawing with time constraints/realism and abstraction in fashion drawing

FASHION DRAWING WITH TIME CON-STRAINTS—THE ADVANTAGES OF MARKERS

The environment that fashion drawing and design takes place in is often highly pressured. Those who work in such environments (who likely will not have had the benefit of learning to draw using colored markers) might be skeptical as to whether there will ever be time to produce drawings to the degree of detail and elaboration found in this book. I would make two points in reply to such skepticism: first, admittedly, highly rendered drawings of finished garments *do* take time, but the time they actually take should be measured against the time-saving (and other) benefits of having, at an early stage, a clearer, more realistic view of how the finished garment will look before investing further in fabrication of a prototype or samples. Two, in learning to draw well, to the level shown in this book (in itself an investment, but not as large as commonly thought, and one that can yield big returns) then, almost as a biproduct, one also learns how to make accurate, effective drawings *quickly*. This book is always mindful of the time pressures involved in the creation of fashion and attempts always to point to the quickest and easiest solution for making a drawing.

The amount of time actually taken to makesome of the elaborate and apparently complex drawings shown in this book however, might come as a surprise to many: a large proportion of the drawings in this book (though certainly not all) were, despite initial appearances, completed in well under thirty minutes. For those motivated to learn and practice thirty minutes is indeed a not-unrealistic goal for drawing all but the most complex and exotic garments within a few months of beginning to learn to draw with colored markers. Such productivity, it should be emphasized, is due in no small part to the speed and ease-of-use of markers.

REALISM AND ABSTRACTION, CLARITY AND INTENT IN FASHION DRAWING

Underpinning this book is the conviction that fashion drawing and design—the presentation of ideas about garments that do not yet exist—is most effective, and ideas are best communicated, if the garments, their component fabrics and materials and the figures they are shown on, are drawn as realistically as possible. Realism has already been mentioned several times in this introduction as a standard in fashion drawing and some comments are in order here as to what is meant by it.

In this book, realism stands for the accurate reproduction in a drawing of how things—fabric, garments, figures, garments on figures—appear in reality. Although this sounds circular, this statement points to the crux of the issue—the secret of accurate representational drawing—which is in being able first to perceive how something appears in reality in a way that those perceived elements can be transferred to paper to create a very similar effect, and then actually making that transfer onto the paper.

The appearance of an object in reality is, in fact, the appearance of how light reflects from its surface and is perceived by the eye/mind: the realistic depiction of fabrics and garments closely represents the way that light is reflected from the surfaces of the garment. This representation of the behavior of light on the surface of a garment is, along with the accurate depiction of the figure, silhouette and details (drawings appear odd if the proportions of the body, the shape of the silhouette or the sizing and positioning of the constructional details are not correct) the key to realism (which in my view is the key to effectiveness) in fashion drawing. For fabrics and garments this accurate depiction of light reflecting from the surface means careful use of shading and highlighting to accurately represent the different shadows that form in different types of crape and the shine, sheen or matt appearance of the parts that are turned to the light.

An accurate depiction of light is, if we make the effort to perceive light and shadows as they really are, quite different from what we might expect it to be. For example, it is quite common to see fashion drawings where the garments are meticulously rendered with a uniformity across the whole surface. In a sense it is correct that the garments are made of fabric that has a certain uniform appearance. That is *not*, however, how fabric and garments appear in reality: in reality light conditions will often determine that at any one time—and a drawing is a frozen moment in time, not a timeless idealized version of that something—a large part of a garment is either in shadow, reflecting little or no light, or in the direct path of light and reflecting all that light: the details of the surface are not clearly perceived in those areas but only in the parts in between the extremes of light and dark. To render the garment as though the surface has a uniform appearance *is* unrealistic and indeed *looks* unrealistic. To render a garment so it *does* appear realistic is to render it as it is most often seen, with areas of light and shade, dark shadows and highlights. Shading is an important theme in this book that is discussed at length in the chapter on fabrics and the explanations of how the individual garments are drawn.

Abstraction—reducing objects to their essential elements of their appearance either by simplifying the overall appearance or omitting non-essential parts—is a useful device for fashion drawing, *provided it is used correctly*. Abstraction can be usefully employed with objects that are familiar and unmistakable: for example, the figure itself is very familiar, and features or whole body parts can be omitted and the eye/mind will easily understand what is intended. It can often be effective, for example, to depict the hair, or even the whole head as abstract geometric shapes to echo design elements in the garments, to depict the skin tone of a figure as a flat graphic application of color to contrast with a complex, highly rendered garment or to omit body parts completely so the attention is not drawn away from the garments.

When drawing *fabrics*, however, which are of many different types and are not as intuitively identifiable as a head or nose, for example, care and caution has to be taken in attempting to reduce appearance to

colors for modern fashion

sir joshua reynolds

Sir Joshua Reynolds
Lady Bampfylde
Tate Gallery, London, Great Britain

colors for modern fashion

how this book is organized

HOW THIS BOOK IS ORGANIZED

The organization of *Colors for Modern Fashion* is quite straightforward, though it should be used in different ways by those with differing levels of skill and experience, as is explained in the next section, HOW TO USE THIS BOOK.

Included below is a brief overview of the various chapters of the book. The main issues raised in each chapter are also discussed at the beginning of each chapter and should be reviewed before embarking on work related to that chapter.

Chapter One: Materials and Technique is a prerequisite for everything that follows and should be carefully reviewed by all.

Chapter Two: Color and Design was included because, despite the existence of a number of books on the subjects, it was felt that the book should itself provide some guidance and be able to answer questions about color and design that arise when making fashion drawings. It was also felt to be necessary to illustrate some of the concepts of color and design theory with examples from fashion drawing so some of the potential applications could be directly seen. Although placed in the beginning of the book, the concepts clearly are for application once the fashion croquis can be drawn well, and the chapter should be referred back to as progress is made in basic fashion drawing skills.

Chapter Three: Fabrics is perhaps the most important chapter in the whole book in terms of its contribution to improving basic fashion drawing skills. Being able to show accurately and realistically how fabrics appear and how they drape on the figure is crucial to fashion drawing and underpins the progess to be made in other areas of the book. The chapter that follows it, Body and Head also presents new approaches for presenting those important features of the body that are so important to the overall depiction of the figure and garments.

Chapter Five: Beginning to Draw shows how simple, basic garments that are more suitable for beginners can be drawn. This chapter acts as a bridge to the final four chapters of the book, where how complex garments are drawn is explained. Studying these drawings can also help the more advanced to improve the speed and efficiency of their drawing.

The largest chapter in the book is Chapter Six: Women's Fashion. This chapter attempts to capture the enormous diversity of women's fashion. My own fascination with superlatively designed high-fashion is clearly apparent here, and I make no apology for it: though we might not have the opportunity to wear them often, the exquisite craftsmanship and brilliant design vision in the creation of these garments is an inspiration to everyone interested, or working, in fashion. Besides illustrating how

how different types of garments and fabrics are drawn, the drawings are also intended as a tribute to the extraordinary, brilliant work being produced by modern fashion designers.

The intention of this chapter on women's fashion is that it serve both as a teaching aide and also a source for reference and inspiration for drawing many different types of garments. Garments are organized according to fabric type, with a number of garments by different designers included in each category. This corresponds with how advanced fashion-drawing-in-color courses are often taught in major fashion schools. A wide variety of garments as well as variations in the way fashion drawings can be composed is included so that the student is given a large amount of information and a huge number of different combinations and possible permutations of fabrics, garments and accessories as well as poses, moods, gestures and compositional variations. I have supplemented the work of great designers with some designs of my own. These designs were usually made to illustrate particular points about specific fabrics or garments where I could not readily find something appropriate by another designer. No direct comparison with the work of the great designers included in the book is intended, but I hope these particular drawings also serve to show to students what a powerful design tool drawing is, and to inspire them to experiment and create their own designs.

The chapters on men's and children's fashion recognize the importance, and increasing importance, of fashion for these groups and the particular requirements for drawing—and designing—effectively.

The Appendix is a collection of croquis and poses of basic garments that can be used—especially by beginners who have not yet developed skills to create their own croquis and poses at will—as starting points for their own drawings. A glossary of the technical terms used in the book is included with a full index that will allow the reader to track down the garment, fabric or topic of interest.

colors for modern fashion

nancy riegelman

Nancy Riegelman
21st Century Lady Bampfylde

colors for modern fashion

how to use this book

HOW TO USE THIS BOOK

This book covers a wide range of material from an intermediate to an advanced stage of fashion drawing. If you are studying alone, outside a college course in fashion drawing, then in order to make best use of this book to progress from your present skill level first decide which of the following most closely describes your present experience and skills and follow the directions for that level.

Level 1. BEGINNERS. No previous experience in fashion drawing and no or little experience in other types of drawing.

Level 2. INTERMEDIATE. Experience in fashion drawing, both in sketching and using color—watercolors, gouache or other media but not colored markers.

Level 3. ADVANCED. Experienced in fashion drawing and using various media, including colored markers. Interested to expand technical and compositional skills.

For all three levels, the parts of the book indicated below should be read and studied and the appropriate exercises (they are divided into beginners and advanced) should be undertaken and practiced before moving to the next part.

LEVEL ONE: BEGINNERS

IMPORTANT. For those who are completely new to fashion drawing and drawing in general, it is important to acquire the basic skills of sketching and a knowledge of the proportions of the figure. Unless a firm foundation is built in sketching and being able to draw the figure and silhouette of the garment then efforts to draw fashion in color will not be successful. First, either take an introductory course in fashion drawing where the basics of sketching and the proportions of the figure are taught, or review in depth *9 Heads—A Guide to Drawing Fashion by Nancy Riegelman* or a similar introductory work on fashion drawing.

Once the figure and simple garment silhouettes can be drawn, *Colors for Modern Fashion* should be used as follows:
A. Begin by studying Chapter One: Materials and Technique. This is basic for everyone learning to draw with colored markers.
B. Work through Chapter Five: Beginning to draw, learning how to draw simple garments on the figure.
C. Work through Chapter Three: Fabrics.
D. Work through Chapter Four: Body and Head
E. Work through Chapter Two: Color and Design to broaden knowledge of composition and color.
F. When speed and accuracy have developed sufficiently begin studying the remaining advanced level chapters.

LEVEL TWO: INTERMEDIATE

For those with experience in fashion drawing and using other color media, it will be easy to adapt markers to the already acquired skills but a number of extra techniques unique to markers should be studied. It is recommended that the parts of the book be studied in the following order:

A. Begin by studying Chapter One: Materials and Technique. This is basic for everyone learning to draw with colored markers.
B. Work through Chapter Four: Body and Head
C. Work through Chapter Three: Fabrics.
D. Work through Chapter Two: Color and Design to broaden knowledge of composition and color.
E. Study Women's Fashion, Men's Fashion, Children's Fashion and Wardrobe Basics.

LEVEL THREE: ADVANCED

Advanced level students should first review Chapter One: Materials and Technique and practice any techniques that are not familiar. The chapters on Body and Head, Fabrics and Color and Design should then all be reviewed before proceeding to the broad ranges of garments presented in the other chapters on Women's Fashion, Men's Fashion, Children's Fashion and Wardrobe Basics.

MATERIALS AND TECHNIQUE

materials and equipment

traditional artistic media/markers

Oils and watercolors.

Pastels.

Over the last decade or so colored markers (more often referred to in this book simply as "markers") have come to be used extensively in fashion drawing. Prior to their use, fashion drawings in color were made (and indeed still are being made) using watercolors, oils and other media. Using these traditional media to make fashion drawings is a longer process requiring more effort: given the speed and ease-of-use of markers it is possible to produce accurate and realistic drawings in color much more quickly; output is increased and more ideas can be developed to a more advanced stage than was usual before they came into use.

To understand how markers are used and appreciate some of their advantages, it is useful to compare them directly with the traditional artistic media that were in use for several centuries before their invention. Some of these media are still used to brilliant effect in fashion drawing today by a number of contemporary illustrators and designers, some examples of whose work are included in this book.

OILS
Oil paint is made of oils and pigments and is diluted in a number of ways, usually with the use of linseed oil and turpentine. There are numerous techniques for applying oil, both with wet-on-wet and wet-on-dry coats.
ADVANTAGES: A wide variety of effects can be achieved, with a full range of hues and values, transparencies and saturations. Oil is the only "paint" that can be applied in very thick layers so that the surface of the painting appears to have a textural depth. The effect of "luminosity" —the appearance of light originating inside the painting—is stronger with oils than any other medium.
DISADVANTAGES: Complex preparation; very slow drying for wet-on-dry application, expensive and difficult to learn and use.

WATERCOLORS
Watercolors are pigments that are soluble in water. They can be applied wet-on-wet or wet-on-dry.
ADVANTAGES: Watercolors are relatively easy to prepare and apply. By varying the degrees of dilution a number of effects can be achieved, including unique transparencies and tonal variations. Watercolors have a special and unique "luminosity", particularly when applied on white paper.
DISADVANTAGES: It is difficult to achieve opaque, highly saturated colors using watercolors. Though not as long as for oil, the drying time between coats can be lengthy.

GOUACHE
Gouache is a water-based paint but with different ingredients from watercolors, and which give it more opacity. It can be applied wet-on-wet and wet-on-dry.
ADVANTAGES: A wide variety of effects can be achieved, from dense opacity to luminosity approaching that of watercolor. Its opacity makes it ideal for covering large areas.
DISADVANTAGES: Gouache tends to crack if applied too thickly. It lightens as it dries, does not have the depth and texture of oil and does not quite achieve the transparency of watercolor. It is relatively expensive.

ACRYLIC
Acrylic is a synthetic paint made of pigments in an emulsion base. It is soluble in water and a number of gels and can be applied dark over light and vice versa.
ADVANTAGES: Acrylic dries quickly, is versatile in use and long-lasting. It is possible to achieve a wide variety of effects with acrylic.
DISADVANTAGES: The preparation for acrylic is complex; it dries more quickly than oils but is still slow compared to some other media. Acrylic is an expensive art medium.

COLORED PENCILS/PASTELS
These are dry media that can be used directly and do not need further media for application onto paper. Colored pencils come in wax-based, pastel-based or water soluble forms. Wax-based are most common. Pastels are either so-called soft pastels— dry crayons of powdered pigment bound in a gum solution—or oil pastels, which are pigment in a wax and fat base.
ADVANTAGES: Quick and easy-to-use, relatively cheap. Blend easily and can usually be easily erased; they produce a range of subtle effects, are good for fine, detailed work, and combine easily with other media, such as markers.
DISADVANTAGES: Do not easily produce saturated applications of color; it is difficult to cover large areas evenly.

COLORED MARKERS
Available with solvent-based inks (permanent markers) and water-based inks (watercolor markers). Markers have a range of felt tips so they can be applied in variety of thicknesses.
ADVANTAGES: Quick and easy-to-use. Easy-to-learn—techniques can be mastered in hours, compared with weeks or longer for other media. Efficient and clean, no preparation and no clean-up is necessary. Markers blend easily with other markers and colored pencils. Markers are available in wide range of colors and produce a wide range of effects including high saturation and luminosity. Color-coded markers can be calibrated to computer colors and color systems such as Pantone®.
DISADVANTAGES: Make a permanent mark that is difficult to erase or change with darker colors.

materials and equipment

markers/purchasing markers

A typical selection of markers for beginners

Selection of markers for more advanced users. Grey tones, neutrals and pastels have been added to the beginner's selection.

MATERIALS AND EQUIPMENT FOR DRAWING WITH MARKERS

Colored markers are a versatile drawing and coloring medium that combine well with a number of other media. In this book markers are used together with other materials and equipment to achieve the effects used to make the fashion drawings shown here. The amount of other materials and equipment needed is relatively small, and is all that is needed to achieve all the effects required for the drawings shown in the book. The additional materials are, most importantly, colored and black (lead graphite) pencils, which add a range of soft and subtle effects to markers; white gel pen for highlights and ink pen for fine contour or detail work. Markers do, however, also combine well with paints of various types, pastels and inks, and the more adventurous might wish to explore some of these other combinations once the main techniques for applying markers and the additional media used in drawing fashion have been mastered.

The materials and equipment used for drawing with markers are described below, and recommendations are given for purchasing an initial supply and for how to add to it. These materials are all available at art supply stores or on-line outlets.

COLORED MARKERS

The markers used in this book are permanent markers—inks in an alcohol solvent base. The marker ink is held in a felt pad inside the body of the marker and flows onto the paper through the tip, which is of two or three different widths. Most markers have a broad beveled tip at one end and a fine tip at the other; some have two fine tips.

When first introduced the range of marker colors was limited. Nowadays literally hundreds of colors are available, often with ranges of values and intensities for specific colors, full ranges of blacks, greys, neutrals and even fluorescents. A number of trends have caused this expansion, one that has been particularly influential being the rise in popularity of Japanese manga comics that has given rise to the development of new ranges of metallic and iridescent colors. Markers are now available that correspond with standard printing colors and, as mentioned, coded to match color recognition systems.

PURCHASING COLORED MARKERS

When purchasing markers, although the color is always indicated on the outside by a name, number, cap color or combination of those, and marker manufacturers provide charts with the range of colors available, it is always best to test the marker before buying to check the color and freshness. A fresh marker will make clean, even strokes with no color or value change over an area of a few strokes. It should not be necessary to press down hard on the marker: markers that require pressure to make a mark, and that "squeak" in use, are partly dried out and will not function as well as fresh markers. It should also be noted that a marker's color will vary according to the paper that is used (see below). If in doubt, the art supply store will usually supply a sample of the actual paper that will be used for drawing

to test the color.

When making a first purchase of markers, it is best to buy a set of twelve markers corresponding to the twelve hues of the color wheel (as shown in the picture at left—the color wheel is discussed in the next chapter of the book) plus black and a grey—perhaps a cool grey 10%—plus a colorless blender. Using colorless blender, a wide range of colors can be achieved by mixing these first markers, and new marker colors can be added over time. More colors mean more flexibility.

Markers are available from a number of companies. The drawings in this book were made using Letraset Tria markers. These markers were chosen for a number of reasons, including the wide range of colors, particularly pastels, ease of use, ease of mixing and that they each have three tips of different widths, giving great flexibility in the type of marks that can be made on the paper. Virtually all the colors used in the drawings of this book, however, can be found in other brands of markers, and the final choice of brand is a matter of personal preference.

RECOMMENDATION: Start with a set of 12 to 15 markers corresponding to the hues on the color wheel, plus black and cool grey and a colorless blender. Add new colors as required (or coveted!).

materials and equipment

papers/colored pencils

Specialized marker paper for final drawings.

Layout drawing paper used to plan the drawing.

Colored pencils are used to draw the initial croquis and silhouette.

A full set of colored pencils.

PAPERS

A number of paper manufacturers make specialized marker paper, and a number of other non-specialized papers can also be used when drawing with markers.

Paper, including marker paper, has three main characteristics: the SURFACE TOOTH, the TRANSLUCENCY and the INK-ABSORPTION RATE AND CAPACITY.

The SURFACE TOOTH of a paper is its roughness—or graininess—which is what determines the appearance of marks on the surface. The TRANSLUCENCY is the amount of light that passes through the paper—how transparent or opaque it is. The INK-ABSORPTION RATE AND CAPACITY is the rate at which ink is absorbed by the paper and the total quantity of ink that can be absorbed.

Papers such as VELLUM have a low surface tooth and feel smooth to the touch. Vellum papers have a low absorption rate and marks made on them with markers and pencils appear soft and of limited intensity.

Papers such as BOND paper have a high surface tooth with relatively high absorption, resulting in intense colors.

Specialized MARKER PAPER is moderately translucent, with a medium absorption rate and capacity and a medium-high surface tooth. It allows for a wide range of tonal gradation and color saturation as well as the precise line quality that is necessary for detailed fashion drawing. The translucency, combined with the absorptive properties allows for pleasing, almost luminous type effects to be achieved.

VELLUM TRACING PAPER has a very low absorbency rate so does not produce intense colors or subtle effects, but it is useful for copying or transferring images—for example, some of the croquis included in this book.

For drawings with markers, on balance it is best to use either a specialized marker paper or a bond paper. The drawings in this book were all made using specialized marker paper, which is particularly effective in creating the range of effects developed in this book, but the choice is one of personal taste and the reader should make a comparison before deciding.

RECOMMENDATION: For the final drawing use a specialized marker paper or bond paper, depending on personal preference. Use a branded layout or other bond paper for layout drawings and a vellum tracing paper for copying silhouettes.

COLORED PENCILS

As mentioned, the principal disadvantage of colored pencils is that it is difficult to achieve deep saturation and smooth, even applications over large areas with them. When used together with colored markers, though, they are an almost perfect complement, adding an important range of delicate and subtle effects: together markers and colored pencils are virtually all that is needed to achieve the full range of effects required for fashion drawing and are used

materials and equipment

mechanical pencils/pens/colorless blenders/gel pens/sharpeners/erasers

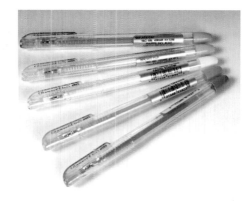

Gel pens.

Black marker, colorless blender, turquoise marker, mechanical pencil, Micron.005 pen, white gel pen, graphite pencil.

Lead for mechanical pencil, erasers.

Electric pencil sharpener. These sharpeners produce better points than manual sharpeners.

extensively in the drawings throughout this book.

Wax-based colored pencils are the most common and are easy to apply and blend. They are sturdy and keep a fine point (it's important to work with sharp pencils at all times—best points are achieved with electric pencil sharpeners). A number of good quality brands of colored pencils are available. Pencils are cheap, so the more the merrier. RECOMMENDATION: Start with a set of 12 pencils in the same colors as markers plus black and grey. Always use an electric pencil-sharpener to ensure fine, long points.

MECHANICAL GRAPHITE PENCILS
Mechanical pencils are easier to use than wood and graphite pencils: the lead does not need sharpening and line thickness is always uniform. Use a 0.5mm lead. A number of brands are available.

INK PENS
A specialty pen such as a Micron .005mm is best for detailed work. Other brands are also available.

COLORLESS BLENDERS
Colorless blenders are markers without the color pigmentation and are important for mixing markers and for a number of effects where the original color is diluted and reduced in saturation. They often come in a white tube and are used extensively for the effects used in the drawings in this book.

GEL PENS
Gel pens are readily available in a number of brands and in different colors. White is the color used in this book for highlights, though other colors can be used for experimenting.

PENCIL SHARPENERS
As mentioned, it is important to draw only with sharp points so fine lines can be achieved (if a wider line is needed a mark can be made with the side of the pencil lead). Plastic pencil sharpeners are almost useless—they make short, stubby points that make short, stubby lines. An electric pencil sharpener is well worth the investment and can greatly enhance line quality. A number of different brands are available.

ERASERS
Erasers should always be kept handy. Mechanical pencils often have a built-in eraser. Kneaded erasers knead into any shape to remove marks clearly and easily without damaging the surface. Pink pearl erasers are good general pencil erasers. Electric erasers are more expensive but can erase large areas more quickly and more cleanly than manual erasers.

marker application and technique

preparing to draw/holding the marker

Holding the marker—usual position.
The marker is held in the middle for a long, smooth mark. This is the most comfortable position for holding the marker.

Holding the marker—short strokes.
The marker is held very close to the tip for shorter strokes.

Holding the marker—nuanced lines.
When the broad tip of the marker is being used, a rotation of the wrist brings the beveled (sharpened) tip into contact with the paper, quickly and conveniently changing the width of the line. (called a "nuanced line").

Holding the marker—detailed work.
The marker is held close to the tip for detailed work.

Holding the marker—fine lines.
A fine line is created using the fine tip of the marker.

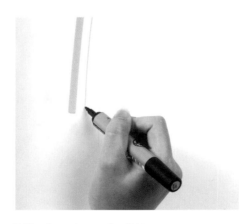

Holding the marker—medium lines.
A medium line is created using the medium tip of the marker.

MARKER APPLICATION AND TECHNIQUE

As with all artistic media—oil, watercolors, gouache and the various others—in order to be able to use markers correctly a number of techniques have to be learned. The following section describes and illustrates in detail these basic and essential techniques, those that are used in making the drawings included in this book. Those who do not already have experience using markers should practice all the techniques illustrated over the next few pages before attempting to make drawings. This will give a good sense of how markers feel and how different effects are achieved with them. ·

To attain true proficiency in drawing fashion in color with markers it is essential to master these techniques so they become second nature. When moving on to study and copy the garments included later in the book continual reference should be made to this chapter when a particular technique or effect is mentioned.

PREPARING TO DRAW

Before starting to draw a number of tasks of preparation should be performed:

1. Assemble everything that will be needed for the drawing: the various papers (marker paper for the final drawing, layout paper for preliminary drawings and tracing paper to copy silhouettes), the markers, blenders, pencils, erasers, pencil sharpener, fabric swatches and images.
2. Practice a few croquis to confirm what the pose will be.
3. If the drawing is to be made with reference to actual fabric swatches examine them and decide how they will fit together; hold them to the light and move them to get an idea of how they will drape.
4. Sketch out possible shapes for the hair and gestures and other elements to be included in the drawing.
5. Select the palette of markers to be used and test each one on scrap paper.
6. Try out some mixes and blended effects.
7. Make sure the points of the markers are clean. If they are not clean rub them on paper.
8. Sharpen pencils.

Sit in a well-lit place, at a table or desk, with an upright posture, in a comfortable chair. In order to be able to control the marker keep the elbow on the surface and the weight on the forearm so that the wrist is free to move across the page. Keep the touch light—pressing too hard spoils markers and makes heavy lines.

HOLDING THE MARKER

The marker is held with the same grip as that used for holding a pen or pencil, that is with the shaft of the marker between the index and middle finger, with the pressure of the thumb balancing and guiding it. The marker is held in different positions according to the mark being made. For most applications the marker is held in the center. This leaves the wrist flexible so a wide variety of lines and marks can be made.

marker application and technique

holding the marker/blending and mixing/colored pencils

The broad tip of the marker is used to create a broad line.

Mixing on a palette. Step 1.
Mixing allows subtle new colors to be produced, often not available directly from the marker. First the colors to be mixed are applied side-by-side onto the acetate palette.

Mixing on a palette. Step 2.
The colors are mixed together using colorless blender. Colorless blender is neutral, without color, so ensures the mix is in proportion to the actual amounts of each color applied to the palette. To see how the mixed color will actually appear it is necessary to apply it onto paper.

For SMALL STROKES hold the marker near the tip.
For LONG STROKES hold the marker in the middle.

As mentioned, most markers have two or three tips. Every marker has a broad tip for wider marks with a beveled, or sliced, edge which allows for slimmer but still saturated applications of color. The opposite end of the marker has a pointed tip for finer marks. Letraset Tria markers have a third point hidden under the pointed tip, a super-fine tip that is used for precise detailing.
For FINE STROKES use the fine tip or super-fine tip of the marker.
For MEDIUM STROKES use the beveled edge.
For BROAD STROKES use the flat edge.

BLENDING AND MIXING TECHNIQUES
In this book "blending" a marker is the term used to refer to the process of diluting a single marker color with colorless blender (in this book colorless blenders are also referred to simply as blenders). This produces a more transparent, less intense version of the original color, depending on the proportions of marker color and colorless blender used.
"Mixing" is the process of mixing two or more marker colors together to form new colors, also using a colorless blender.

In general the best effects are obtained using markers directly, without having to alter their color, and given the large ranges of marker colors now available this is often quite feasible. It will however at times be necessary to blend or mix markers to obtain new colors, either because (i) the selection of markers available is limited, or (ii) the required color is not available, or (iii) because a subtle color variation outside the available range of colors is required (particularly to show the gradation of tone necessary to depict the shading of drape, as used extensively throughout this book).

The main blending and mixing techniques are described below. Experimenting is fun and can yield interesting results. Remember that best results are obtained by mixing colors close to each other—the further apart they are the more they will tend to "muddy" (as described in Chapter Two: Color and Design).

MIXING—MARKERS-TO-COLORED PENCIL
Markers can be mixed with colored pencils (especially wax-based pencils) to create subtle variations in hue and value ("hue" is another word for color; "value" is the technical term for referring to the level of darkness or lightness of a color and is discussed at length in the next chapter). For example, adding blue pencil to a yellow marker base results in a new greenish hue; a dark brown pencil when added to a light skin tone creates a shift in value in the original skin tone, making it darker. Colored pencils can also be used with blended marker colors (as described below) to yield even more subtle color variations.

MIXING—MARKER-TO-MARKER (THE KISSING TECHNIQUE)
When only a small amount of additional color is needed it is possible to create this by combining the inks of two markers directly by rubbing their broad tips together: a coat of the new color emerges on both tips. After applying the new color, clean the marker tips by continuing to scrub them on scrap paper until the original color reappears.

MIXING AND BLENDING ON A PALETTE
When a sizeable amount of a mixed or blended color is required it is possible to blend one marker color with colorless blender or to mix the inks of two or more markers on a palette and then apply directly to the paper. Palettes can be made of any material that does not absorb marker ink, such as tracing vellum, which has a very low absorption capacity, or acetate sheet—usually the best option as it is light, stiff and transparent. Applying marker inks onto a non-absorbent surface spreads the inks, making them more transparent. This carries through to the blended colors, making the technique particularly suitable for obtaining subtle colors.

To mix colors using a palette, first place the palette on a flat surface. If using transparent acetate sheet, place a white piece of paper underneath so that the true colors can be seen. Gauge how much mixed-marker ink will be required for the task in hand and apply an appropriate amount of the first marker onto the surface of the palette with a rotating motion of the wrist. Lay down the second color next to the first and continue with further colors until all the chosen colors appear side-by-side on the palette. Next, the colorless blender is used. Colorless blender is pure marker solvent without color that will dilute and mix regular markers. A colorless blender is used in the same way a wet brush is used to dilute and mix watercolors: insert the colorless blender into one of the marker colors, "drag" it to the other colors and mix. Further amounts of either color can be added until the desired color emerges. Test the color on paper to see if it is the desired color and if so apply to the drawing with the tip of the colorless blender.

Using a blender allows a range of gradated tones to be achieved. This is particularly useful where softer colors are required and for detailed shading. Using only a small range of colors, with colorless blender it is possible to produce an almost limitless range of colors.

A considerable, and unique advantage markers have over other media when blended is that the blended color survives on the palette almost indefinitely. Even when the alcohol base has evaporated, the pigments remain, and an application of blender brings them instantly back to life. If colorless blender is not available, it is possible to refresh dried marker using any light-colored marker, though the resulting blend will of course contain that color.

COLORED PENCILS
An additional valuable blending technique can be achieved by blending colored pencils together. They can be blended the same way as markers, using colorless blender, but must be blended on paper, as they do not make a mark on acetate or vellum. Once the pencil is mixed with blender, however, it can then be transferred onto a palette or vellum.

marker application and technique

blending marker/blending colored pencil/mixing—marker-to-marker/mixing on a palette

Blending marker on a palette. Step 1.
"Blending" is diluting a color to obtain a more transparent version that can be used for delicate applications. A quantity of marker ink is applied onto the acetate with a circular motion. The color is "pulled out" using a colorless blender.

Blending marker on a palette. Step 2.
The blended color is transferred from the acetate onto the marker paper. The darker area is where a double layer has been applied.

Blending marker on a palette. The final effect.
A less saturated, more transparent version of the color results (seen here alongside the original color).

Mixing markers, marker-to-marker—the "kissing technique".
When a small amount of mixed color is needed markers can be mixed directly by rubbing the broad tips together. A small amount of the new color is left on the tip of each marker.

Blending colored pencil.
Colored pencil cannot be applied to acetate so is applied to marker paper and then mixed with colorless blender, making the color from the pencil less granular.and more ink- like. Blended colored pencil is used when a pastel or delicate transparent color is required.

Gradation of tone with colored pencil.
Colored pencil is applied to paper and then "pulled out" using the colorless blender to give progressively less-saturated tones. This technique is useful in creating shading in very light colors.

Mixing marker and colored pencil on a palette. Step 1.
A liberal quantity of marker of the chosen color is applied onto the acetate palette.

Mixing marker and colored pencil on a palette. Step 2.
The marker ink is "pulled out" with a "to-and-fro motion" of the wrist, moving the hand towards the body, resulting in a more transparent "blended color."

Mixing marker and colored pencil. Step 3.
Colored pencil is applied to the paper and diluted using another (clean) colorless blender, creating a light, transparent color.

marker application and technique

layering/drawing croquis and silhouette/shading /sheen/highlights

Mixing marker and colored pencil. Step 4.
Blended marker ink (red) on the end of a colorless blender is added to diluted colored pencil to create a new mixed color (orange). The new mixed color is applied onto marker paper.

Layering. Step 1.
Layering gives variations of color, depth and complexity. Three blended colors are applied on top of each other.

Layering. Steps 2 and 3.
Step 2. Further colors (blended red, violet) are applied. Adding extra colors gives even greater depth and color complexity. Step 3. Applications of further colors give even more subtlety, depth and luminosity to the drawing.

Filling in the silhouette using a scrubbing motion.

Drawing the croquis with a light-colored pencil.
Light-colored pencils give a clear line and do not "muddy" the color of the markers.

Drawing the silhouette.
The silhouette of a garment is drawn with a grey or other light-colored pencil.

Shading with pencil.
Creating heavier line weights in areas where the body bends gives a sense of depth.

Creating soft white sheen with pencil.
Sheen is seen on the surface of fabrics with luster such as leather, cottons, velvet, crepes and others. It is drawn in using the side of the pencil.

Creating white highlights with the tip of a white pencil.
Highlights are brighter, sharper whites than sheen and appear in highly reflective fabrics such as patent leather, satin, taffeta, lycra and others.

basic techniques for applying color

shading/adding detail/saturating color/layering

Deepening the value of a color.
Shadows in folds are indicated using the side of a black pencil over the color of the fabric. The pencil is held from above so downward pressure can be applied. For shorter strokes the pencil is held close to the tip.

Adding Detail.
Detail is applied with the tip of a pencil. The pencil is held close to the tip for precision control.

Creating saturated color. Step 1.
Color is applied to the front side of the paper. In this example black is used, for which it is often difficult to achieve good saturation, but the technique is the same for all dark colors.

Creating saturated color. Step 2.
Color is next applied from the reverse side of the paper, further saturating the color. This technique also has the effect of evening out the color and obscuring any streaking or uneven application of color.

Creating saturated color. Step 3.
The paper is turned back to the front side and a third layer of marker is added resulting in an even application of deeply saturated color.

Layering with the same color and different medium.
Adding black pencil over black marker to give depth and texture. This technique is often used for tweeds and velvets.

BASIC TECHNIQUES FOR APPLYING COLOR

SHADING—DEEPENING THE VALUE OF A COLOR

Shading is used to express changes in surface appearance where a fabric drapes and parts bend in (become concave) causing a shift into shadow (see Chapter Three: Fabrics for detailed explanations of drape and shading in different fabrics).

To achieve the effect of dark shadow on a colored surface, apply either black marker or black pencil in the areas where shadows are to be indicated. Black markers will create a flat tone as the ink is absorbed into the paper. Applying black pencil over the black marker will give a slight reflective quality to the shadow, giving the impression of black shadow on a contoured, three-dimensional—as opposed to a flat—surface.

CREATING SATURATED COLORS

To achieve highly saturated color effects with markers, after making the first application of marker on the surface of the paper, reverse the paper and apply marker again from the underside using a firm scrubbing motion. Another layer can then be added to the top side of the paper. When dry, a beautiful saturated color will result. This technique works particularly well with dark-valued colors such as black, blue and red.

LAYERING

Layering is the application of a series of colors in sequence, each successive color being applied over the preceding color, but leaving part of the preceding color uncovered so that the progression of colors can be seen. Layering is a technique that can be used with the same (or very similar) color to achieve a subtle gradation of value of the same hue (as in skin tone for example) or with different colors, where the effect is to give a richness and luminosity to the resulting color as more colors are layered in. Layering different colors yields new colors, according to the principles of color mixing, but with layering a "memory" of the original colors survives the process and is perceived in the resulting layered color.

In layering, the edge of each applied color is visible, almost like slices of ham on a platter. This is distinct from the effect of gradating tone, discussed below, where no edges are visible and the color shift is seamless. When layering colors, start with the lighter colors and progress to the darker colors.

basic techniques for applying color

adding shine, highlights, detailing / skin tone on body and face

Adding shine, highlights and detailing.
White gel pen is brighter than pencil and is used to add light anywhere on a composition in the form of shine or highlights—pinpoints of light. It can also be used for details such as top-stitching, beading, sequins, paillettes and shines on patent leather and metallic surfaces. White gel pen is also useful for erasing mistakes makde on white paper.

Adding skin tone and shading to the body. Step 1.
Skin tone is applied to the figure with medium strokes of a beige marker held in the middle.

Skin tone and shading. Step 2.
Deepen the color of the skin tone by adding shadows with a blended color applied with a colorless blender.

Skin tone and shading. Step 3
The remaining skin tone is filled in with beige marker. Marker is applied with horizontal strokes in the torso and with vertical strokes in the legs and arms

Adding skin tone and shading to the face. Step 1.
Once the contours of the face are drawn, skin tone is added with even strokes of a beige marker. To avoid streaking do not lift the tip of the marker from the page

Adding skin tone and shading to the face. Step 2.
The planes of the face are defined by adding shadows with a beige marker to the areas that recede from the light.

ADDING SHINE AND HIGHLIGHTS

An object has highlights—or "shine"—at those points where light strikes it and is reflected, as opposed to the parts where light is absorbed and the object appears to have color. Highlights are indicated by applying white pencil over the underlying color. White gel pens can also be used: these contain an opaque white ink and are effective in creating very strong, almost luminescent white marks. Gel pens are also available in a range of iridescent colors which can yield intriguing effects.

GRADATING TONE

To achieve a gradation of tone—a gradual darkening or lightening shift in the tonal value of a color, often used in shading draped garments—a technique is used where a color is applied and then "dragged out" to become progressively more diluted. First the original marker color is applied to the paper, and, when dry, colorless blender is added, moved backwards and forwards to loosen the pigments and then "dragged" in the intended direction. The color becomes more transparent and the result is a continuous, seamless progression of color from darker and more saturated to lighter and less saturated. This technique was invented by Leonardo da Vinci in the 16th century and is known as *sfumato* —literally "shaded off"—from the Latin "fumare", to smoke. The effect is similar to seeing an object through mist or smoke and is particularly useful in shading fabrics.

basic techniques for applying color

sfumato/stippling/luminosity/tints/shades/neutralizing colors/drawing lines

Sfumato. A smoky effect created by gradating tones using colorless blender, traditionally used as a background. Different gradated colors can be layered to increase the impression of depth.

Stippling.
Stippling is a spotted or speckled effect created by up and down movements with the marker held vertically. Stippling is used to create texture of fabrics with threads of uneven thickness and an uneven surface—tweeds, raw silk and others.

Luminosity.
A vibrant, luminous effect is created by adding a bright color from the reverse side of the paper.

Creating a tint by diluting a color with colorless blender to allow the white of the paper to show through.

A shade (a darker version of a color) is created by adding to the original color blended grey (or black) marker that is darker than the original color using colorless blender on a palette. The colorless blender is used here to mix the colors.

Neutralizing a color (making it less colorful by adding a neutral color—white, black or grey—or mixing it with its complementary color). The colorless blender is used here to mix the colors.

CREATING SHADES
Shades are the variations that result from adding black to colors, darkening (reducing the value) and lowering the saturation of the original color. To create shades with markers, black, or a grey that is darker than the color to be darkened, is added to the original marker color using colorless blender on a palette. The more black or darker grey that is added, the darker the shade of the original color becomes. With black pencil, apply to the paper, add blender and transfer the resulting color to the color to be shaded on the palette. Shades created with pencil do not dilute the original color as much as black marker.

CREATING TINTS
This is the opposite of creating shades. Tints are lighter versions of a color (often pastels) and are achieved by the addition of white pigment. The effect can be achieved in two ways: either mixing white pencil directly with another color on a palette using colorless blender, or diluting a color directly with colorless blender on the paper, creating a transparent color which, applied to white paper, allows the whiteness of the paper to show through, yielding a tint/pastel effect.

NEUTRALIZING COLORS
Neutral colors have no "color"—or "chroma"—they are, technically, the "achromatic" black, white and greys, though dull, muddy colors with a small amount of color are also commonly referred to as neutrals. To "neutralize" a color is to remove some of its color. This is done by adding black, white or grey or mixing it with its complementary color. A fuller description of neutralizing colors and complementary colors is included in Chapter Two: Color and Design.

NOTE ON DRAWING LINES
A line made with a single sweeping gesture is usually more elegant than a line made up of a series of small lines, sometimes referred to as "chicken scratches". Being able to draw elegant, expressive lines is a technique that requires practice to master. To draw graceful lines, it is important to sit gracefully, upright and perpendicular to the page. Keep the weight on the elbow and draw from the wrist. Focus on achieving precision and control—the qualities that need to be developed so that the lines of a garment can be drawn quickly and accurately. It is difficult to draw well when fatigued or upset.

mastering technical fashion drawing

do not do's of fashion drawing with markers

DO NOT DO. When too many colors are mixed the result becomes muddied and dull. Adding a small amount of an unmixed, pure hue to the composition as an accent will bring the drawing back to life.

DO NOT DO Left figure, do not draw one side of the figure and then the other—they invariably do not match up. Right figure, do not outline the figure in heavy black—it flattens the drawing, making it appear two-dimensional.

DO NOT DO. Left figure, hands are too small; right figure, the head is too large. It is essential to keep body proportions correct as the eye is sensitive to the smallest discrepancies.

MASTERING TECHNICAL FASHION DRAWING

Fashion drawing is a form of technical drawing: its purpose is to communicate information, both technical information about construction and detail and also less precise ideas about overall style and appearance. Like so many highly evolved human activities (ballet, synchronized swimming, gymnastics and opera singing spring to mind) technical drawing is (for the vast majority of us) not a naturally instinctive activity.

To make precise technical drawings whether they are of fashion or in other areas of design —architecture, product design, automobile design, for example— it is essential to develop a set of drawing skills and to practice constantly to refine these skills. In order to be able to draw objects accurately the eye has to be trained to see clearly shapes, shifts in hue and value, and details. It is important always to keep in mind that technical drawing is a visual language used to communicate ideas. In the same way as it is necessary to speak or write clearly to be understood, in drawing too it is always necessary to present ideas clearly.

DO NOT DO's OF FASHION DRAWING WITH MARKERS

There are many pitfalls in the road to mastering fashion drawing— or any type of drawing in fact— and many of them have to be experienced first hand in order to learn how they are to be subsequently avoided. Some of the worst mistakes can be avoided, though, by studying the following "DO NOT DO's" and "DO's". These "moral commandments" of fashion drawing with markers are the hard-learnt lessons of many years experience in making and correcting mistakes and can save the reader much frustration and expenditure of fruitless energy.

DO NOT try to fill in one side of an object (e.g., a garment) completely and then fill in the opposite side attempting to match it to the original side. Things almost never line up so easily, even with the simplest poses.

DO NOT use a heavy black outline around objects or figures unless a two-dimensional effect is intended.

DO NOT outline noses in black.

DO NOT make hands very small.

DO NOT make heads very large.

DO NOT use too many neutral colors or the palette can appear muddy.

DO NOT shade with lines.

DO NOT keep several markers open at the same time.

DO NOT eat, drink or smoke around markers. They are toxic and flammable.

mastering technical fashion drawing

applications of technique/do's of fashion drawing with markers

Application of technique: saturated color.
A deep, saturated color created with using a scrubbing motion of the marker from the front and reverse sides of the paper.

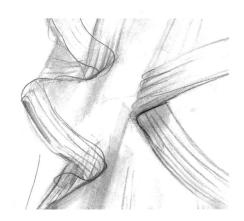

Application of technique: shading with blended color.
Blended colors are used to indicate shading as they are softer, less-saturated colors that can be easily gradated. Shadows fall on the undersides of these transparent cascading folds.

Application of technique: indicating contour with nuanced lines.
Nuanced lines show the subtle texture of the petals of a flower. The fluidity of gesture in the line quality in this drawing expresses the delicacy of the flower.

Application of technique: sheen.
White pencil is applied over the base color to show sheen-here on fringe.

Application of technique: layering of colors to show texture and shadow.
Layered colors are used in representing saturated colors: colors appear brighter and more saturated when layered in coats as opposed to single flat applciation. Here saturated colors are achieved by using colored pencil over marker.

Application of technique: saturated color.
Rich, saturated color is achieved by applying marker from both sides of the paper and deepening the shadows with black marker.

DO's OF FASHION DRAWING IN COLOR

DO try to work in a well-lit environment: either in daylight or, if working at night, using a light-source that is not too yellow or blue.

DO apply colors from light to dark.

DO always check that a marker is clean before applying it to a drawing.

DO apply color by using a scrubbing circular motion of wrist to avoid streaking.

DO be careful when using black—it is unforgiving and usually cannot be reversed.

DO observe work from a distance of at least three or four feet every twenty minutes or so—some effects are difficult to judge from close-in.

DO use layered color for beautiful rich effects.

DO make sure to cover up markers, as open they expose the user to fumes and dry out.

DO close all markers tightly at the end of the work session or they will dry out.

DO keep pencils sharp. Start each session with sharp points.

DO remember that the first drawing is not always the final drawing. It takes a while to warm up, and it is usually necessary to draw for a while before one begins to draw well.

DO stop and rest when fatigued.

DO apply color from front and back of paper for extremely saturated color.

DO remember to breathe.

DO keep the work area ventilated.

practice and exercises

1. Following the instructions for holding markers, fill a page with thin, medium and wide lines.

2. Make a series of lines that change width by rotating the marker.

3. Apply areas of yellow, red and turquoise marker to acetate or vellum. Dilute each color separately with colorless blender and apply the new color onto marker paper. (Note: clean off the tip of the colorless blender between colors by rubbing it on paper until the color disappears).

4. Choose three colors and apply onto acetate or vellum. Pick up each color in turn with a colorless blender and apply to marker paper to create a constant gradation of tone from the original color to its most transparent form.

5 (i) Apply a yellow, green, orange and pink colored pencil to marker paper. Blend each with a colorless blender. Transfer to marker paper and experiment mixing combintations of colors. (ii) Mix the different blended colored pencil colors separately with light blue and light green markers.

6. Copy (by tracing or drawing freehand) a croquis from the Appendix and fill in with any colored marker using a scrubbing motion.

7. Copy a croquis from the Appendix and fill in with a light beige marker. Apply layers of blended pink and finally blended orange over the first layer.

8.(i) Copy one of the croquis from Chapter Five: Beginning to Draw using light grey colored pencil. (ii) Copy one of the croquis with simple outfits from the Appendix also using light grey pencil.

9. Copy a croquis with clothes from the Appendix and add shading in the folds of the fabric using colored pencil.

10. Copy a croquis with clothes from the Appendix. Fill in with a medium to dark color. Using a white pencil add a. highlights on the surface of folds b. sheen on the broad surfaces of the fabric. Using a colored pencil add stippling to any area of the fabric to create a texture resembling tweed or raw silk.

11. Copy the silhouette of any garment in this book. Create a *sfumato* background using layers of blended color.

12. Copy the silhouette of any garment in the book and fill in with saturated color by applying markers from the front and reverse sides of the paper.

COLOR AND DESIGN

modern fashion drawing

great masters of fashion drawing/fragonard

Fragonard, Jean-Honoré (1732-1806)
The Stolen Kiss.
Hermitage, St. Petersburg, Russia

modern fashion drawing

great masters of fashion drawing

MODERN FASHION DRAWING

Fashion drawing as it is known today, is a relatively recent development, dating from around the turn of the twentieth century. Prior to that time, drawings or paintings showing fashion garments were made as works of fine art—usually portraits of nobility in their finery or in sporting or religious scenes. Many of the portraits and scenes drawn and painted by the great European masters from the Renaissance onwards, (and American artists from the 19th century) include highly skilled renderings of beautiful high-fashion garments. These works of art often served to introduce the work of a particular couturier or dressmaker to a wider public and to inspire copies and similar designs from other dressmakers (a process that continues to this day).

In modern times fashion drawing has narrowed in scope and purpose and is now primarily used as a tool for fashion design rather than an art form (mention should be made, though of a small number of fashion artists/illustrators, some examples of whose work is included in this book). A modern fashion drawing is usually executed in two or three hours at most, often much less, and very rarely approaches the scope and complexity of paintings by Fragonard, Goya or Whistler, for example, which of course took much longer to complete.

Even though its purpose is now more often functional than purely artistic fashion drawing is, nevertheless, still "composed", and embodies a number of design decisions that play a crucial role in determining the success of the drawing. Whether drawn for art or for commercial illustration, the purpose of fashion drawing is to present beautiful garments in as appealing a manner as possible. To achieve this end the drawing itself should be made as appealing and attractive as possible.

The modern fashion drawing is now based on the nine-head figure—an idealized version of the human form (which is naturally equivalent to about eight heads in length) that flatters both the figure and the garments, making them appear larger than life. Good composition of the drawing based on the nine-head figure is one of the vital ingredients in making a drawing attractive and securing its overall success.

Color is a central part of vision and how the world appears. In art and design it is a powerful, complex and unique design element. When fashion drawings are made in color, not surprisingly color plays a major role in their composition beyond that of simply indicating the color of the garments. A knowledge of the properties of color and the way colors combine and interact is an important part of a preparation for learning to make sound decisions on the use of color in the composition of fashion drawings and, by extension, the use of color in fashion design. This chapter reviews the basic principles and elements of good composition, the properties of color and the main theories of how colors contrast and interact with each other.

Whistler, James Abbott McNeill (1834-1903)
Harmony in Grey and Green: Miss Cicely Alexander, 1872-1874.
Tate Gallery, London, Great Britain

modern fashion drawing

composition and design

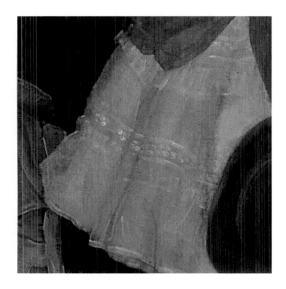

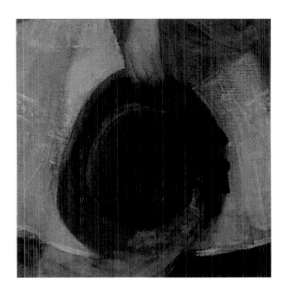

COMPOSITION AND DESIGN

In the other chapters of this book the term "design" almost always refers to fashion design—the design of the garments. In this chapter the term "design" is used with its broader meaning, equivalent to "composition." Fashion design is indeed simply a branch of the larger field of "Design" that covers virtually every type of object or activity made by man, from architecture to automobiles, from interior and product design to the design of industrial devices, from computer graphics to books. Since the time of Leonardo da Vinci and the Renaissance, efforts have been made to create rules that apply not just to one field of design but across all of them.

The composition—or "design"—of a drawing or painting is the range of decisions made about how the subject matter—the "content"—is presented. This presentation of the content—the purely visual aspects of a drawing or painting—is referred to in art as the "form" of the drawing or painting. In fashion drawing the principal content is the garments themselves (the figures and other elements being secondary content) and the form the way that they are presented.

Drawings are often made with different purposes and audiences in mind and have different emphases. As in the case of fashion drawings, some focus more on technical aspects such as construction and details, others on capturing the beauty of the design. No matter, though, what the intended purpose or audience for a drawing, a drawing is always more effective if it feels balanced, engaging, easy on the eye and easy to understand. If a drawing displays these qualities it will capture the viewer's attention and seduce the eye.

A large part of what makes up a compelling drawing is the quality of the drawing itself, and showing how to draw well in color is the main purpose of this book. The composition of the drawing, though, is a significant part of the final product. If its various elements have been assembled with care and consistent regard for the principles of good form and color composition it is more likely to succeed in its purpose than otherwise.

Although *every* drawing is "composed", time constraints mean that often no more than a few moments can be taken to plan a quick concept sketch. More sophisticated drawings or drawings for more advanced stages of presentation, however—when making a detailed drawing of a final design, a drawing for a portfolio, or an editorial illustration for a magazine, for example—require considerable prior thought and planning if they are to be successful.

composition

croquis

The nine-head croquis is the basis for all modern fashion drawing. The legs are longer and the pelvis shorter than in real life. The figure is symmetrical about a central axis line.

Simple composition with nine-head croquis. The elongated legs and arms make the clothes appear larger than life.

composition

principles and elements of design/fashion drawing black and white v. color

Figure based on nine-head croquis in a composed setting.

PRINCIPLES OF DESIGN/ELEMENTS OF DESIGN

The results of the study over the centuries of the ideas and methods underlying good art and design have been distilled by artists and educators into a body of guidelines, or prescriptions, generally known as the PRINCIPLES OF DESIGN. These principles are: HARMONY/UNITY, FOCAL POINT/EMPHASIS, BALANCE, SCALE AND PROPORTION These principles are not rules or laws as in science (there are no firm rules in art and design) but are guidelines for making designs that present content in an effective and pleasing way.

The tools used in making art and design—LINE, SPACE, SHAPE, VALUE, TEXTURE, and COLOR—are generally referred to as the ELEMENTS OF DESIGN.

The application of the principles, and use of the elements of design in fashion drawing is, along with topics in color theory and design, discussed in detail in this chapter.

FASHION DRAWING—BLACK AND WHITE v. COLOR

Black and white drawing—line drawing using pen and/or ink on paper—allows for garments to be drawn with a high degree of accuracy: the silhouette of a garment, its drape, the type and weight of fabric used in its construction, the detailing, how the fabric wraps around and falls from the body—these key characteristics of a garment can all be expressed with no more than a pencil and paper.

Fashion drawing in color produces all of the effects of black and white drawing but adds a powerful new dimension, allowing a truer, more complete representation of the clothing to be made. Color is a strong defining feature of a garment, and the use of color in a fashion drawing supplies the main piece of information absent from a black and white drawing.

Color is also a valuable tool for accurately and convincingly representing the three-dimensional reality of a garment, as it allows subtle gradations of hue and value to be shown in the drape of the garment and in the figure. The ease with which, in almost any medium, color can be applied to large areas, and the effectiveness of a solid block of saturated color compared to a solid block of greyscale pencil or ink shading means also that a whole range of superior effects can be achieved with color.

As well as increasing the accuracy and realism of a drawing, the addition of color, when well done, allows the direct emotional, sensual, and cultural impact of the clothes that is directly related to their color to shine through. The drawing becomes exciting and engaging, arousing the interest and attention of the audience in a way it is difficult for a black and white drawing to do.

principles of design

composition in fashion drawing

COMPOSITION IN FASHION DRAWING

A fashion drawing is "composed" at a number of different levels and stages and design decisions have to be made at each. In most instances, though, a number of decisions are "given" or already made, and others are made quickly and intuitively. These generally include the design and colorways of the garments to be included in the drawing ,the combination of garments and choice of accessories. Very often a drawing is made with reference to a swatch of the actual fabric the garment is to be made of.

The variables in the drawing that are usually within the sphere of decision of the artist/designer are: (i) the pose, gestures and coloring of the basic figure drawing of the croquis with the subject garments and (ii) the composition of the figure or figures on the page, the background elements, skin tone, make up and hair, objects and empty (or"negative") space. This chapter is concerned mainly with the type of decisions described in (i) and (ii)— the composition of the figure itself and the composition of the figure or figures on the page. These topics recur repeatedly throughout the various chapters of this book.

PRINCIPLES OF DESIGN APPLIED TO FASHION DRAWING

For those beginning to draw fashion, and particularly for those who have no formal training in art and design, it is useful to become familiar with the principles of design and to develop an awareness of how and when they can be applied in drawings. The following section of this chapter reviews both the principles and elements of design, with illustrations of how they are applied in fashion drawing.

Unity. This drawing is unified in a number of ways: the silhouettes of the figures and garments are very similar; the figures are in almost identical mirror poses, close together and bending towards each other; the contrast between the dark and light pants provides a tension that further unifies the elements of the drawing.

principles of design

harmony/unity/proximity/repetition

Repetition. These figures are unified in the composition by repetition of color and shape—the hair color and skin tone, pose, styling of accessories, styling of the garments and proximity.

HARMONY/UNITY

The closest to a "golden rule" in design, as in art, is the concept of harmony, or—what is essentially the same idea—unity. The individual parts of a drawing must "fit together" in a unified, harmonious whole, or it will appear awkward and disjointed. Fashion drawings as mentioned, incorporate design decisions on a number of different levels, covering many different elements. All these many elements should fit together so as to form a coherent, unified composition.

With so many variables in play, many of the decisions to be made regarding whether certain elements "fit together" in a drawing are subjective, and numerous situations arise where there are no hard and fast rules indicating how best to proceed. A number of graphic devices do exist, though, to help unify a drawing. These are particularly useful if the elements to be included in the drawing do not seem to fit together naturally. The main device that are employed for unifying drawings are the following:

PROXIMITY

Elements placed close to each suggest unity. The eye does not have to travel large distances between the different elements and encompasses them all with ease.

REPETITION

Repetition of shapes, colors or effects can suggest unifying links. The repetitive themes of a line of clothing, for example—which can be emphasized to ensure the theme is noticed—can often of themselves bring unity to a composition.

principles of design

demetrios psillos

Demetrios Psillos
Breeds Apart

principles of design

harmony/ unity/ continuity/ variety/ focal point/emphasis

Continuity. A number of repeated but varying elements in this composition give continuity to the line of figures: hair-styling, skin-tone, fabric and color, accessories, details of the garment styling (top-stitching, bar tacks), cool and warm variations of the white fabric and the continuous dark/light contrasts within each outfit.

CONTINUITY

Continuing a line or the direction of a line, a series or sequence, or placing objects in a line—"aligning them"—can unify elements that might be distant from each other and would not otherwise immediately appear to be similar or connected. In a fashion drawing, for example, a series of shoes or other accessories might appear unconnected; drawing them on croquis wearing similar clothes, though, can introduce a unifying continuity into the composition.

VARIETY

Adding variety—making subtle differences among objects—can also draw attention to the similarities, and unity, between the same things. A drawing showing a number of different garments from a line will also display a number of common features that makes it feel like a unified line: garments with similar silhouettes, for example, might display a number of variations in lengths of the hem or sleeves or in other detailing.

FOCAL POINT/EMPHASIS

A drawing should catch the viewer's attention so the eye is attracted and encouraged to explore further. A device that helps achieve this is a focal point. A focal point is a point in a drawing to which the eye is drawn. Once the attention has been engaged the eye is led to the other parts of the drawing

In fashion drawing the garments themselves are usually made the focal point so that the eye will immediately be led to them as the most important aspect of the drawing.

A focal point is usually created by emphasizing one or more elements in a drawing—creating a contrast by making them differ from the others. This contrast or emphasis is often as simple as including a noticeably different shape or color, but can also include value contrasts, differing textures, changing the size or scale of objects, changing the scale or directions of patterns, changing line weight, changing the angles of planes, adding abstraction into a naturalistic setting (or vice-versa) or switching from rectilinear (straight-lined) to curvilinear (and also vice-versa).

A further way of creating emphasis or a focal point is through the placement of the elements in the drawing: for example, particular elements can be emphasized by arranging them in a pattern, or one element can be placed in isolation from the others. In the drawing opposite by Demetrios Psillos, the dog on the left serves as a focal point because of its size and location; the lines of the dog leashes then lead the eye around the other elements of the drawing.

It is not always essential to create a focal point in a fashion drawing, but there are a number of situations where it is a particularly useful device. If a drawing is complex, a focal point can create a point of entry, so simplifying the task of interpretation. Another example is where a drawing has many similar repeated elements—a white wedding dress for example. The addition of a contrasting section or

principles of design

balance/symmetry

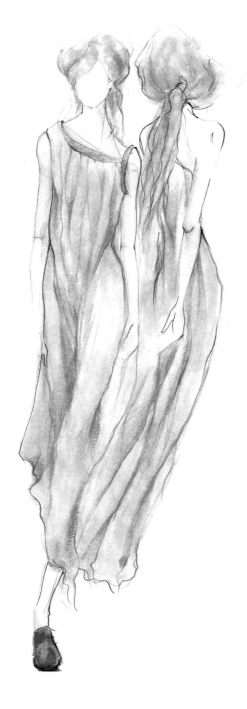

bright dash of color can serve to draw the eye into the picture to examine the different elements.

BALANCE/SYMMETRY

Balance is the relative weight between the elements on the left and right sides (and sometimes between top and bottom) of a drawing. The eye quickly senses if a drawing is not in balance: balance occurs when the eye is equally attracted to the components on each side of a composition. A "balanced" picture appears graceful and pleasing to the eye, so unless there are good reasons not to do so (if a disturbing effect is intentionally sought, for example), then a drawing should appear balanced.

Balance can be achieved in a number of different ways. The most obvious form of balance in a drawing is SYMMETRICAL BALANCE. This is where the two sides of the drawing are (in the extreme case) identical, or, more usually, contain similar elements of similar shapes and proportions. In a fashion drawing, for example, similar figures could be placed on either side of the page to create a satisfactory—though not necessarily interesting—sense of balance.

The human form is symmetrical. When the figure forms an asymmetrical pose—moving the hips to one side for example—there are offsetting moves both away from and back to the vertical center-axis line so that the figure always appears to maintain a "balance" (the eye also immediately senses if a figure is balanced or not). Just as with the actual human form, the left and right sides of the nine-head fashion figure are symmetrical—a hypothetical vertical center-axis line divides the drawing into two "mirror image" parts.

Asymmetrical balance. The two lighter colored figures on the left are in visual balance with the single dark-skinned figure on the right.

principles of design

asymmetry/balance

Asymmetrical composition. The figure on the right has a darker, more voluptuous dress that visually balances the two figures on the left

ASYMMETRY/BALANCE

A drawing cannot always be symmetrical, containing an even number of elements distributed evenly between its left and right sides. Fashion drawings in particular will often contain uneven numbers of figures—one, three or higher—that cannot be placed symmetrically on either side of the page as with two or four figures. It is important, though, that even if a drawing cannot be balanced by symmetry, it nevertheless appears balanced; that although objects on either the side of a drawing are dissimilar they hold an equal attraction for the eye. This type of balance can be achieved in a number of different ways and is referred to as "asymmetrical balance."

If a single figure is to be drawn it is often placed in the middle of the page. To add interest the head or one of the other parts of the body can be placed to one side, or some other element—a different movement or drape in the clothing or hair, or a subtle gesture or shift in expression—might be included. This creates an asymmetry in the figure which could cause a feeling of imbalance. To restore the sense of balance in the drawing an off-setting gesture is added that leads the eye back to the figure.

In a drawing with more than one figure—three figures, for example— two might be placed together in relatively simple vertical poses while the third figure might have a more extended pose and occupy a space similar in area to the other two figures.

A drawing can be "balanced"—meaning "brought into balance—by varying its main elements in a number of different ways. COLOR plays a major role in achieving balance and is discussed later in the chapter. VALUE CONTRAST—the difference in value—darkness and lightness—between two or more colors is also an important device to achieve balance: the eye is attracted to dark-light contrasts and a strongly contrasting combination of colors in one part of a drawing can offset larger shapes with a lesser degree of contrast in another part (for example, a patent leather handbag with high contrast between the high value of the white highlights of the shine and deep black of the body, held out from the figure might be used to offset a combination of garments of a single, or similar colors without shine).

TEXTURAL CONTRAST—using an interesting or detailed texture over a relatively small area can offset larger shapes with less pronounced texture.

Leading the eye away from shapes concentrated in one part of a drawing (to which it is naturally attracted) through the use of line or other means is another device also frequently used to bring balance to an asymmetrical composition. This effect can also be seen in the drawing by Demetrios Psillos earlier in the chapter.

elements of design in fashion drawing

line/contour drawing

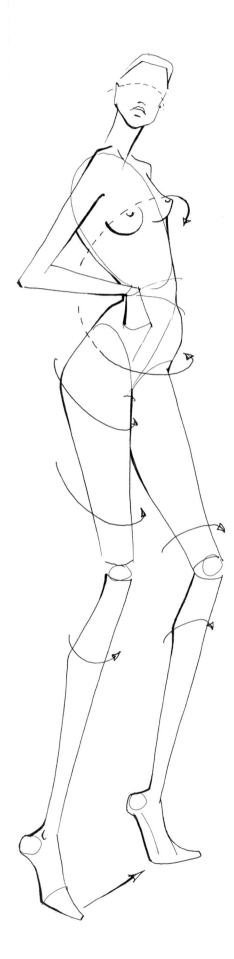

Nline-head croquis line drawing. The arrows highlight the three-dimensional cylindrical shapes on which the figure is based.

ELEMENTS OF DESIGN IN FASHION DRAWING

LINE

Lines are the most familiar elements in art and design and are present with us all from an early age in the form of drawing and writing.

In its purest form a line is the path traced by a point set in motion—it has length and no thickness. A line is also a physical mark on a surface—paper or some other substance —with a length greater than its width.

A line—a line on paper or another surface—is defined by a number of different variables: THICKNESS, LOCATION, DIRECTION AND QUALITY. The thickness of a line can vary greatly and is a most important variable in fashion drawing, as is line direction—whether a line is straight, curved, zigzag or angled, to name but a few of the possibilities. Line quality refers to the medium that is used to make the line and the weight, texture, speed and expressiveness of the line in that medium—the uniquely personal way different artists use line.

Line is important in art and design for a number of reasons, the principal reason being its ability to describe shape–the edges of objects. Drawings where lines are used to show the edges of objects are known as "contour drawings." Contour drawings are particularly important in fashion drawing, where the outside edge—the silhouette or contour— of a garment is usually a defining feature, and the other edges of shapes within the garment—seams, pleats, details—are also important. Flats, for example (flats are technical line drawings that serve as blueprints and contain critical data on shape, size and structure of a garment, similar to an architectural drawing) are extreme examples of contour drawings.

Line is also used in numerous other ways besides defining the shapes of objects: Line is used extensively to indicate the aspects of objects that make them appear three-dimensional. At the simplest level, for example, lines can be used in the form of "cross-hatching"—parallel lines of varying thickness and density—to create simple shading. In fashion drawing line is used in a number of ways to indicate the presence of the body under the garment, the curve of a garment around the body, different fabric types and more. These uses are discussed in detail in this chapter and also in the chapter on fabrics and are continually referred to in the explanations of drawings throughout the book.

Another type of line, important in art and design generally, and fashion drawing in particular, is the "implied line." This iš not an actual line but a line that is suggested by the continuation of a series of objects lined up in a drawing or the continuation of a gesture or glance. Implied lines can be useful for leading the eye around a drawing or, as mentioned, in balancing disparate elements.

elements of design in fashion drawing

line/line drawings

Vik Muniz
Rochas (Pictures of Wire), 2004

elements of design/use of line

use of line in fashion drawing/line thickness and weight

line curves to fit dress around shoulder

dark line, dark shadow

thin line, button hole

soft line indicates shadow on body

soft lines of torso under garment

shadow under buttonhole

seam

nuanced line

wide line to indicate shadow

dark, thick line for leather shoe

Use of different types of lines to express different features of a garment (here a wedding-dress by Ray Kawakubo).

LINE POSITIONING

Lines are themselves the result of movement and, in turn, to the eye they can suggest movement. This is an important characteristic for fashion drawing where it is often appropriate to capture the appearance of a garment when the body is in motion. The direction and positioning of lines can lead the eye and reinforce the sense of movement and vitality in a drawing: whereas horizontal lines suggest lack of movement, stability and equilibrium, for example, diagonal lines suggest movement and vitality.

LINE AND COLOR

In line drawing—drawings made with lines, usually created with a pen or pencil—the information in the drawing is conveyed solely by the use of line. As lines sometimes have to convey more than one type of information, the use of line has to be very precise in order to avoid confusion. When color is used, much of the information conveyed in a line drawing of a garment by line is conveyed, without line, through use of color: shading, for example, is expressed through gradating color through shades and tints and not through cross-hatching. This means that line can be used more selectively to bring additional information to a drawing, such as the position and shape of seams, slits, pocket detailing, pleats, trims and so on- or for stylistic effect.

USE OF LINE IN FASHION DRAWING

Information provided by line on shape, size, proportion and detail is conveyed mainly by the location and direction of straight and curved lines. A further type of information, beyond the information on the shape the line encloses, is communicated by the width of the line and weight of the ine itself.

Varying width and weight of line is a particularly useful device in fashion drawing, as it is well-suited to representing the differences between fabrics and the subtle visual effects of three-dimensional garments on the figure: drape lines, nuanced lines indicating depth and shadow and lines within the garment.

The principal ways to vary width and weight of line and their applications in fashion drawing are as follows:

LIGHT, THIN, CRISP (CLEAN EDGED) LINES, drawn with a sharp, hard graphite or mechanical pencil are useful for indicating light, crisp fabrics such as linen, taffeta, laces, tulle, polished cottons.

LIGHT, SOFT (FUZZY-EDGED) LINES drawn with the edge of a softer pencil are useful for indicating knits, bouclé, angora, embroidery, ribbing.

LIGHT THICK LINES can be used to indicate the fit of a garment- the position of the figure under the garment.

DARK, THIN, CRISP lines can be used to draw seams, shadows under buttons or other small details such as sequins, edges of jewelry, joints in accessories and shadows in crisp fabric.

elements of design/use of line

conventions for line use

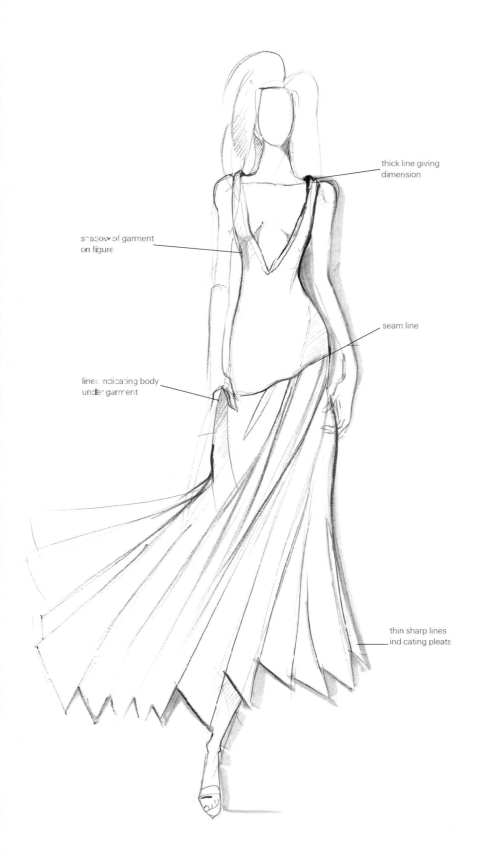

thick line giving
dimension

shadow of garment
on figure

seam line

lines indicating body
under garment

thin sharp lines
indicating pleats

Use of different types of lines to express different features of a garment, shown here in a dress by Versace.

DARK SOFT LINES can be used for soft fabrics in shadow and other items that are soft such as thick wool, quilts, heavy shoes, purses.

NUANCED LINES are lines that change in thickness and weight along their length, switching from light to dark, to thick to thin, to crisp to soft-edged, sometimes disappearing and reappearing as the line moves into and out of areas of light.

CONVENTIONS FOR LINE USE IN FASHION DRAWING
Besides the use of different types of line that realistically represent different type of fabrics or aspects of drawing the figure, there are also a number of "conventions" for line use in fashion drawing. Here the use of a particular type of line is, as much as it is a realistic representation of the visual reality, symbolic—in varying degrees—a psychological association with a quality of a fabric or garment. The main conventions for line use in fashion drawing are:

THIN LINES in general suggest lightness of weight, delicacy and detail.

THICK LINES in general suggest shadow—distance from the light source, weight and solidity.

LIGHT LINES in general suggest light—an object being lit.

To draw fashion effectively it is necessary to be able to draw lines in the different ways outlined above, as the situation demands. These variations in line, though, are independent of style and line quality—the overall way line is used.

There is considerable variation in use of line and line quality: for example, some artists, fashion illustrators and caricaturists (or cartoonists) are often-able to express a great deal about a facial expression or attitude, or the drape or line of a garment using little actual line—displaying what is referred to as an "economy of line." The opposite technique— a dense application of many lines—can also be used with excellent effect.

Notwithstanding these variations in style and usage, no single style of line is naturally superior to any other: the great fashion illustrators display a wide range of line quality and style. As with many other areas of art and design, the only requirements are that the final product is clear and aesthetically pleasing.

A line made with a single sweeping gesture is usually more elegant than a line made up of a series of small lines, sometimes referred to as "chicken scratches." Being able to draw elegant, expressive lines is a technique that requires practice to master. To draw graceful lines, it is important to sit gracefully, upright and perpendicular to the page. Keep the weight on the elbow and draw from the wrist. Focus on achieving precision and control—the qualities that need to be developed so that the lines of a garment can be drawn quickly and accurately. It is difficult to draw well when fatigued or upset.

color

primary/secondary colors/additive color process

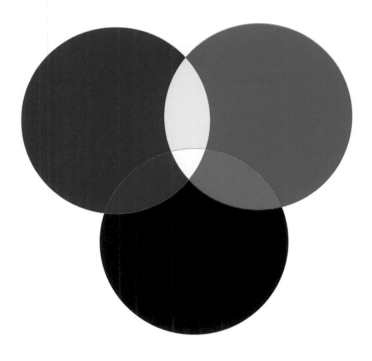

Combining the three primary colors of white light—red, green, and blue (RGB)— to form white and the three secondary colors, cyan, magenta and yellow (CMY). Note that the primary blue of white light almost appears more violet than blue.

The three secondary colors of white light—cyan, magenta and yellow—are also the primary colors of process color.

COLOR

White light is formed of rays of light of different colors, as can be demonstrated with a prism, which separates white light into its component hues, like a rainbow (note that "hues" is the term usually used to refer to colors in their "pure" state, though elsewhere in the book the terms "hues" and "colors" are used interchangeably). The hues of light, often called spectral hues—the hues of the spectrum—are red, orange, yellow, green, blue, indigo and violet (though some color experts do not now consider that indigo is part of the spectrum and prefer to recognize only the other six hues).

Although objects are commonly referred to as "being" a particular color, color is in fact not a property of objects but is the perception, by the human eye and brain in coordination, of light of various wavelengths reflected from objects. These different wavelengths of reflected light that are perceived by the human eye and brain correspond to different "colors". When white light falls on an object the object absorbs all the rays of white light except those corresponding to its "own color", and the object is then perceived as being of that color. A red object absorbs all the rays except red light; a blue object absorbs all the rays except blue and so on.

Objects of different textures—different types of fabrics for example—reflect light in different ways. A shiny fabric, no matter what its color, will tend to reflect all light at its highest points; no rays of light are absorbed and all the white light is reflected, so white highlights appear. Matt fabrics like wool absorb and reflect light uniformly and in consequence display a regularity of color across their surfaces, in contrast to the variations in color of shiny fabrics.

PRIMARY COLORS/SECONDARY COLORS/ADDITIVE COLOR PROCESS

Primary colors are colors that cannot be obtained by mixing other colors. The primary colors of white light are red, green and blue. Secondary colors are obtained by mixing two primaries together—blue and green gives cyan, red and green gives yellow and blue and red gives magenta.

Light mixes in a different way to pigments (the material that gives paints and inks their "color"). The primary colors of light—red, blue and green—can be added back to each other to recreate white light. This way in which colored rays of light combine is called an "additive" color process, or system, as shown in the illustration. TV, computer monitors and other visual projection technologies all generate ranges of colors through mixing of colored light according to the additive process (so called RGB— red, green and blue).

PIGMENTS/PROCESS COLORS

Pigments, the material that is the colored ingredient of paint, markers and other color media, mix together in a different way to rays of colored light, as do the colors used in printing and photography (these last activities are referred to when talking about

color

pigments/process colors/ subtractive color process

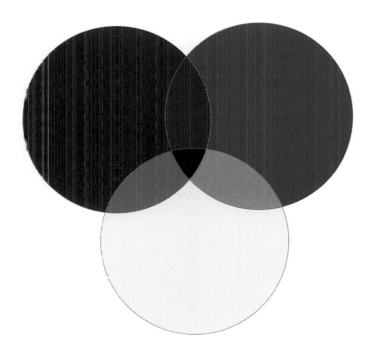

Mixing the pigment primaries.
The pigment primaries—red, yellow and blue, combine in pairs to form the pigment secondaries-orange, green and violet. Pigments combine in a "subtractive color process". The combination of all three pigment primaries, in theory, filters out all colors forming black. In practice, impurities bring about a result that is not pure black.

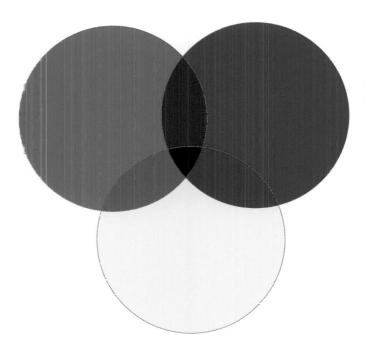

Mixing the process primaries.
The process primaries—cyan, magenta and yellow—combine in pairs to form the process secondaries—orange, green and violet—the same as the pigment secondaries. Process colors, like pigments, combine in a "subtractive color process." The combination of all three process primaries in theory filters out all colors forming black, but again in practice the result is not pure black but more mud-colored.

color as processes , and the colors associated with them as "process colors"). The primary hues of traditional pigments are red, yellow and blue, and the primary hues of processes (the process primaries) are cyan, magenta and yellow, referred to as CMY (CMYK is CMY + black, for which K is a symbol). CMY are also the secondary colors of the primary additive system of white light, that is, the secondary colors formed by mixing pairs of the primaries red, green and blue.

SUBTRACTIVE COLOR PROCESSES

Pigments and process colors combine in what is known as a "subtractive" color process (or color system) and mixing colors produces different results from those obtained by combining light of those same colors. The results of mixing the pigment and process primaries to give their secondaries is shown in the illustration. Note that the secondaries of both pigment and process primaries are the same—orange, green and violet. The process is known as subtractive because of the nature of pigments: their "color" comes from their properties of filtering out all the components of white light with the exception of their "own color". Combining two pigments is in effect the same as placing one set of filters on top of another—"subtracting" a further set of the components of white light from the first. This is why paints (in their many forms) lose intensity—or saturation, as it is often called—when mixed together, forming "neutrals"—browns or greys. Mixing all three primaries together filters out the whole spectrum of white light, leaving, in theory, black, though in practice pigment impurities and differing solvent concentrations mean the result is not pure black.

Mixing processes for markers, as for all other pigments, are subtractive, so mixes tend towards black—in actuality though, resembling mud more than coal—as more colors are added.

color

value/value keys

Draped fabric with a wide range of values.

PROPERTIES OF COLOR

VALUE

Value is the technical term used to refer to the lightness or darkness of a color. Lighter versions of a color are said to have higher values, and darker versions lower values. Adding white to a color makes it lighter, increasing its value and producing what is known as a "tint." Adding black darkens a color, lowering its value and creating what is known as a "shade." Mixing colors will result in a new color somewhere between the original colors in value. "Blending" a color—diluting it with its solvent (colorless blender for markers)—makes it lighter, increasing the value. Examples of altering the value of a color are shown in the section on mixing colors in Chapter One: Materials and Techniques.

Value is an important characteristic of color for fashion drawing. Fabric, when made into garments that are then hung on the figure, drapes naturally, displaying a range of color values the breadth of which varies according to the type of fabric. A garment with a lot of drape, and deep folds, will display high color values on its flat surfaces and ridges, possibly even a shine or sheen, the highest value of the color—white; in the folds the color will decrease in value, often appearing black—the lowest value of the color—in the deepest recesses. This phenomenon, the gradual shift in value from high to low and low to high, is, referred to in this book as "gradation of tone," as has already been seen in Chapter One. How gradation of tone appears in different fabrics and types of drape and how it is rendered in fashion drawing with markers is covered extensively in the chapter on fabrics.

Different colors have different intrinsic value levels, and are commonly known as light and dark colors. Yellow is light, higher in value than blue, which is dark, lower in value than yellow.

VALUE KEYS

Value keys are groups of different colors of the same value—all with the same degree of lightness or darkness. Designs sometimes make use of colors of similar value and/or saturation levels, as described below in the section on color schemes.

properties of color

saturation

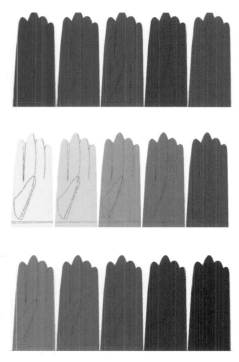

Adding progressive amounts of grey of the same value level to colors reduces the saturation of the colors, finally resulting in grey.

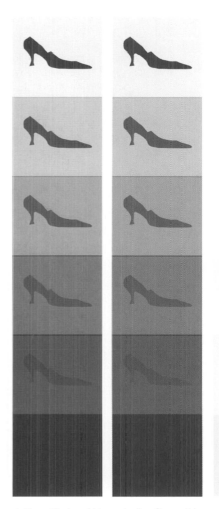

Adding white to red, blue and yellow. Red and blue are lower value colors and their values increase significantly and saturation decreases with the addition of white. Yellow is a high value color and its value changes less as saturation decreases with the addition of white. The shoes in each column are of the same value and saturation levels.

SATURATION/INTENSITY

One of the main properties of color is its "saturation," or "level of saturation." When used in describing color, "saturation" has the same meaning as "intensity" or "purity".

Saturation can be easily understood by visualizing the process of *lowering* the saturation of a color: Lowering saturation is achieved by adding grey of a similar value. As more grey is added the color loses saturation (though keeping the same value) eventually giving way to pure grey. Adding grey to a color results in what is called a "tone"—a less saturated version of the color. The saturation of a color can also be decreased by mixing it with its complementary color, resulting in an increasingly muddy, neutralized version.

Increasing the saturation of a color, on the other hand, is achieved by adding more of the same color, displacing greys and neutral elements or adding an already more saturated version of the same color. (A common misconception about colored markers is that they cannot create intense, saturated colors, such as those that can be achieved with oils, gouaches or acrylics. Highly saturated colors can in fact be created quite easily with markers as is shown in Chapter One: Materials and Technique.)

CHANGING VALUE AND SATURATION SIMULTANEOUSLY

The value of a color is changed, as mentioned, by adding white, black or grey, to produce tints, shades or tones. Changing the value also changes the saturation level—the purity or intensity of the color.

Making a color more saturated by adding a purer version of the same color to it, or making it less saturated by adding grey also changes the value of the color according to whether the pure color or grey being added is higher or lower in value than that to which it is added.

properties of color

decreasing color saturation—increasing value

Decreasing saturation, increasing value. Here, the blue of the dress becomes lighter—higher in value— as its saturation decreases through addition of white pencil and colorless blender. The resulting lighter blue color at the left of the drawing is a "tint" of the original blue.

properties of color

decreasing color saturation–decreasing value

Decreasing saturation, decreasing value. Here the blue of the dress becomes darker—lower in value—as its saturation decreases through addition of black marker. The resulting darker blue color at the left of the drawing is a "shade" of the original blue.

color wheels

additive/subtractive color wheels

The additive color wheel showing the three primary colors of white light—red, green and blue (RGB)— and the three secondaries—cyan, magenta and yellow (CMY). (P = primary color, S = secondary color.)

The traditional subtractive system color wheel. The wheel shows the position of the three primaries, RYB, the three secondaries, OGV and the six tertiaries, RO, RV, YO, YG, BV and BG . (P = primary color, S = secondary color, T = tertiary color.)

COLOR WHEELS

Color wheels have been in use for several hundred years as tools showing the separation of the colors of the spectrum into distinct colors—or "hues" as the colors of the spectrum are known in their pure states. Color wheels are a way to display the spectrum of colors so that the relations among them become clearly apparent.

Different color wheels exist to show color relations for pigment and process subtractive systems and for additive systems. The color wheel for additive systems—the component rays of white light—show the three additive primaries—red, green and blue— and the secondaries—cyan, magenta and yellow— as shown in the illustration.

The traditional subtractive system color wheel has twelve segments representing the three primary hues, three secondaries and six tertiaries. The wheel shown here is based on that devised by Johannes Itten (1888–1967), an artist from the German Bauhaus school working in the second half of the twentieth century. The three subtractive primaries—red, yellow and blue—are shown as equidistant segments with their secondaries, orange, green and violet lying mid-way between the primaries. The tertiaries—red-violet, red-orange, yellow-green, yellow-orange, blue-green and blue-violet— lie between their component primaries and secondaries.

Artists and designers are interested primarily in the pigment subtractive wheel as an aid in predicting the results of mixing colors of paints or inks. The additive system wheel is also directly relevant as it shows the relations among the component colors of white light, of use when considering the results of interactions among perceived colors, which reach the eye as rays of light, and how to combine colors harmoniously. Because both subtractive and additive mixing processes are of relevance to artists and designers, sometimes red, blue, green and yellow are all considered as primaries—the combination of the additive and subtractive primaries.

It is important to note that the traditional subtractive color wheels showing the primary and secondary subtractive are guides and do not usually give accurate predictions of the results of direct mixing of colored pigments, due to variations in pigments, the type of solvents they are used with and different concentrations. Constant experimentation is necessary and mixed colors should always be tested before being applied.

color wheels

color wheel relationships/color values/complementary colors

Inherent values of colors. Colors are arranged from the highest value—the lightest— on top, to the lowest value— the darkest— at the bottom. The position of each color in this diagram is also equivalent in height to its position on the color wheel.

As was seen in the demonstration of mixing marker colors in the chapter on technique, when the mixing process is a subtractive one, the results, particularly if the colors are distant from each other on the color spectrum, are usually muddy—the colors have tended to neutralize each other rather than produce vibrant new colors. Better results are obtained when mixing colors closer to each other in the spectrum, or by using blender, white or grey or black to achieve the effects of more transparent, more neutral, darker or lighter values or less saturated versions of a color.

(When markers were first produced color ranges were limited; now, however, there are hundreds of colors available. If budget permits—and a marker collection can be built up over a period of time so the cost can be spread out—then it is always best to use the marker with the pure pigment closest to the desired color. It will almost invariably be brighter and more saturated than a mixed color).

COLOR WHEEL RELATIONSHIPS

COLOR VALUES
The different colors on the color wheel have different values—degrees of lightness and darkness. The color wheel is usually drawn with the highest value color—yellow—at the top. The colors on both sides of the wheel become progressively darker—lower in value—towards the bottom of the wheel, where the darkest hue, violet, is situated. In the diagram on the left the colors of the wheel have been re-arranged in two columns with the highest value colors at the top and the lowest at the bottom.

COMPLEMENTARY COLORS
Colors opposite to each other on the color wheel are known as complementary colors, so called because they "complement"—or complete— each other. With additive, light-based color processes, when complementary colors are combined they form white. With subtractive, pigment-based processes complementary colors "neutralize" each other and tend to black.

The complementary color relationship is central to understanding color and making color decisions, in all areas of art and design as well as in fashion drawing and design.

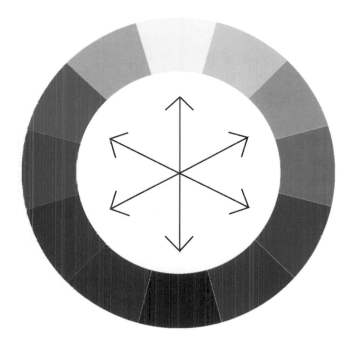

Complementary colors—colors opposite to each other on the color wheel.

color wheels

analogous hues/color temperature

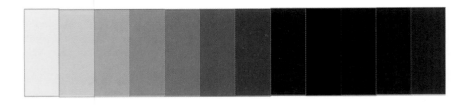

Adding complementary colors to each other in progressive amounts. At the point where similar amounts of each hue are mixed the colors are "neutralized" and the result is a "muddy" color.

ANALOGOUS HUES
Analogous hues, sometimes referred to as color families, are groups of two or three hues next to each other on the color wheel.

COLOR TEMPERATURE
The hues on the color wheel are almost equally divided between what are commonly referred to as warm colors and cool colors. Warm colors—those adjacent colors spanning from red to yellow—are supposedly associated with warmth and light; cool colors—those from green to violet—are supposedly associated with cold and dark. Yellow-green and red-violet are on the borders between warm and cool, and can take on either characteristic depending on their context. Variations of the primary colors can appear either warm or cool depending on whether they are mixed with warm or cool colors. Whites, greys and neutrals are known as warm or cool if the colors they are mixed with are warm or cool.

Although referring to colors as warm and cool is a widely used convention in design, in both fashion and other areas, and is used extensively in this book, it should be noted that this classification into cool and warm is essentially psychologically and culturally based: the association is not in fact made in all cultures and its validity is questioned by some experts in color.

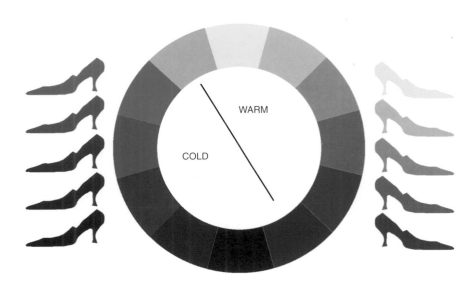

The color wheel is almost equally divided between the so-called cold and warm colors.

color wheel relationships

color chords

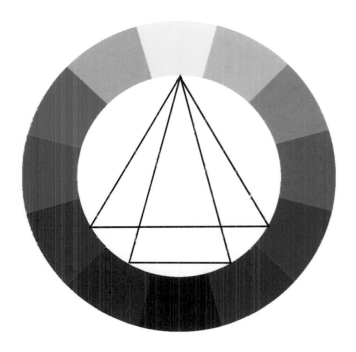

Triadic color chords, based on three colors. The chords are defined by either equilateral (all sides are equal) or isosceles (two sides are equal) triangles. The triangles can be rotated to any position on the wheel to indicate triads made up of other color groups.

COLOR CHORDS

Certain groups of colors spaced out on the color circle are known as color chords. These are groups of colors that, using the musical analogy, combine in a harmonious fashion, each with a different character.

Chords are formed of two, three, four or more colors, with each color in its group standing in a geometric relation to the other color. For two colors, chords are directly opposite each other on the color wheel, being pairs of complementary colors, for example yellow and violet. These pairs are known as complementry dyads, "dyad" meaning "two."

Color chords of three colors are known as triads (meaning "three"). Triads are either equidistant colors, in configurations of equilateral triangles (triangles with sides of equal lengths) for example red, green and blue—the additive primary triad—or form isosceles triangles (triangles with two sides of equal length). Triads that form the shape of an isosceles triangle are composed of a color at the apex of the triangle matched with the two colors lying on either side of its complementary color, known as "split complementaries."

Color chords of four colors form squares or rectangles (tetrads, for example orange, red, green and blue).

The geometric shapes of color chords can be rotated within the color wheel to give numerous color chord combinations.

A similarly harmonious result to that of color chords, is also said to apply to colors of the same hue but different, equi-distant levels of saturation or value. These and harmonious color combinations in general are discussed later in the chapter in the section on color harmonies and schemes.

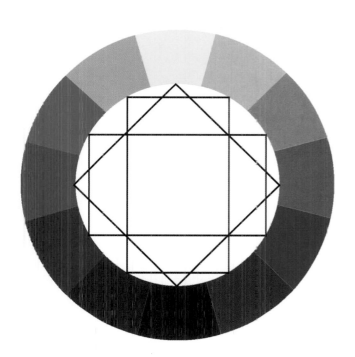

Tetradic color chords, based on four colors. The chords are defined by a square or rectangle inside the color wheel. Square tetrads are composed of two pairs of complementary colors.

composition in color

color chords

The colors in this outfit form a tetrad on the color wheel— blue-green, yellow, red-orange and violet.

The colors in this outfit form a complementary dyad on the color wheel—yellow and violet.

The colors in this outfit form a triad on the color wheel—blue-violet, red-violet and yellow.

composition

color chords

The colors in this outfit form a dyad on the color wheel—yellow and violet.

The colors in this outfit form a tetrad on the color wheel— blue-green, yellow, red-orange and violet.

The colors in this outfit form a tetrad on the color wheel— yellow-green, yellow-orange, red-violet and blue-violet.

color relativity and contrast

interaction of colors

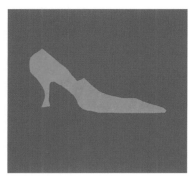

Color relativity. The shoes are all the same color but appear different against backgrounds of different colors.

COLOR RELATIVITY AND CONTRAST

Colors are rarely viewed alone, in isolation, but are generally seen together with other colors. The appearance of a color varies according to the conditions in which it is viewed—the conditions and direction of the light—and the colors that are adjacent to it. Artists have always been aware of this relativity of color and it has been commented on since the time of Leonardo da Vinci.

The French chemist Michel Eugene Chevreul (1786–1889) was one of the first to explore color relativity. Chevreul was the director of a factory that produced tapestries. He found that the color of a dye would often appear to change between the design stage and the actual printed fabric. Upon investigation he discovered that the problem was not related to the dyes but was optical, due to the influence of one color placed directly against another. Chevreul called this phenomenon "simultaneous contrast."

The artist, educator and writer on color, Josef Albers (1888–1976) in his book *Interaction of Color* believed that it is rare to see a color that is not influenced by the presence of other colors. He compared the relative sensations received by the sense of sight with the relative sensations received by the sense of touch. As an illustration he suggested the experiment of placing the left hand in cold water, the right in hot, then moving both hands to a container of lukewarm water. To the left hand that had been in the cold water, the lukewarm water feels hot; to the right hand that had been in the hot water the lukewarm water feels cold. Albers claimed that colors interact with each other in a similar way and appear different depending on the colors to which they are adjacent.

The interaction of colors is highly relevant in fashion drawing, where often a number of colors will be present in the drawing and a large number of possible color combinations from which a unique selection has to be made are possible. Fabric colors and combinations of fabrics of different colors, skin tone, hair, facial skin tone, make-up, accents, background colors all have to be chosen with reference to each other and in such a way that everything appears to fit together.

To make effective and coherent choices about combining color, it is important to be aware of the principal ways that colors interact with each other. These ways in which colors interact are the basis of formal color "schemes", where specific combinations of colors are selected, as well as being present in any color composition, whether the colors are presented in a "scheme" or not.

The interactions of color have been described and classified in a number of different ways, and the process is on-going, with new books about color and color interaction appearing with regularity. To provide a brief, explanatory framework for the different ways in which colors interact, the principal conclusions on the topic of Josef Albers and another great colorist, Johannes Itten, already referred to

interaction of colors/color contrast

contrast of hue

above, are summarized below.

Although Albers and Itten's views are their own personal opinions, and there is not clear supporting scientific evidence for them all (as is very often the case for theories that attempt to explain phenomena that are based on individual subjective perception) their views, nevertheless, do provide a clear, comprehensive and concise way of thinking about how colors interact. Albers' approach in the classroom was in fact to develop his students' sensitivity to colors through extensive experimentation before teaching about charts and tables. For those studying color in order to make more informed color decisions in fashion drawing and design developing a direct sensitivity to color relations is as important, (or moreso) as an awareness of the scientific knowledge and theories of those relations.

In his book *The Art of Color* Johannes Itten lists seven types of color contrast. These are:

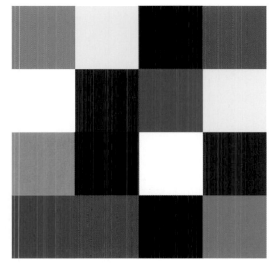

Contrast of hue.

CONTRAST OF HUE
LIGHT-DARK CONTRAST
COLD–WARM CONTRAST
COMPLEMENTARY CONTRAST
SIMULTANEOUS CONTRAST
CONTRAST OF SATURATION
CONTRAST OF EXTENSION

CONTRAST OF HUE
Although the strongest contrast in colors is between black and white, black and white are not, strictly speaking, colors, but "achromatics"—meaning "without color". Among true colors (the "chromatics") the highest degrees of pure contrast of hue are between pairs of the additive primaries—red, green and blue—and pairs of the subtractive primaries—red, yellow and blue. This is because primaries are pure hues and do not contain color elements from the other primaries. Secondary colors also contrast, but less than primaries as they always have one primary color element in common. In general, the colors that contrast most with each other are those that are furthest apart on the color wheel—meaning they have fewer component colors in common.

Detail of fabric showing contrasting hues.

interaction of colors/color contrast

light-dark value contrast/cold-warm contrast

Light–dark contrast. The pairs of shoes in each row are the same color but appear lighter against a dark background and darker against a light background. Note this effect also works for the achromatic grey in the bottom row.

Cold–warm contrast.

LIGHT—DARK VALUE CONTRAST

Light and dark colors contrast. The greatest light-dark value contrast, as for hue contrast, is that between black, the darkest color, and white, the lightest. Contrasts also exist among the chromatic colors , according to how far apart the colors are on the color wheel, as shown in the diagram of the ordering of colors by value.

If a color is placed against a darker background the contrast in values will make it appear lighter; if it is placed against a lighter background the contrrast in values will make it appear darker.

COLD—WARM CONTRAST

As discussed, some colors seem warm, suggesting warmth and light, and others seem cool, suggesting cold temperatures and darkness. On the color wheel approximately half the colors are warm and half are cool.

Warm and cool colors also influence other colors when placed together, warm primaries and secondaries making other colors warmer, cool primaries and secondaries making other colors coolers. Warm and cool colors can present interesting contrasts, accentuating the temperature of each other as well as the particular hues.

In fashion drawing a decision is often made to make the overall color scheme, or parts of it, cool or warm. If a cool color scheme is opted for, various elements can be made "cool": for example, light beige skin tone can be made cool by the addition of a small amount of blue. Conversely, red or another warm color can be added to the skin tone or to the shadows of a white garment if a warm color scheme is desired.

interaction of colors/color contrast

cold-warm contrast

Drawing based on cold–warm contrast (red- and blue-based colors).

color relativity and contrast

complementary contrast/simultaneous contrast/contrast of saturation

Complementary contrast. The complementary colors in each pair accentuate each other and vibrate against each other.

COMPLEMENTARY CONTRAST

Complementary colors are "opposite" colors—those that are directly across from each other on opposite sides of the color wheel. For the subtractive color wheel, complementary colors are traditionally the pairs of the three primaries, red, blue and yellow, with their non related secondaries, green, orange and violet, and for the additive colors, red and cyan, blue and yellow, green and magenta.

Complementary color pairs accentuate each of the colors—a simultaneous contrast of colors—causing them to vibrate next to each other, sometimes an interesting effect for a drawing. A large area of background color with a small area of its complement in the middle makes the complement seem brighter and more saturated.

SIMULTANEOUS CONTRAST

Chevreul use the term "simultaneous contrast" to refer to the general phenomenon of the interaction of colors. Itten developed this idea and related it to the "afterimage effect" noted with complementary colors: If the eye stares at an area of saturated color for a while and then looks away to a white wall or blank sheet of paper, the complementary color appears. The eye simultaneously "requires" the complementary color to appear and generates it spontaneously if it is not present. Stated in another way, a color provides its own complementary color as a contrast even though that color is not actually present in a physical form on the surface.

CONTRAST OF SATURATION

Contrast of saturation is the contrast between saturated, highly intense colors and dull, neutralized colors. As mentioned, the saturation levels of colors can be changed by adding black, white, grey or the complementary color, resulting in shades, tints, or neutralized versions of the original color. These different levels of saturation of the same hue provide an interesting contrast that is frequently used in fashion drawing.

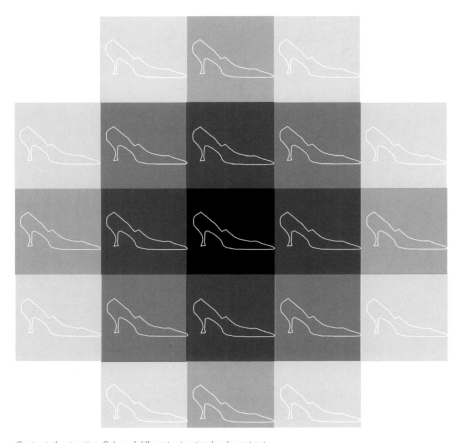

Contrast of saturation. Colors of different saturation levels contrast. The more saturated colors here are also darker, and so dark—light contrast is also present.

color relativity and contrast

contrast of extension

CONTRAST OF EXTENSION

High value colors such as yellow are brighter, and have more visual prominence or impact than low value colors like blue. To combine two colors of differing values so as to give a sense of balanced composition the proportions have to be varied. The numerical values recommended for combining colors by the famous German poet, playwright, novelist and philosopher Johann Wolfgang von Goethe (1749–1832) who also published a work on color theory—*The Theory of Colors*—are (as adapted by Johannes Itten):

Yellow   3
Orange   4
Red   6
Green   6
B ue   8
Violet   9

This weighting system would suggest that in order to achieve balance for an orange and blue composition, for example, the colors should appear in the proportion of 4/8—twice as much blue as orange; for green and violet 6/9 and so on. The drawing opposite is made using Goethe's proportions.

Gretchen—an homage to Goethe.
Contrast of extension. This composition contains colors in the proportions recommended for color balance by Goethe—violet and yellow in the proportions 9/3.

color relativity and contrast

bezold effect/subtraction

The Bezold effect—changing the dominant background color alters the relative appearance of the other colors in a composition.

Subtraction. Top, the dominant green background (G) "subtracts" itself from the yellow-green shoe (Y+G), making it appear closer to yellow. Below, the dominant red background (R) "subtracts" itself from the violet (composed of red and blue (R+B) shoe making it appear closer to blue.

THE BEZOLD EFFECT

The Bezold Effect, named after Wilhelm von Bezold, a nineteenth-century German textile chemist, is a color effect of great importance to the textile and fashion manufacturing industries and also relevant in fashion drawing. Bezold manufactured rugs, and discovered that changing one of the colors in a pattern in rugs changed the overall color appearance of the pattern. The effect is seen more strikingly when the dominant color is changed, particularly in patterns, where colors are directly adjacent to each other, than in composed drawings, but even in drawings the effect is important. The effect is particularly relevant when printing patterns on fabrics using different color variations.

SUBTRACTION

This effect, discussed, by Josef Albers in his book Interaction of Color , suggests that a dominant color—a color "ground," as he called it—will "subtract" itself from the less dominant color so the less dominant color appears different than it would against a neutral background. This concept can be understood by looking at the components of colors. For example, in the illustrations on the left, if green is the dominant color and yellow-green the less dominant, green (G) is subtracted from yellow-green (Y+G) to give the yellow-green more the appearance of yellow (Y). If red (R) is the dominant color and violet (V) is the less dominant, violet being a mixture of red (R) and blue (B), the red subtracts itself from the violet giving it a more blue appearance.

color harmonies and schemes/simple harmony

monochromatic/analogous/achromatic schemes

Monochromatic color scheme.

COLOR HARMONIES AND SCHEMES

Color schemes are guidelines for choosing groups of colors that will harmonize, forming combinations that are pleasing to the eye. Formal color schemes are based on combinations of colors from the color wheel, selected according to various rules.

There are three types of formal schemes: Schemes based on a limited number of colors or neutrals are often referred to as SIMPLE HARMONY SCHEMES.

Schemes based on opposite or contrasting harmonies, using colors from different sides of the color wheel or temperature contrasts, are often referred to as CONTRASTING HARMONY SCHEMES.

Schemes based on color chords—equally-spaced colors on the color wheel—are referred to as BALANCED COLOR HARMONY SCHEMES. As balanced color harmony schemes often embrace colors distantly spaced on the wheel they are sometimes also in fact contrasting, as well as balanced harmonies.

SIMPLE COLOR HARMONY SCHEMES

Simple color harmony schemes group colors that are close together on the color wheel or of similar levels of value and saturation. A common simple color harmony scheme for example is neutrals of different hues but similar saturation levels. These schemes generally yield safe, predictable results, but can be wanting in range and excitement, though atypical uses can be striking. Sometimes the dominant color of a composition or design is referred to as its "tonality." Paintings of Picasso's so-called Blue Period, for example, have a marked blue tonality. Both monochromatic and analogous color schemes, described below, usually display a particular color tonality.

MONOCHROMATIC COLOR SCHEMES
Monochromatic color schemes are schemes based on a single hue, e.g., red or blue. These schemes have only value and saturation contrast, no (or very little) hue contrast, and display a certain "tonality," as referred to above.

ANALOGOUS SCHEMES
Analogous schemes are based on analogous colors—colors from the same family of two or three neighboring hues on the color wheel. Analogous schemes are extensions of monochromatic color schemes, also displaying little hue contrast, with the exception of yellow-orange and yellow-green. Often with analogous color schemes one of the colors dominates the others, in which case these schemes also display particular "tonalities".

ACHROMATIC SCHEMES
Achromatic schemes are based on pure achromatics—white, black and greys or chromatic neutrals resulting from mixing complementary colors or mixes of earth colors and black and/or white.

color harmonies and schemes/ simple harmony

analogous/ achromatic schemes

Analogous color scheme. The colors in this drawing are
three hues adjacent to each other on the color wheel.

Achromatic scheme. This drawing is based on "greyscale"
achromatic colors—black, white and greys.

color harmonies and schemes/contrasting harmony

cool-warm schemes

Color scheme based on cold–warm harmonious contrast.

CONTRASTING COLOR HARMONIES AND SCHEMES

As opposed to simple color schemes where the colors are close to each other on the color wheel and provide little contrast of hue, when contrasting colors are used in schemes the potential for clashing colors is greater and more care has to be given to ensure the combinations are harmonious.

COLD-WARM COLOR SCHEMES

These schemes are based on combinations of a pair of adjacent hues from the "cold" (blue) side of the color wheel and an adjacent pair from the "warm" (red) side. The colors can be from anywhere on their side of the wheel, and can appear as tints and shades, so the scheme is quite flexible.

SPLIT COMPLEMENTARIES.

Split complementaries are schemes based on three colors where a color is linked with the two colors adjacent to its complementary color on the color wheel. For example, red, whose complementary color is green, could be linked with green's adjacent hues, yellow-green and blue-green. Split complementary schemes display color balance—equal distances between colors on the color wheel—as well as contrast of hues, an often pleasing combination.

DOUBLE COMPLEMENTARIES

These schemes use two adjacent hues with their complementary pair. As with cool-warm schemes, the hues can appear in varying levels of saturation and value. The expanded color range softens the stark contrast of saturated complementaries.

COMPLEMENTARY DYAD SCHEMES

These color schemes are based on two contrasting complementary colors on the color wheel—either one primary and the opposing secondary or two opposing tertiaries. Chromatic neutrals are also examples of complementary dyad schemes—they are groups of neutralized versions of pairs of complementary colors.

color harmonies and schemes/balanced

triad/tetrad schemes

A color scheme based on a triad—green, violet and orange.

A color scheme based on a tetrad—blue-green, violet, red-orange and yellow.

A color scheme based on the primary triad—blue, red and yellow.

A color scheme based on a triad—green, violet and orange.

color harmonies and schemes/balanced schemes

triad/tetrad schemes

A color scheme based on a tetrad—blue-green, violet, red-orange and yellow.

BALANCED COLOR HARMONY SCHEMES

Balanced color harmony schemes are based on colors equidistant on the color wheel which harmonize like equidistant notes in a musical chord.

TRIAD SCHEMES

Balanced harmony triads are three equally spaced hues, forming equilateral (equal-sided) triangles based on the three primaries, three secondaries or two combinations of the six tertiaries. Each hue in a triad of this type is exactly between the other two hues, so triads are always vibrant with maximum contrast of hue. Triads—groups of three colors—that are not of this type, such as split complementary triads. are contrasting, but not balanced harmonies.

A variation of a triadic scheme commonly used is to employ two of the three colors from a triad, for example red and yellow from the primary triad red, yellow and blue.

TETRAD SCHEMES

Tetrads have also been discussed in the section on color chords. Tetrad schemes are four-color schemes based on two pairs of colors where the distance between the colors in each pair is the same. In geometric terms, this means four hues which form a square or rectangular shape on the color wheel. Tetrads have a wide variation in hues and the best results are usually obtained by combining them with another scheme such as value or saturation keys.

color harmonies and schemes/contrasting harmony

split complementary scheme

A color scheme based on a split complementary. Blue, whose complementary color is orange, is combined with the colors adjacent to orange—yellow-orange and red-orange.

color harmonies and schemes/balanced harmony

color keys

COLOR KEYS

Color keys isolate one property of a color—hue, value or saturation. Keys based on one hue where the value or saturation is varied are also monochromatic schemes. Colors of similar value levels or saturation levels can also be grouped together in a unified manner, irrespective of their relative positions on the color wheel.

Scheme based on a color key—the level of saturation. The colors have the same level of saturation.

color harmonies and schemes

color accents/other schemes /color order

Color accents.

COLOR ACCENTS
Color accents are not, strictly speaking, color schemes, but are uses of relatively small amounts of colors against dominant background colors. The accents usually contrast with the background in one of the color contrast ways discussed, and are also usually relatively higher value and/or colors of higher saturation than the background colors. A common use of color accents, for example, is dashes of a bright color against a muted, neutral or achromatic background. If the quantity of color used in the accent increases then the accents tend to lose their piquancy.

OTHER COLOR SCHEMES
Besides color schemes that fall within the three types of formal schemes where the combinations of colors are chosen according to rules, a number of informal harmonic schemes also exist where the rules are more flexible. The simplest schemes are based on varying a group of two to four colors by producing tints, shades and tones.

A number of schemes isolate one aspect of a color such as value or saturation, referred to above. Other schemes are based on tonal (value) gradations within one or more colors, gradation of saturation levels and gradation of hue. A number of these schemes are employed in the drawings throughout this book.

COLOR ORDER AND SERIES
Color order and series—large topics in themselves—are schemes that encompass color combinations over extensions greater than the single page. They are more relevant, for example, to the ordering of pages in a portfolio or placement of colors on a presentation board than to individual compositions.

Color orders suggest logical ways to arrange objects of different colors. Colors can be ordered according to position on the color wheel, value, saturation and then distributed according to horizontal, vertical or diagonal grids.

color harmonies and schemes

subjective color and discord

Discordant colors.

SUBJECTIVE COLOR AND DISCORD

Color schemes are useful as guidelines for producing harmonious color combinations. Color combination is not an exact science, and as the number of variables involved in color composition and the ranges of values of each of those variables are great, it is quite possible to produce harmonious compositions outside of the guidelines of the formal color schemes. Once the artist/designer steps outside these color scheme guidelines, however, it is necessary to have a well developed sense of color, as there is a greater risk of committing mistakes and arriving at discordant color combinations.

DISCORDANT COLORS

Discordant colors are colors that have no real affinity to each other: they are not analogous, do not share similarity of value or saturation, nor do they balance each other as complementary contrasts or color chords. What is a discordant pair of colors in isolation, though, might not be discordant in a context where several other colors are present—or at least the discord might be offset by other effects.

Color discord is sometimes an intentional device in art and design, used in cases where the subject itself is unsettling or uncomfortable, and in fashion drawing too discord can also be employed to create an unsettled tone, of use, for example, for emphasizing the "edginess" of a particular garment.

composition in color

putting the elements together

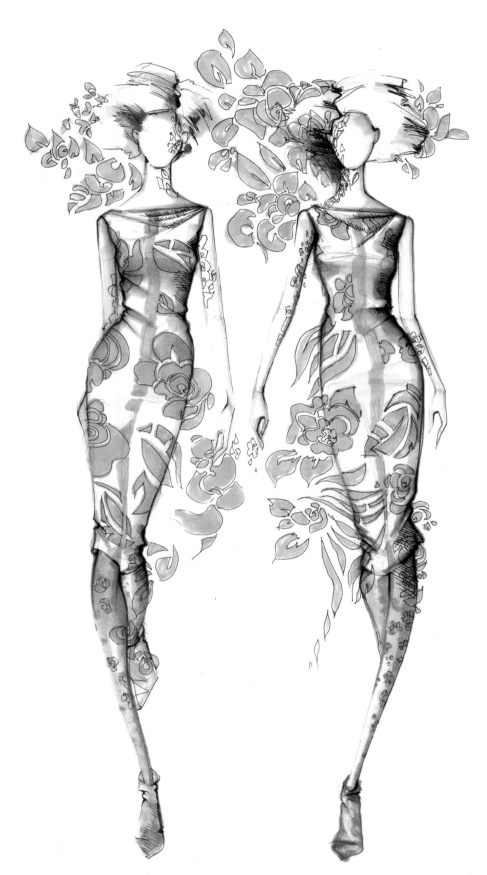

COMPOSITION IN COLOR

The different aspects of the facts, theories, principles and practices underlying color and design have been discussed separately. When making an actual fashion drawing all the decisions about color and design have to be made quickly and in rapid succession.

Color brings a new dimension to a drawing. Color can be used as a powerful tool for conveying information, expressing ideas, moods and emotions and as a way for unifying and enhancing the overall design. Color also adds an extra level of compositional complexity, however, and generates a further set of design decisions. The process of putting all the elements together successfully in a color drawing can be a challenging one, and in many cases there will be a number of equally plausible compositional options to choose among. In these situations instinct, preference and taste will determine the final choice.

Although in many situations numerous outcomes are equally possible, it almost always turns out to be the case that when making color and compositional decisions the more informed the decision-making and the greater the understanding of the principles of design and properties and behavior of color, then the better the final results will turn out. Many designers and artists do make decisions intuitively, but many of these intutions were developed after a solid educational grounding in art and design and many years of practical experience. Even though the design-decision process at some point becomes intuitive, however, there will still be times when a drawing has not turned out as hoped for but it is difficult to pinpoint exactly where the problem lies. In these cases, subjecting the work to a critical examination in the light of the principles of design and color combination often sheds light on how a problem can be solved.

This book contains many examples of fashion drawings in color ranging from simple to highly complex. Each drawing is accompanied by a detailed description of the techniques used and, in many cases, a comment or two about the compositional decisions regarding color and design. Studying the drawings and the accompanying descriptions, along with a familiarity with the contents of this chapter will assist in developing a skill in composition in color as well as learning the techniques used to draw the particular garment or fabric being described. With constant practice and experimentation these skills will develop and improve and good design and color decisions will become second nature.

composition in color

initial compositional decisions/elements to include/grouping

Grouping. The same dress styled for three different occasions. This is an asymmetrical composition: the red color accents of the figure on the left balance the larger rendered areas of the two figures on the right, whose garments are in black and neutral colors.

PUTTING THE ELEMENTS TOGETHER

The remainder of this chapter reviews the sequence of design decisions involved in the composition of a fashion drawing, both the practical decisions relating to the presentation of the garments themselves and then the application of the principles of design and color combinations discussed in the first part of the chapter.

INITIAL COMPOSITIONAL DECISIONS

The fashion drawing is, first and foremost, an illustration. As mentioned at the beginning of this chapter, before considering the various issues of the overall composition of the drawing a number of initial decisions have to be made about the presentation of the subject matter. To recap, these initial decisions are:

1. The design and colors of the garments to be included in the drawing and the combination of garments and choice of accessories (many or all of these decisions will be givens from the start).
2. The pose, gestures and coloring of the basic figure drawing of the croquis with the subject garments.
3. The composition of the figure or figures on the page, the background elements, skin tone, make-up and hair, objects and empty (negative) space.

Once these decisions have been made, (or mostly made—for example, final decisions about hair, make-up. skin tone and accessories, or the background color can be left until later) the compositional design and color elements can be considered and the drawing planned out. These decisions are presented and discussed in the order in which they usually (but not always) occur.

ELEMENTS TO INCLUDE IN THE DRAWING— THE NUMBER OF GARMENTS AND FIGURES

The first decision to be made about a drawing is what it is to include. If a number of garments are to be illustrated then the different ways the garments can be combined (whether on the same or on different figures) has to be considered, and decisions made as to which option would make for the best presentation. This often entails further decisions as to the number of figures to be included in the drawing.

GROUPING

Decisions on grouping (or not-grouping) figures are based on whether the clothes are related to each other, and whether they are best shown together or separately. Clothes from coordinated collections can be placed together to reinforce their common design elements or to show the idea of a particular theme—a type of garment, fabric, or silhouette for example. Two figures are often used in a drawing when establishing a theme; three or more figures are used when a large number of garments are included in a collection, such as often happens in sportswear. How to create an attractive and balanced drawing with varying numbers of figures is discussed and illustrated later in the chapter.

composition in color

grouping

Grouping. A group showing examples from a line of casual wear. Note the color combinations in each figure and across the group. The gestures of the hair, hand in the third figure and leg in the fourth figure lead the eye around the composition.

composition in color/other elements to include

backgrounds/figure and pose/decisions on pose

Croquis against background. The addition of the leaves in the background enhances and unifies the drawing in a number of ways, providing an attractive grounding for the figure and garments, which are simple and sparse and might otherwise lack impact. The shape and color of the individual leaves closely echo the shapes and colors of the garments and parts of the figure, and the shift in values also reflects the way the figure is shaded. The leaves are blowing in an "S" curve that suggests movement and also adds diagonals and movement to the drawing, counterpoising the curves and diagonals in the figure. The figure appears to be floating gently downwards along with the leaves.

OTHER ELEMENTS TO BE INCLUDED IN THE DRAWING/BACKGROUNDS

Decisions concerning what other elements, in addition to the subject garments, should be included in or excluded from a drawing are made taking into consideration the number and complexity of the garments and what will create a pleasing and balanced final drawing.

If the subject garments are simple—bikinis for example—a decision might be made to include additional visual elements in order to give the drawing a more finished and balanced look—perhaps some accessories or relevant (sometimes irrelevant) props or backgrounds. If, on the other hand, the garments are complex and detailed, it might in fact be necessary to omit some inessential elements, such as the details of the features of the face, complicated accessories, or even parts of the figure, so that the drawing does not become cluttered and the attention stays on the garments themselves.

FIGURE AND POSE

Once decisions have been made on the subject matter of a fashion drawing—the garments to be represented and the other elements to be included—many of the other decisions about the overall composition often (though not always) fall easily into place.

The next set of decisions to be made concerns how best to depict the garments in the drawing for the given purpose and audience in mind. This will depend on the type of garment being presented, its function, its intended market and sex/age range as well as whether it is to be presented alone or grouped with other garments.

DECISIONS ON POSE

The first aspect of this overall depiction of the garments to be considered is the pose or poses of the figure or figures. There are three main considerations when deciding on the pose of the figure:

FIRST, the pose should be appropriate to the type of garment: either its function or "mood". For example, an active sportswear garment, or range of garments, might be drawn in an action pose to show how they fit when being used as intended; a "street" garment might be drawn with a relaxed pose typical of the body language associated with the street; evening wear might be depicted using figures with elegant, interesting poses.

SECOND, it is important always to consider the basic silhouette and construction of the garment and to choose a pose that emphasizes the key areas of the garment. For example, pants should be drawn with the legs apart so the garment is not confused with a skirt; a wide sleeve is best shown with the arm held out from the body so the full extent of the fabric can be appreciated; heads should not cover a structured collar; with a full skirt the pose should reveal the extent of the drape.

THIRD, the choice of pose should suit the elements of the garment to be emphasized in the drawing. To draw attention to a detail at the hip, for example, placing a hand there will draw the eye to it.

composition in color

figure and pose

Pose. The choice of a side view pose allows the width and fullness of the skirt of this elegant evening gown to be fully appreciated while at the same time creating a slim profile of the figure as an attractive contrast.

composition in color

figure and pose/decisions on pose

Note that for most poses, symmetry and balance in the pose will tend to make a figure appear at rest and peaceful; shifting the weight to one side of the body gives more sense of movement and energy; stretching the arm above the head elongates the figure if a slim silhouette is to be emphasized.

Poses and gestures should be chosen also so that there is a natural movement of the eye from one element to another inside the drawing and the eye is not led outside the composition. Gestures or faces pointing or looking off the page should be avoided, as they draw the attention away from content of the drawing.

Another important consideration in deciding on the pose for a figure is a practical one: whether drawing skills are sufficiently developed for the task in hand. It is necessary to assess this realistically: for example, three-quarter views of the body, with limbs bending and extending in different directions usually involve perspective and fore-shortening and can be tricky to draw. If drawing experience is limited it is usually best to choose a less ambitious pose than risk an awkward-looking, technically incorrect drawing.

Once the pose of the figure or figures has been chosen the next decisions to be made include positioning on the page, scale/consistency of scale, lighting, skin tone, hair, accessories and accents. Most of these decisions are interrelated and should always be made with an eye to the main visual themes of the drawing and with consideration given to what interaction they will have with the other elements.

Decisions at all stages, particularly if the drawing is not progressing smoothly, should be subjected to a test of whether they conform with the basic principles of good design, a process that becomes intuitive with practice and experience.

Pose. This is a dynamic pose based on angles: the eye is led around the composition and picks up the many details. Note the shape of the hair and flowers echo each other. Attention can be drawn to a detail in the garment with a gesture of the hand, as is seen here.

composition in color

position on page/negative space/pose

POSITION ON THE PAGE/NEGATIVE SPACE
If there is a limited amount of space on the paper—if, for example, the drawing is to be placed on a presentation board together with flats, fabric samples, colorways and other information, then the choices regarding positioning may be limited; in some instances limitations of space may in fact dictate a simpler pose than the one that was originally considered.

If garments are being shown on a single figure, it is important that the figure fill as much of the available space as possible, allowing for an inch to an inch and a half on top and a little more beneath. Small drawings make it seem as though ideas are being explained in a whisper: to make sure drawings receive the attention they deserve it is best to make sure they are sufficiently large.

The positioning of the figure on the page determines the way the eye moves around the page. The figure should be placed so that the eye is not led away from the page and remains viewing the subject matter of the drawing. Consideration should be given to the shapes created in the drawing by the subject matter and its surrounding space: varying the size and shapes of the negative spaces (the spaces around the figure) can be more interesting than making symmetrical or similarly-shaped negative space and can contribute to the balance, rhythm and unity of a drawing. Background color and other elements can be added to the negative space to help further unify the drawing, as is discussed further below.

Pose/Position on page. A pose should be chosen that shows off the garments as well as capturing their mood and indicating the market they are designed for. Facial expression, body language and styling provide further information that reinforces the drawing of the garments on the figure. The figure placed on a diagonal across the page creates a feeling of movement and breaks up the page into interesting variations of negative space.

composition in color

position on page do not do's/scale/consistency of scale/lighting position/color

DO NOT DO. The figure occupies too small a portion of the page.

SCALE/CONSISTENCY OF SCALE

Consideration has to be given to the relative scale of different drawings, both on the same page and on different pages.

If figures are being placed on a number of pages of similar size—a portfolio or book for example—then an effort should be made to keep the sizes of the figures as close as possible, while, as mentioned, at the same time filling as much of the page as possible. If it is necessary for reasons of space or layout to include figures on a different scale it is best to keep the variation in scales to a minimum. Varying scales can cause confusion appropriate in Surrealist paintings but not as a rule in fashion drawing.

LIGHTING POSITION/COLOR

A decision should be made as to the lighting treatment to be used. A simple "neutral" frontal lighting is often sufficient when drawing simple garments. Single-source lighting from the side or below can create dramatic effects of shading and highlights revealing a full range of color values and the complexities of the drape (shading is covered at length in the next two chapters). When making a decision about the *color* of the lighting, the color to be used in the various parts of the drawing has to be considered—the skin tone of the figure, the hair and background objects included as accents to the drawing. If the actual colors of the garments themselves need to be clearly identified in the drawing, a lighting treatment should be selected that avoids confusion.

DO NOT DO. The figure occupies too large a portion of the page.

composition in color

lighting position

Figure lit from front.

Figure lit from below.

composition in color/planning out the drawing

skin tone, hair, accessories, accents/application of design principles and elements

Repetition and accessories. The repetition of the same garment unites the drawing and at the same time provides a convenient way to show off different accessories. The accessories in turn provide additional information about the garments. In the figure on the left the garment is accented with classic accessories; the accessories with the center figure are for a more contemporary look and the figure on the right has artistic and distinctive accessories that suggest bold, designer-market styling.

SKIN TONE, HAIR, ACCESSORIES, ACCENTS

In fashion drawing everything other than the garments is secondary in importance and is present in the drawing solely to enhance the appearance of the garments. This applies to the skin tone, hair, accessories (except in cases where they themselves are the subject of the drawing) as well as to the other unrelated elements that show up from time to time.

SKIN TONE is an important topic in itself, covered in the next chapter. Skin tone can be treated in effect as an accent of color in the drawing, and broad license taken in the colors chosen to represent it, both natural and artificial, or, alternatively, a color can be chosen that is naturalistic or part of the overall color scheme of the drawing.

HAIR should be treated as an accessory to the clothes and the decisions regarding its shape and color made to reinforce the shapes and colors in the garments.

ACCESSORIES are useful in adding information about a garment—for example, a tennis racquet is an easy device to show that a skirt is a tennis skirt. Accessories can also be used to highlight a color or shape, but again should never overpower the figure and garment, except, as mentioned, where they are themselves the subject of the drawing.

COLOR ACCENTS can be used to unify a composition—for example a particular color of reflected light used throughout the drawing can pull together garments of disparate shapes and colors, and can also be added when a drawing is in need of dash of spice.

PLANNING OUT THE DRAWING
APPLICATION OF DESIGN PRINCIPLES AND ELEMENTS

Once the decisions about content and layout of the drawing have been made, the overall composition should be thought through in terms of its own design integrity and effectiveness, and decisions made as to how best to apply the principles of design and how to choose the elements of design in order to execute the drawing. The purpose of the drawing is to represent the garments realistically and make them appear as attractive as possible. Unless all the other elements in the drawing are "just right" and the overall composition is harmonious and balanced, the garments will not appear at their best.

In general, the same design principles should be applied to a drawing in color as to a black and white drawing, and then, as a second stage, the principles for color composition applied as an additional set of guidelines. Although there are some differences in the ways they are used and the ways they are executed between color and black and white line drawings, line type and quality, value contrast, symmetry, asymmetry balance, repetition, focal point and emphasis are equally important for both.

composition in color

applying design principles/repetition/value contrast/symmetry and asymmetry

Repetition. This group of figures are wearing garments from a line that features a blue ribbon motif. The blue ribbon contrasts with the other muted colors of the garments (the overall color scheme is one of colored accents against neutral backgrounds) and acts as a strong unifying device in the composition.

REPETITION

In black and white drawing repetition is of similar shapes or patterns, or, sometimes. similar value levels or value contrasts. In color, repetition can be introduced independently of shape or pattern, and used in addition to or as an alternative to those elements.

Repetition in color can be achieved in a number of different ways, ranging from repetition of exactly the same color to repeated occurrences of different tints, shades and tones of the same hue. Repetition of the same color in a composition can serve to unify disparate elements in a composition. If a large proportion of the colors in a drawing consist of the repeated color then the drawing may begin to appear as though it has a monochromatic color scheme. If this is not the intention then use of the repeated color should be limited.

VALUE CONTRAST

As a compositional device value contrast is as important in color drawing as in black and white. When drawing with color, however, value contrasts occur within the variations of a single hue—particularly in fabric—as well as between different hues, so value contrast occurs across a wide range of colors and color combinations.

Value contrast in color is used in a very precise way when showing variations of value within a small color range, as often happens when rendering draped fabric three-dimensionally. These value contrast effects are usually localized, occupying a relatively small area, and limited to the fabric color and a range of shades and tints of that color. When value contrast in color takes place on a larger scale in the drawing, and between different colors, then in planning the drawing its effect also has to be weighed in the context of the overall color scheme. In these cases the other types of color contrast and interactions that are present have all to be taken into consideration.

SYMMETRY AND ASYMMETRY

Symmetry and asymmetry have to be considered for achieving balance in color drawings as well as black and white, but color is a powerful tool that can be used to balance an asymmetrical composition. High value and/or saturated applications of color on one side of a composition can balance larger shapes of lower values and/or saturations on the other, as is mentioned in the description above of the weightings given to different colors by Goethe, and is discussed below in the section on color proportions and dominance.

compos tion in color

asvmmetry/types of line/ line quality

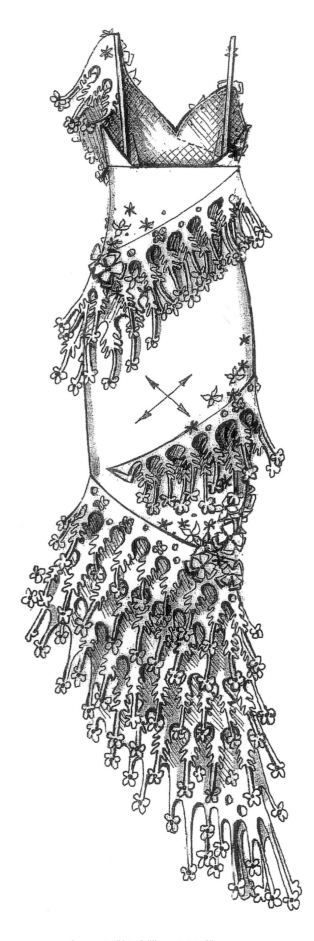

Asymmetry/Use of different types of line.
This technical "flat"—an ink drawing of an elaborate asym-metrical cress—uses a number of types of line: thin line is used for the silhouette, cross-hatching is used to indicate shading, and a wider line is used to indicated the deeper shadows.

TYPES OF LINE/LINE QUALITY

Line is an important element of all fashion drawings and in planning the drawing thcught should be given to how line will be used and what tools will be required.

As has been discussed, when using color, shading can be incicated withcut the use of line, so line can be conveniently used to show construction, detailing and drape. The type of line to be used in the drawing will depend on the fabrics of the garments and the type and quantity of detailing to be included. The rendering of different fabrics and the particular use of line in each is covered in detail in the chapter on fabrics.

composition in color

color decisions/light/color backgrounds/color design/fabric color

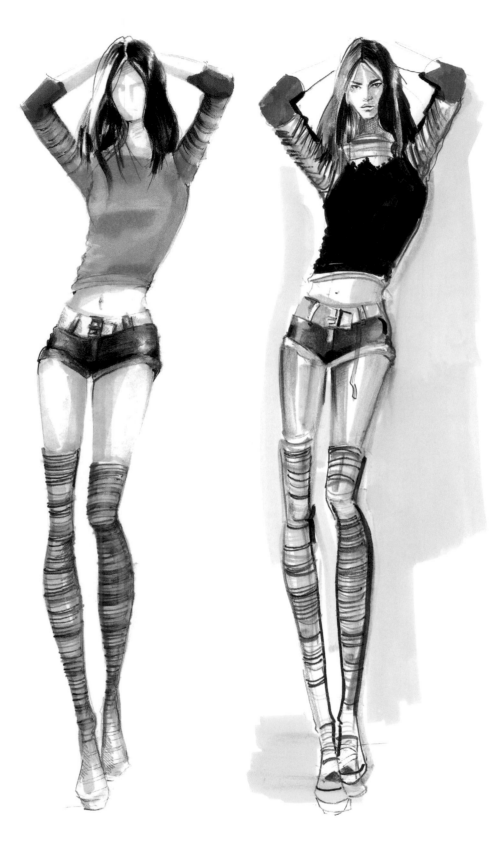

Background color. The figure on the left is placed against a white background and softly lit for a pale, soft look. The figure on the right is shown against a yellow background that reflects onto the body and clothes, providing strong color contrasts for a more dramatic presentation.

COLOR DECISIONS

COLOR BACKGROUND

It is usual to present colored fashion drawings against a neutral background—white, grey or black. Colored backgrounds have an effect on all the colors in a drawing (the Bezold effect comes into play) and the color interactions should be carefully evaluated before making a final decision.

For the sake of simplicity and clarity it is recommended that a white background be chosen, but the addition of a colored background can also be used to unify or add interest to a composition.

COLOR DESIGN AND FABRIC COLOR

The color of the fabrics to be used in a fashion drawing is usually a given, as color is one of the main variables that shifts as fashion changes, and whole collections are often designed around a particular color palette. As a result the color design for the skin tone, hair, make-up, accessories, reflective and background colors is usually created with reference to that color palette. It is important however that, although secondary, the color treatment for the elements of the drawing that are not garments is chosen to show the garments to best effect.

There are a number of ways to approach the color design of a drawing. It is possible to opt for one of the formal color schemes discussed earlier in this chapter, and base these schemes around the color(s) of the garments. As mentioned, employing a formal color scheme to a drawing will virtually ensure a harmonious result.

composition in color

color proportion and dominance/color balance and symmetry

COLOR PROPORTION AND DOMINANCE
A dominant color—a color that asserts itself more
than the other colors in a drawing—can itself be part
of a formal color scheme, and can unify a drawing,
as well as creating mood. As discussed, the choice
of dominant color has a strong effect on all the
other colors in a drawing, so the choice should be
made which reinforces the intended effect of the
drawing—for example, romantic, energetic, or
provocative. The dominant color in a composition
can be the color that is naturally dominant among
the elements of the drawing by virtue of its extent
and brightness or can be a color that is made to be
the dominant color by adjusting saturation/value or
repeating the color in accents, backgrounds and
so on.

COLOR SYMMETRY
Color can be used in order to bring asymmetrical
compositions into balance by varying the relative
proportions and placement of colors with different
impacts. A drawing is seen to balance if there is
equality in visual impact between its two sides,
between its top and bottom and sometimes along
its diagonals. For example, a dark shadow extending under a figure at the bottom of the page might
feel as though it is being pulled down by gravity,
giving the viewer an uncomfortable reaction. To
counter this a bright color or combination could be
placed in the upper portion of the drawing, for
example, in the hair, in a hat of as a background
accent.

Repetition and variation. The hair color, print patterns and details (bows) are repeated, and work
to unify the drawing, while variations of color and in the silhouettes of the garments themselves
add variety and interest.

composition in color

fashion drawing and composition

FASHION DRAWING AND COMPOSITION

The attractive and harmonious presentation and combination of all the elements in a fashion drawing is important for the drawing to be effective, and color schemes and choices and the overall compositional decisions are a key part of this. It should always be kept in mind, though, that fashion drawings are first and foremost technical drawings, providing information about the garments. Figures and garments must be presented accurately and realistically: correct color schemes or compositional balance cannot compensate for a poorly drawn figure or a garment drawn so it is not clear what fabric it is made of, how it drapes on the figure or what the constructional details are.

Once drawing the garments on the figure is mastered, though, good design of the colors and composition of a drawing can move the drawing to a higher level where its impact, and that of the garments it shows, can be greatly enhanced.

composition in color

practice and exercises

1. Draw a front view croquis using a nuanced line.

2. Select a croquis with clothes from the Appendix. Copy this croquis using (i) a light line and (ii) a heavy line.

3. Draw a figure and garment using five different types of line. The lines can represent shading, cast shadow, crisp fabric, soft fabric, seams, details, hems, the figure under the garment or other aspects of the clothing and figure.

4. Draw the silhouette of a blouse made of (i) linen and (ii) silk. Refer to the chapter on fabrics for the characteristics of these fabrics.

5. Draw a croquis. Create a background for the croquis by pasting objects cut out of magazines. Put a simple garment on the figure that relates to the background.

6. Draw two figures wearing dissimilar outfits and add (i) accessories, (ii) make-up and (iii) hair to create continuity between the two.

7. Draw three figures with overlapping arms or legs.

8. Draw two figures. Fill in the top of one and the bottom of the other with saturated colors. Fill in the unfilled bottom with a tint of the saturated color of the top; fill in the unfilled top with a shade of the saturated color of the bottom.

9. Draw a t-shirt and a skirt on a croquis. First fill in the t-shirt with a low-value color and the skirt with a high-value color and then repeat switching the t-shirt to high value and skirt to low value.

10. Draw a t-shirt and skirt on a croquis. Fill in the t-shirt with horizontal stripes using a saturated color for the uppermost stripes, making them progressively less saturated lower on the garment. Make the color less saturated by mixing in grey.

11. Draw three croquis and silhouettes of garments. Fill in the first croquis with a pattern based on complementary colors; the second croquis with a pattern based on secondary colors and the third based on tertiary colors.

practice and exercises

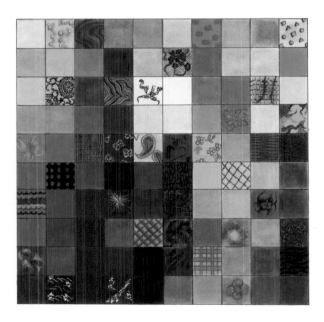

12. Draw a croquis in an active pose using (i) a fine line, (ii) a dark line and (iii) a light line nuancing to a dark line where the figure bends.

13. Draw a group of three figures with some limbs overlapping, wearring black, white and grey garments. Unify the group using (i) colorful accessories and (ii) different garment design details such as buttons, fringe, pockets, shirring and so on.

14. Make a balanced composition consisting of three figures wearing dresses of different lengths. Balance the composition by varying (i) sizes (e.g., two short and one long skirt), (ii) value (e.g., two light skin tone figures and one dark) and (iii) position and gesture.

15. Draw two or more figures wearing active sportswear garments. Create a focal point for the composition using (i) a graphic device (e.g., a cartoon character, image from nature, symbols) on one of the garments, (ii) a design element on one of the garments, (iii) an accessory and (iv) an element related to but not on the figures (e.g., clouds reflecting the colors or shapes in the clothing).

16. Draw three croquis with silhouettes of full skirts. Fill in the garments with a leaf pattern using warm and cool colors.

17. Draw three figures wearing dresses. Fill in the first dress with a print based on a complementary dyad, the second with a print based on a triad and the third with a tetrad.

18. Draw a blue evening gown and add color accents in lavender or red, (i) where they are integrated into the outfit (e.g., appliqués, trim, embroidery), (ii) in the hair and skin tone, and (iii) as accessories.

19. Draw two croquis wearing tops and pants, facing each other. Fill in one of the croquis with a color scheme based on analagous colors and the other with a scheme based on split complements.

20. Draw a grid of 100 squares of 1" on marker paper. Fill in the first two columns with variations of warm colors using marker and colored pencil. Fill in the next two columns with cool colors, the next two with neutrals, the next two with pastels, the next two with pretty colors and the last two with ugly colors. Practice drawing some patterns in the squares with colored pencils in contrasting colors, making the colors as saturated as those of the backgrounds. The grid at the left is an example of a completed exercise.

21. Draw a skirt and top with a palette of colors based on those taken from any diagonal of boxes in the grid made in the last exercise.

22. Draw groups of three figures united by pose and gestures (i) in a beach setting, (ii) at a party, and (iii) practicing a sport. The group of figures on this page is an example of such a group.

FABRICS

defining the body under the fabric

body shadow map

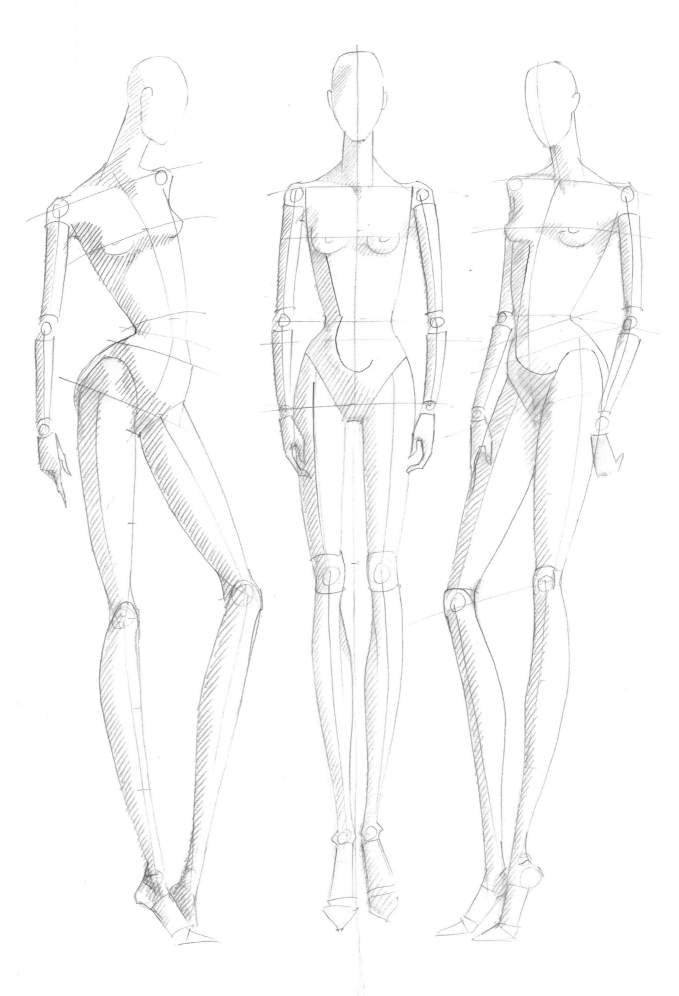

Areas where shadows form on the unclothed body—body lit from right side.

defining the body under the fabric

body shadow map

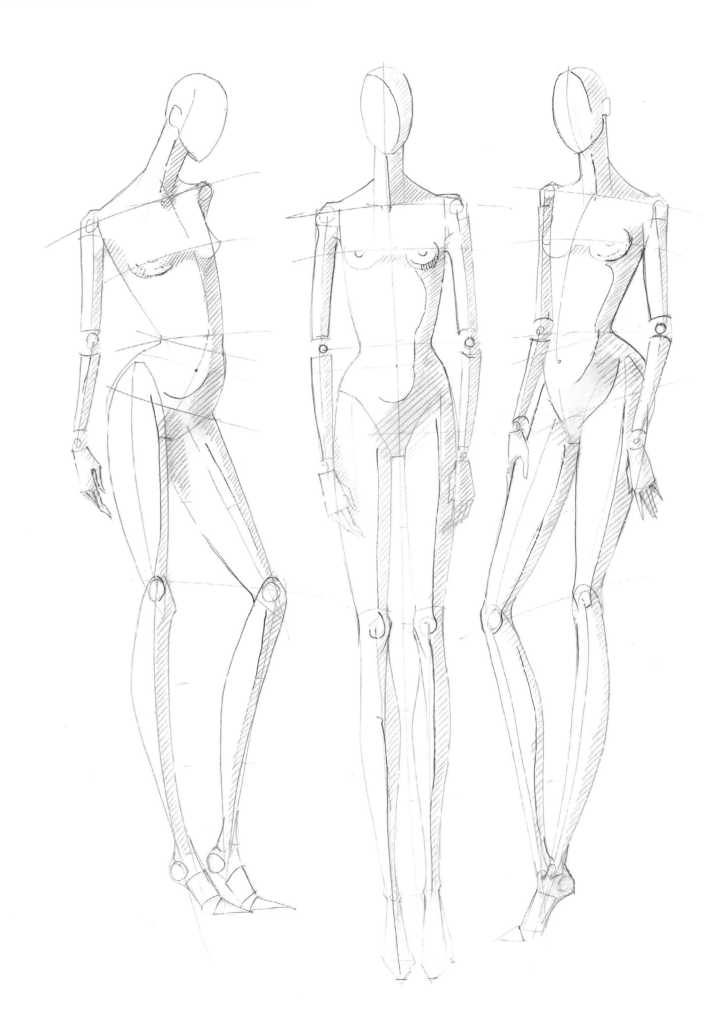

Areas where shadows form on the unclothed body—body
lit from left side.

defining the body under the fabric

fabrics

Silhouette of garment on body. To understand shading in fabric it is necessary to understand the shading of the body , as can be clearly seen here under the garment. This is a female three-quarter figures lit from the front; shadows form from the neck to collar-bone, underarm area to outer arm, around the bust-line, rib-cage, tummy, pelvis and leg.

FABRICS

Much of the excitement of fashion is the feel of a fabric, its sensuality, whether it is soft or crisp, transparent or opaque, loose or tight; the way it makes us feel protected, relaxed, elegant or seductive. The way fabrics form a skin over our bodies transcends function alone and makes a garment an objects of beauty: this is why those who truly love fashion spend so much of their time, effort and resouces on buying or making clothes. A beautiful fashion drawing, well-conceived, technically correct and executed with style and flair recognizes and is itself a tribute to the beauty of fashion.

Fabric is at the very heart of fashion. To draw fashion well it is essential to draw fabrics well, and to draw fabrics well means capturing their visual essence, of which there are two basic aspects: one, the surface appearance—how the fabric "looks"—and two, the way fabric drapes on the body. If this visual essence is successfully captured in a drawing, then it will be possible almost to feel the fabric in the drawing as well as recognizing it visually.

The surface appearances of different fabrics vary greatly according to their intrinsic texture and the way in which they reflect light. Fabrics also drape differently according to weight, weave and the construction of the garment into which they are made. To draw fabrics so they can be immediately and unmistakably recognized it is essential to identify and clearly represent these distinguishing visual characteristics, leaving no confusion as to what the fabric is and how it will look in the finished garment.

Although many of the illustrations in this chapter are of finished garments, the focus is on the fabric itself rather than on design and construction. The chapter is organized as follows: first, *simple* shading of garments using one layer of color is covered, followed by *complex* shading where two or more layers of value are applied. The shading of fabrics of different intrinsic color values and ranges of values is then examined, followed by a review of pattern and drape in fabric and finally an in-depth review of how a wide range of different fabrics are drawn.

Focusing on fabrics in isolation and learning how they are drawn aids considerably when drawing finished garments. For quick concept drawings it is not practicable or necessary to make detailed renderings of the fabric of a garment (although it is necessary to be familiar with the physical properties of the fabric, as these are reflected in the silhouette and constructional detailing of even a quick concept drawing). When making a more complete drawing of a garment, though, for the drawing to be considered successful the fabric of the garment has itself to be drawn realistically so its texture, color, surface appearance and drape are all clearly perceived. If it is possible to tell from a drawing, on appearance alone, what fabric has been used in the construction of a garment and how the fabric will look when made into the finished garment, this is a major step in helping to understand how the finished garment will actually look. From the point of view of the artist/designer, the better a drawing is

defining the body under the fabric

fabric on the body

The body before draping. This is a male frontal figure with light falling on the face from the right and on the body from the left side. Shadows fall around the sides of the face, under the chin, around the side of the neck, at the collarbone, chest, stomach to crotch, and around the sides of the leg.

understood, the more effective it will be and the greater its chances will be of achieving the purpose for which it was drawn.

FABRIC ON THE BODY

Fabric by its nature is almost without structure: although it can be shaped to a limited extent independently of the body through use of devices such as shoulder pads, corsets and hoops, fabric derives its structure from the support of the figure underneath. The following basic principle of fashion design and construction should always be kept in mind when drawing from the imagination without visual reference material: Wherever it is not directly supported, fabric will drape according to the laws of gravity. These operate in very similar ways in Paris, London, Milan, New York, Tokyo, Seoul, Los Angeles and all points in between!

For fabric to appear realistic when drawn on the body the following conditions must be met:

1. The body under the fabric must be defined with shading.
2. The fabric itself must be defined with shading.
3. The interactions between the body and the fabric must be shown.

How these three conditions for drawing fabric realistically can be met is explained in the text and drawings of this chapter.

DEFINING THE BODY UNDER THE FABRIC

There are two separate aspects to the shadows that form in a clothed figure: one is the shadows caused by the body under the fabric of the garment and the other is the shadows of the crape of the garment as it falls from the body. These two different aspects of shading have to be represented separately in a drawing, but there is also an interaction between them, and this too must be captured for the drawing to appear realistic.

In order to understand how the body under the fabric causes shadows, it is important to understand where shadows fall on the unclothed figure. With skin-tight clothing, the shadows that appear are almost the same as on the unclothed body (which is why tight blouses or shirts can raise eyebrows!). With looser clothing the shadows that appear do so where the fabric crapes, that is, where it falls away from the body.

As mentioned, fabric has no structure without the body underneath. *Generally speaking, the parts of the garment where the body touches the fabric appear lighter in value than the parts where the body does not touch the fabric and where the fabric drapes.* This is because at the points where the body has contact with the fabric of the garment it raises and flattens the fabric, moving it towards, and so catching the light, in the same places as in the unclothed figure. Excess fabric tends to fall away from these raised, lighter areas so that, in general, more shadows will form in areas where the body is not present directly underneath the fabric. When these shadows are shown in a fashion drawing the intention is to show how these shadows define the

defining the body under the fabric

side view figure

Female side view figure. In the unclothed figure on the left shadows fall under the hair, along the side of the face, the side of the neck, under the chest, around the tummy, around the sides of the leg and arm. The figure on the right shows where additional shadows form when fabric is draped on the body.

defining the body under the fabric

male three-quarter figures

boundaries of the shapes of the body under the garment—the roundness of the tummy, the cylindrical shape of the arms and so on. Shadows are indicated usually by applying a second coat of the color of the garment, if the fabric is light to medium in value, or a dark shade or black if the fabric is itself dark. Shadows also tend to form around the bust-line, the line from the arm-hole to the bust-line, at the waist and around the tummy, at the crotch, around the side of the leg, at the knee, around the side of the arm and elbow.

Shadows should be applied in the direction of the body shape to be defined: for example, *around* the bust rather than in a straight line. Long vertical strokes are used for the longer more vertical parts of the body such as the upper torso and the legs. The edges of shadows should be clean, clear and even. Note that shadows are directly affected by the position of the light source and will lengthen on the opposite side from the light source.

One of the most common mistakes in shading the fashion figure is to use a black or dark line to indicate shadow under the bust-line. This usually reads incorrectly as a seam or scar—a definite DO NOT DO. The bust-line is soft and does not have a sharp edge; it is drawn with soft, diffused shadows.

The body looks different under garments depending on whether clothes are transparent, opaque or tailored. For TRANSPARENT FABRICS the body is seen under the fabric and shading is of the body itself. Tiny shadows show in the drape where there are folds and excess fabric. For OPAQUE GARMENTS shadows appear where there is excess fabric. TAILORED GARMENTS are structured so that the body holds up the garment but does not affect the shape of the garment and as a result there is no clear definition of the body underneath. *Only where the body affects the shape of a garment do shadows appear that define the figure.*

Where clothing touches the body, shadows appear in the same places as in the unclothed body. On the clothed form on the left, shadows appear across the chest, under the arm and along the legs. The figure on the right, for reference, shows where shadows form on the unclothed body.

rendering fabric on the body

shading draped fabric

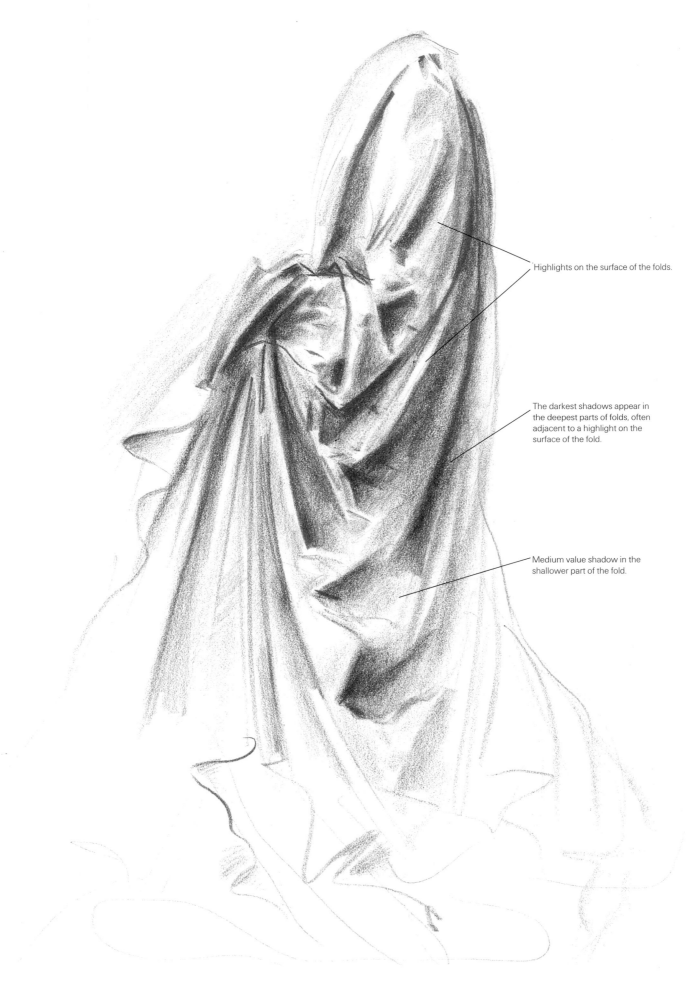

Highlights on the surface of the folds.

The darkest shadows appear in the deepest parts of folds, often adjacent to a highlight on the surface of the fold.

Medium value shadow in the shallower part of the fold.

Shading of draped fabric.

rendering fabric on the body

shading draped fabric/fabric around leg/fabric around arm

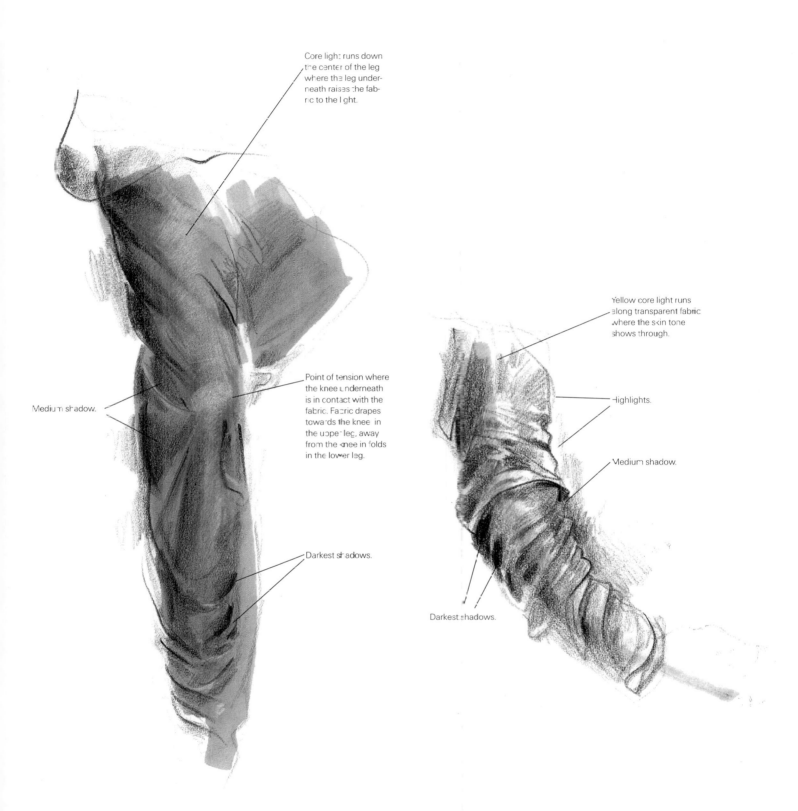

Core light runs down the center of the leg where the leg underneath raises the fabric to the light.

Yellow core light runs along transparent fabric where the skin tone shows through.

Point of tension where the knee underneath is in contact with the fabric. Fabric drapes towards the knee in the upper leg, away from the knee in folds in the lower leg.

Highlights.

Medium shadow.

Medium shadow.

Darkest shadows.

Darkest shadows.

Shading of draped fabric. Left, fabric around a leg; right, fabric around an arm.

rendering fabric on the body/shading draped fabric

close to torso/away from torso/details/cascade drape/ beads/diagonal drape

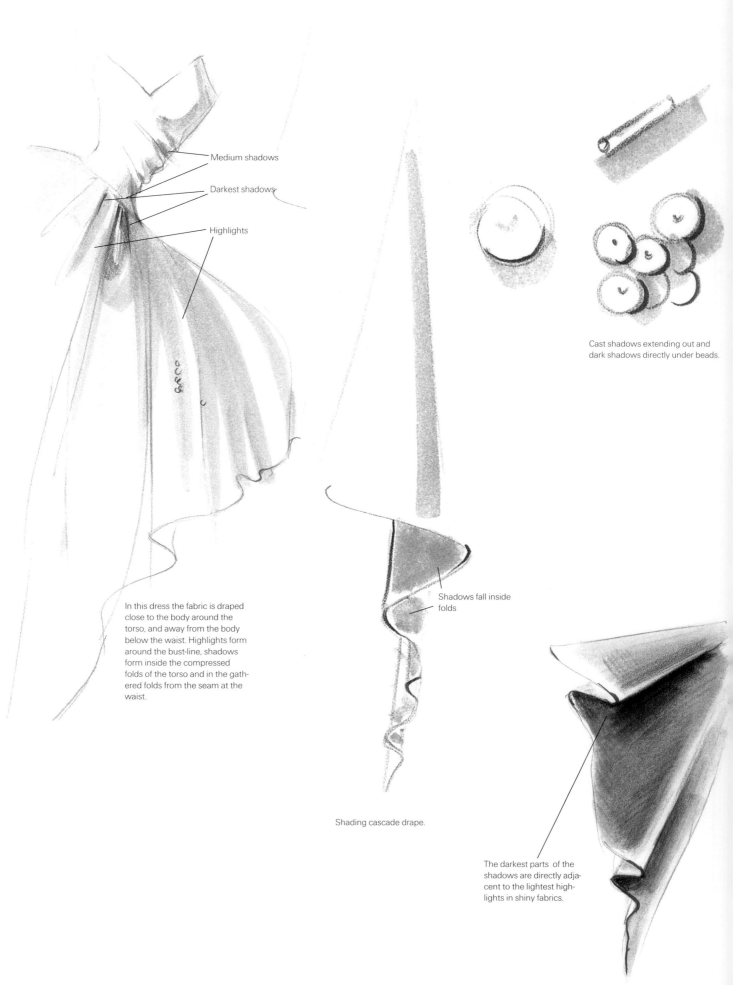

Medium shadows

Darkest shadows

Highlights

Cast shadows extending out and
dark shadows directly under beads.

In this dress the fabric is draped
close to the body around the
torso, and away from the body
below the waist. Highlights form
around the bust-line, shadows
form inside the compressed
folds of the torso and in the gathered folds from the seam at the
waist.

Shadows fall inside
folds

Shading cascade drape.

The darkest parts of the
shadows are directly adjacent to the lightest highlights in shiny fabrics.

Shading diagonal drape.

rendering fabric on the body/shading draped fabric

shadows in garments: pants/shorts

Silhouettes of pants and shorts showing drape and folds and where shadows typically fall with neutral, front lighting.

rendering fabric on the body/shading

shadows in garments: jackets/sweater

Silhouettes of jackets and sweater showing drape and folds and where shadows typically fall with neutral, front lighting.

rendering fabric on the body/shading

shadows in garments: jacket/blouse/t-shirts/constructional details

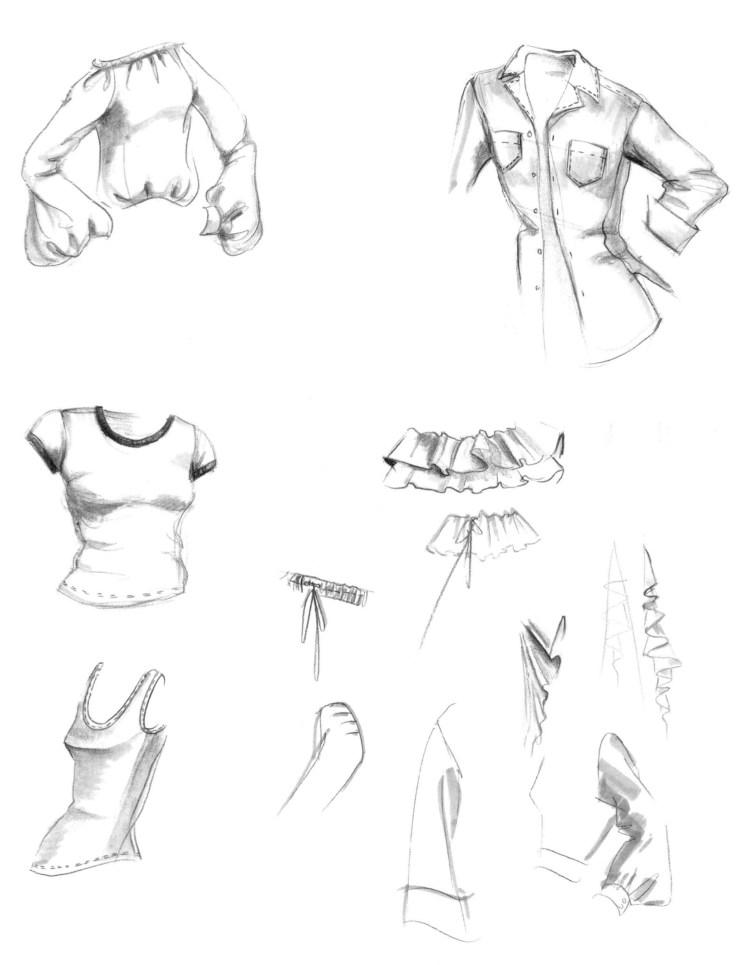

Silhouettes of garments and constructional details showing drape, folds and where shadows typically fall with neutral, front lighting.

simple shading and drape

pants/jackets/coat

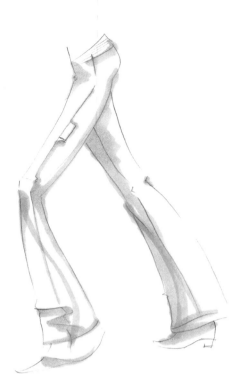

Pants. Shading is added around the waistband, around drape at the hip, under the thigh, at center-seams, from knee to ankle, at folds around the ankle. and in the inside of the garment.

Tailored jacket. Shadows appear under the lapel, around the sides of the torso, along the inner side of the arm, at the drape at the elbow, under buttons and flaps of pockets and in the inside of the garment.

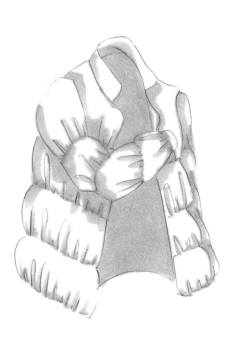

Quilted jacket. Shading is applied around the collar, seams and the gathers of the sleeve and body of the jacket.

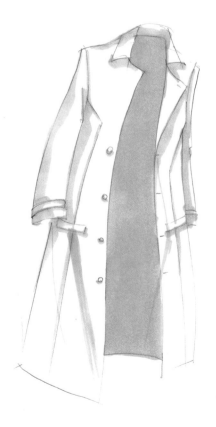

Tailored coat. Shadows appear around the collar, sides of sleeves, band of cuff of sleeve, along the princess line and pockets and under the buttons.

SIMPLE SHADING OF GARMENTS

The pants and coats shown in this section, on this page and the page opposite, can be drawn as simple shapes that fit the body and extend away from the body, sometimes in the same garment. The examples show the simple basic shadows of garments on the figure and the variations of shadows cast by the various parts of the different garments.

The shading of these garments is relatively straightforward and can be completed with one application. This form of simple shading of garments is useful when time is of the essence and drawings have to be made quickly and a complete understanding of the fabric of the garment is not essential but it is still necessary to give a realistic impression of how the garment fits the body. Unless stated otherwise, garments are lit from the front .

When defining shadows in a garment begin by focusing on its silhouette or outline. The silhouette shows where the fabric bends and folds at its edges. Shadows fill in areas that are away from, or receding from, the light source. If the silhouette has a protrusion or ridge, then that is where it will receive the light; an indentation or valley will be in shadow. Shadows also appear along seams or structural elements, under lapels, pockets, cuffs and buttons. Some of the areas of different garments where shadows typically appear can be seen on the preceding page.

Shadows are never equal in size and vary according to the area to be filled and the light source. Shadows tend to fall from the knees to the ankles in pants and from armpit to the bust-line, across the crotch, at the elbows, around the neck and wrists. When drawing shadows use a very light touch and a color slightly darker than the actual color of the fabric. Shadows are soft accents and should appear like a soft cloud: they are not linear in nature, and do not contain hard or broken edges. Blended color is effective in drawing shadows as it is possible to achieve the subtle gradations of tone observed in the folds of fabric.

simple shading and drape

trench coat/bicycle shorts/duffle coat//jacket over blouse

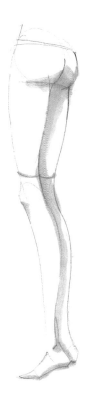

Trench coat. Shadows fall under lapel, under button at waist, around cap of sleeve, under insides of sleeves and drape at elbow, around bottom of sleeves, around belt at waist. The shadow on the right side defines the edge of where the figure would be under the coat.

Bicycle shorts, three-quarter back view. Shadows fall under bottom, around inside of thigh, under the hem.

Duffle coat. Shadows appear in the drape of the hood, under button, around sleeves and drape of sleeves, at side seams of sleeves, at side seam of coat, under pocket. Note that the drape at the back of the jacket falls to the waist.

Casual jacket over blouse. Shadows appear around collar of blouse, around collar of jacket, define spherical shape of bust, along side of jacket, in folds of sleeve. The bust can be thought of as two spheres with cast shadows.

complex shading and drape

blouse and sweater/dress/skirt/tailored jacket

Ruffled blouse and sweater. Shadows appear in the valleys of the folds of the blouse, under the ruff, under the center of the sweater, around the belt, around the buttons, in the ribs at the base of the sweater and in the numerous folds that occur around the arm and sleeve of a knitted garment.

COMPLEX SHADING AND DRAPE

Where fabric contains numerous folds of varying depths, or separate garments are layered in an outfit—such as a sweater over a blouse or a jacket over a sweater—then a wider range of shadows is observed than with fabrics of limtied drape or single layers of garments. To represent the value range of the shadows of such fabric and garments accurately more than one value of a color has to be used: this is complex shading. In the examples of complex shading shown in this section, two values of the color used for the drawing (blue) have been used, but it is common to use three or even more values to give an accurate rendering of a garment or fabric.

With complex shading the shadows appear in the same areas as with simple shading, the difference being simply that a darker value is used in the deepest recesses of the folds. Complex shading is used in those situations—when more time can be allotted and a more finished illustration is called for—when it is necessary to identify the particular fabric used in the construction of the garment. Although only two values are used in complex shading, it is—along with silhouette, construction, drape and detailing—one of the defining features in the accurate depiction of the fabric and garment.

The drawings on this and the following pages show a wide variety of silhouettes and can be used for reference when it is necessary to check where shadows appear in different types of garments. Some of the silhouettes contain additional diagrams to explain how difficult parts of the garment are drawn.

Knee-length dress of medium-weight fabric. Shadows form around the ruffle of collar, under the facing, around center-front seam, under buttons, under the. bow, around the sleeve and drape at the base of the sleeve, around the waistline, under the flap of and under the pocket, around the sides of the leg as they appear under the dress and in the fold of the hem.

Straight skirt of medium-weight fabric. Shadows define the waistband and crotch, continue along the sides of the legs and begin to fall across the body at the right knee.

Designer tailored jacket over turtle-neck sweater. Shadows appear in ribs of collar of sweater, under lapel, at princess lines, around decorative belts and buttons, around sleeves and under the excess fabric of the bell sleeves.

complex shading and drape

double breasted jacket/halter dress/satin pants/asymmetrical blouse

Double-breasted tailored jacket with high collar. Shadows appear under the roll of the collar, under the spread of the collar, under lapels, under the pockets, under buttons, at the belt, around the drape of the sleeves and at the cuffs. The drawing at top right shows the roll of the collar.

Lightweight halter dress. Shadows appear under the gathering at the neckline, around the armholes, at the bust line, in the drape at the waist and in the generous folds in the skirt. The diagrams at left, right and bottom show the shading of different parts of the drape.

Satin pants with high waist. Shadows fall under the loop of the belt under the buttons, in the folds at the zipper, in the folds that form drape of gathers in the inseam and outer edge of the pants. A core light—a long highlight—runs along the center of both legs.

Softly draped, asymmetrical blouse. Shadows define the neck-line, fall around the bust, in the interior of the sleeves and along the side of the arm under the sleeve, and in the drape at the waist.

complex shading and drape

pants/gathered top/pleated skirts

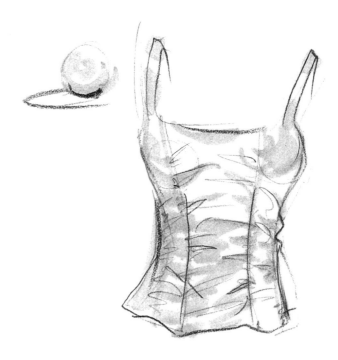

Softly draped pants. Shadows define pockets, crotch, zipper, shadows fall from crotch to knee and from outside knee to ankle and the flair of the pant at the ankle. The legs can be thought of as cylinders with a sphere at the knee, as shown in the diagram next to the right leg.

Gathered sleeveless top. Shadows define the bust line, princess seams and shearing throughout the top. The bust can be thought of as two spheres with cast shadows, like the sphere shown at the top left.

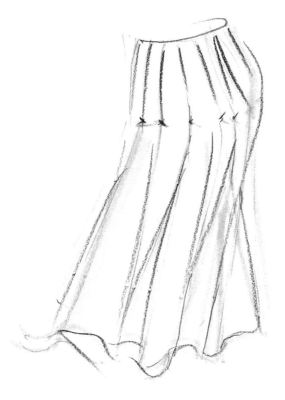

Skirt with inverted pleats. Shadows fall within seams, along drape and inside inverted pleats.

Five-gored fitted skirt with box pleats. Shadows fall along seams, in the drape at the hip and inside the box pleats.

complex shading and drape

short skirt/pleated skirt/slip dress/ruffled collar

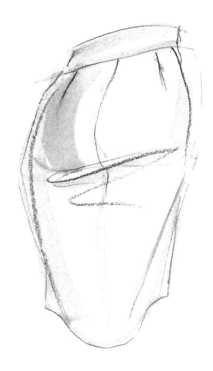

Short fitted skirt, back view. Shadows fall along waistband, tucks, center-back seam, around the bottom and around the sides of the legs.

Tight skirt with knife pleats at sides. Shadows fall under each pleat and at the folds at the crotch.

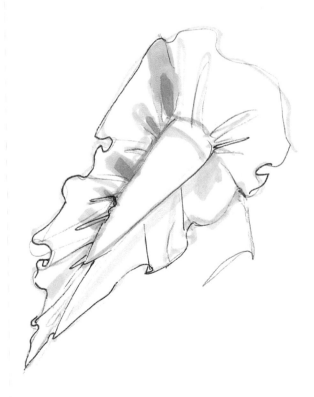

Slip dress. Shadows appear at strap, around bust-line, at side of torso and under tummy and where drape falls across the figure.

Ruffled collar. Shadows form in gathers at neckline, under ruffled edge and inside drape.

complex shading and drape

cascading fabric/layered pleated skirt/full skirt/knotted fabric

Cascading fabric. Shadows fill in folds and drape.

Layered, pleated skirt. Shadows fill in planes and ridges of pleats.

Softly draped skirt. Shadows fill in the drape which falls vertically from waist to hem and horizontally at base of hem.

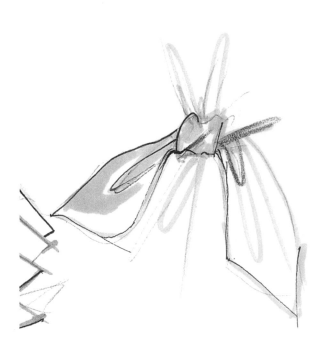

Knotted fabric. Shadows appear at edges of knot, inside the gathers of fabric behind knot, inside gathers of ties and under the ties.

complex shading and drape/lightweight fabrics

long skirt/ruffled skirt/do not do

Long skirt of lightweight fabric. Shadows form along the drapes which fall diagonally across the body from the hip.

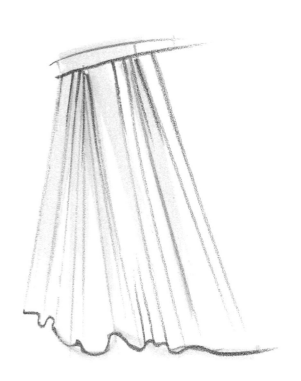

DO NOT DO. Incorrectly drawn gathers. Gathers should line up exactly with seams.

Strapless, lightweight fabric dress with numerous ruffles. Shadows appear under and around the bust-ine, along the right side of the garment, along the drape of the waistline, inside folds of ruffles of skirt and along the folds of the ruffles that cascade from the hemline.

complex shading and drape

sleeveless dress/skirt/palazzo pants

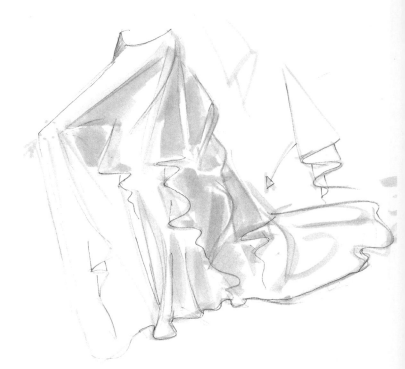

Complex draped skirt with folds falling from knee and extending back in complex drape to train. Shadows appear under thigh, flair out from knee like a flower and cascade in complex drapes that form from the hip. Note that the fabric falls in a horizontal as well as vertical drape.

Fitted, sleeveless dress with cowl neckline. Shadows fill in drape of cowl, princess lines, edge of upper torso of dress, under belt, the drape of the crotch and around the sides of the front leg. The legs can be thought of as cylinders, as shown in the diagram under the dress.

Palazzo pants. Shadows define the side of the legs, under the knee and in the drape of the flare of the pants.

complex shading and drape

full skirt/blouse/shorts/cape

Full skirt with elastic waistband. Shadows fill in folds of the elastic and in the gathers that flar out from center of elastic like a flower.

Cape with mandarin collar. Shadows fall inside and under the collar and fill in under the drape and inside the seams of the cape.

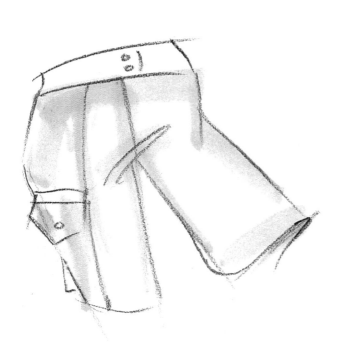

Shorts. Shadows fill in under waistband at seams and at crotch line.

Blouse with shawl collar, bell sleeves and bow. Shadows fill in drape of shawl collar, under collar, sides of bell sleeves, sides of blouse, tie of bow and the bow.

complex shading and drape

stripes

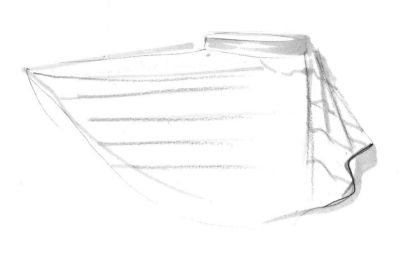

Circle skirt with horizontal stripes. Skirt is seen flattened out—stripes appear horizontal and parallel.

Circle skirt with horizontal stripes. Excess fabric at sides is draped and stripes become diagonal and broken at the folds.

Full skirt, gathered at waist with vertical stripes. Vertical stripes appear closer together at sides of skirt, wider at the center of the skirt. The vertical lines break and fall out of alignment as they bend around the folds. Shadows fill in the gathers of the skirt and the drape that falls from the hip-line diagonally across the skirt.

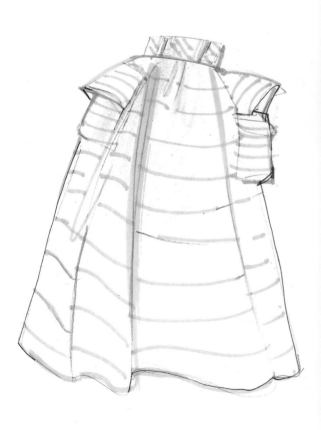

Full skirt with horizontal stripes. Stripes should follow the curve of the drape at the hem of the skirt. Stripes are parallel to the curves of the hem of the skirt. Shadows fill in the folds of the drape that bends from the waist.

complex shading and drape

chiffon evening dress/three-paneled skirt/strapless top

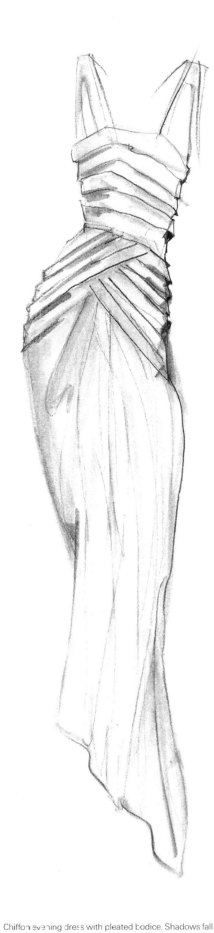

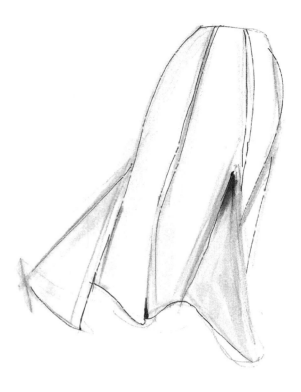

Three-gored skirt with inverted pleats. Light shadows define all of the vertical style lines and fill in the area of the inverted pleat. A second application is made with a darker-marker in the interior of the inverted pleat

Chiffon evening dress with pleated bodice. Shadows fall under each pleat and are applied from both sides of the garment with a light grey marker—10% grey might be the best choice—leaving the white of the paper to show through as a narrow vertical strip in the center, indicating shine. In the skirt of the dress vertical shadows are filled in in the folds of the soft drape with the same marker. A second application of shadows is applied with a darker marker —perhaps 40%—at the edges of the pleats to indicate an increased depth in the fabric and to give a more realistic appearance.

Strapless top with fabric draped on the bias. Shadow is applied with light marker around the bust-line and the interior of the fabric drape. A second application is made with a darker marker along the straps, at the edge of the bust and in the deepest interior of the fabric drape.

complex shading and drape

riding jacket and jodhpurs/tailored, double-breasted jacket

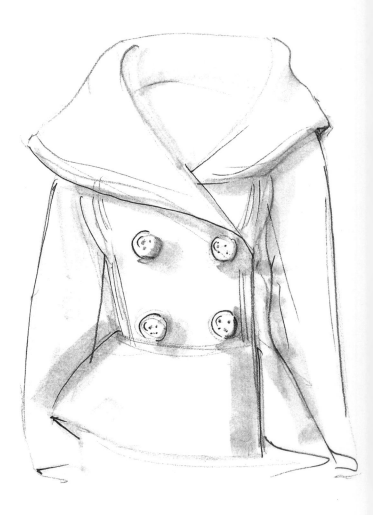

Tailored double-breasted jacket. Light marker is used to define the shadows around the drape of the collar, the sleeves, the contour of the jacket and under the buttons. A second application of darker shadows is applied under the buttons, along the silhouette at the base of the jacket and where the jacket front panel overlaps.

Riding jacket and jodhpurs. Light marker is used to show shadow in the following areas: under the collar, around the inner edge of the sleeves and cuffs, along the outer edges of the jacket, around the button and along the drape of the jodhpurs, including the crotch, knee and silhouette edge. A second application of a darker marker is made in the interior of the jacket front, along the outside of the collar, in the inner sleeves and inner silhouette of the jacket, around the button and where the center-front of the jacket overlaps, along the sides of the jodhpurs and around the knee.

complex shading and drape

teenage outfits

Left: Jacket, shirt, sweater and long shorts with fedora-style hat and sandals. Light shadows are applied around the sides of the hat, around the contour of the face and neck, under the collar, around the neck-line of the sweater, under the lapels, around the crape of the sleeves of the jacket, in the drape of the fabric at the belt-line around the belt loops, around the pockets in the shorts, around the zipper, at the crotch and in the excess fabric of the legs of the shorts where the fabric falls away from the legs and around the legs themselves. Darker shadow defines the area under the hat, the hair the collar, the lapels, the interior of the jacket and the contour of the shorts.

Right: Blouse, tie sweatshirt, two-layer gathered mini-skirt, knee length bicycle shorts, baseball hat and sneakers. Light shadows define the side of the face and neck, the sides of the sweatshirt sleeves and the silhouette of the sweatshirt, the drape of the mini-skirt and the sides of the bicycle pants. Darker shadows define the seams and sections of the baseball hat, around the neck, under the collar of the blouse, the edge of the tie, the hood of the sweat-shirt, the drape of the inner sleeve of the sweatshirt, the zipper on the sweat-shirt, the deepest area of the folds of the skirt and the edge of the sneakers.

shading fabric of different values/ different ranges of value

black fabric/matt solid color fabric

SHADING DARK AND LIGHT FABRICS
With dark fabrics most of the shadows do not have to be differentiated from the fabric color, and only the lighter parts—sheen and highlights—have to be drawn in over the top. Shading with darker color is only used to accentuate the very deepest of shadows. When drawing sheen and highlights keep the pencil sharp!

Black and other dark-colored garments. With dark garments it is the highlights on top of the dark fabric that have to be indicated rather than the shading that appears in lighter garments. After filling in the garment color from both sides of page to get an even application, highlights are applied on ridges of folds using a sweeping motion with a white or light-colored pencil. Shadows within the drape can be deepened in value, if necessary, by adding black colored pencil.

Solid color garment of medium-light value. With a fabric of a solid color of a light to medium value, first define the edges of the silhouette with the medium point of the marker and fill in the interior of the garment with a scrubbing motion. To ensure the application of color is even, apply a second coat from the reverse side of the paper. Shadows should be defined in the interior of the drape using a slightly darker value of the garment color.

shading fabric cf different values/different ranges of value

transparent fabric/white fabric

Transparent or semi-transparent garment. With transparent or semi-transparent fabrics shadows tend to be lighter than with non-transparent fabrics. They are lightest where the fabric extends beyond the figure. Folds are filled in with light-colored marker allowing for lots of white of the paper to show through on ridges of folds. The position of the body as it appears through the fabric is indicated with beige marker applied from the reverse side of the paper.

Warm white garment. Warm white can be shaded with a beige marker. Shadows fall within the wide, soft folds, with the darkest part of shadows at the edges of folds. Here, the darkest shadows are created with beige marker mixed with purple colored pencil and applied with colorless blender. This mixture is applied directly adjacent to the highlights on the ridges of the folds. As the hand moves away from the ridges the color issuing from the colorless blender becomes more dilute and shifts to lighter tones.

fabrics/three-dimensional rendering

fringe

Fringe is the term used for any fabric with loose threads, either bunched into tassels or twists, or separated. Fringe can be made from practically any fabric, including leather, beads, silk, chiffon, yarn wools, lace or linen. Here the fringe is light-colored over a black undergarment. Fringe is usually drawn with colored pencil to capture the stringy quality, but can also be drawn with the fine tip of a marker. Make sure fringe is drawn with a swing! Shadows can be applied to show the deeper parts of the fringe.

fabrics/three-dimensional rendering

paillettes/glass beads/jewels

Paillettes, beads, jewels and other adornments are drawn unevenly in scattered patterns as, even if they are placed regularly on the garment, they appear to disperse in the folds of the fabric.

Each bead is drawn by filling in with a blended color, and a cast shadow is added underneath. It is important to show the beads appearing in profile at the sides of the garment to indicate the beads continue all the way around the fabric.

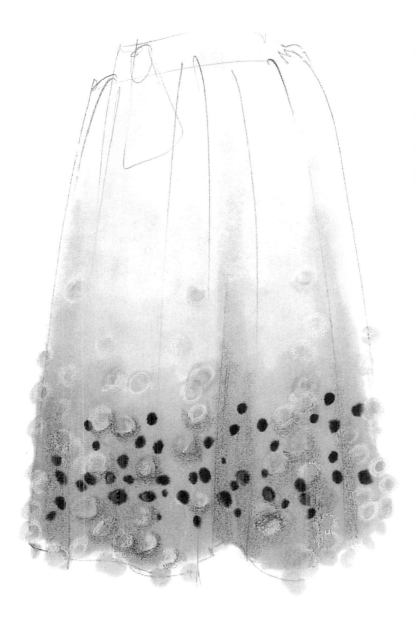

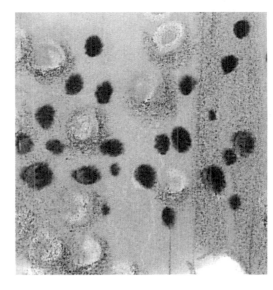

fabrics/three-dimensional rendering

fur/herring-bone/quilting/corduroy

Fur is drawn with short, staccato strokes working from light to dark with darker values where shadows form under the fur. Highlights, scattered throughout the fur, are accented with a gold or apricot-colored marker. The individual hairs of fur are drawn in using the sharp point of colored pencils. Darker color is applied at the edges of the fur and white pencil is used to indicate sheen and highlights in the middle of the fur.

With a herring-bone pattern the base color of the fabric is filled in and the chevron pattern is drawn using the fine point of a marker of a darker shade of the base color. A second application of the pattern with an even darker shade gives the impression of texture and depth to the fabric. Pattern can be applied with colored pencil.Shadows are applied using the side of a black pencil.

Quilting is drawn with stripes of light-colored marker accented with thin point of a marker or a colored pencil of darker value where the stitching gathers the fabric. Soft shadows are applied to the pucker of the quilt.

Corduroy or ribbed fabric is drawn by first filling in the silhouette with an even application of the base color. The ribs of the fabric are then drawn in with a white pencil. A black pencil is used for shading.

Collar—fur; dress—quilting; jacket—herring-bone wool; leggings—corduroy.

fabrics/three-dimensional rendering

lace/stripes/embroidery

Lace. The silhouette of the garment is filled in with light cool grey marker, and light warm grey is used as a shadow inside the shearing, around the bust line, at the side of the torso and in the crape of the sleeve. Using warm grey gives the appearance of the skin under the garment. The pattern of the lace is drawn with a .005 pen. Soft shadows are applied to the interior of the folds with the side of a black pencil and highlights added to the areas of the torso closest to the light source with a cream colored pencil.

Striped cotton shirt. Stripes are drawn to curve around the body. When stripes meet drape they break up in the contours of the drape.
Embroidered skirt. The embroidered motifs are built up with sequence of short strokes using the fine point of the marker. Pattern is denser at the side to indicate foreshortening as the fabric bends.

fabrics/three-dimensional rendering

knits/tulle/tweed

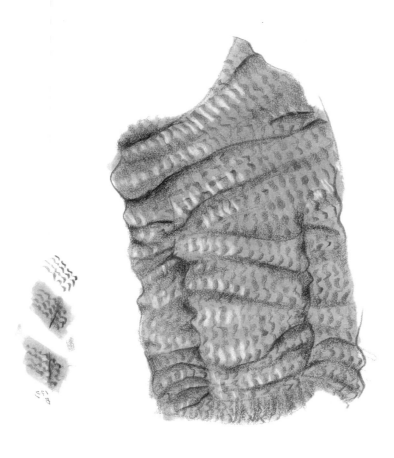

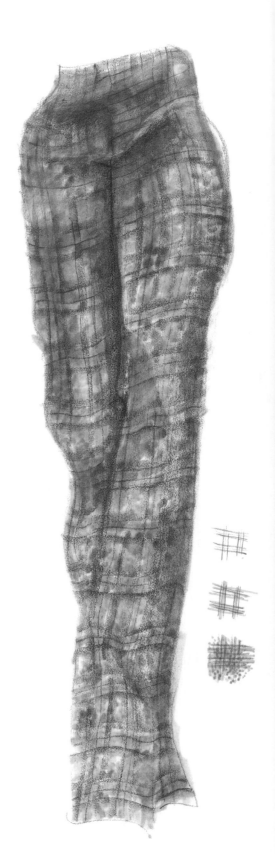

Knits are drawn by first making an even application of the color of the garment as a background. The stitches of the knit are then indicated using the side of a dark-colored pencil with semi-circular strokes. White pencil is used on the top of the folds to show sheen and soften the look of the stitches.

Tulle, faille or grosgrain (fabrics with a subtle, linear, ribbed texture) are drawn by applying an even color with marker then adding vertical, horizontal or diagonal strokes—depending on the direction of the weave—with a very sharp-pointed colored pencil.

Tweed often has a pattern, which is first drawn in with colored pencil. For this plaid, first draw in the horizontal lines as they bend around the body then add the vertical lines, also following the curve of the body and breaking in the folds. The thicker lines of color in the plaid are then applied with a marker. To show the texture of the tweed add lots of small dots in two or three layers using the color of the wool, and some black and white dots for final accents. See also the note on plaid on the page opposite.

fabrics/three-dimensional rendering

plaid/cotton

Plaid. This plaid is a tartan—a Scottish plaid. Plaid is a complicated, chequered pattern based on horizontal and vertical bands and stripes and has to be carefully planned out using a sharp colored pencil. Plaid can be drawn using one of two methods. Method one is to first draw in the widest horizontal and vertical bands with marker (note in this example there are only horizontal bands) then to apply the thinner horizontal lines of the plaid pattern and then the thinner vertical lines of the pattern using colored pencil or gel pen. Method two, which was the method used to draw this garment, is first to draw in the underlying pattern—here the checks of yellow and green—leaving the rest of the garment white, and then to apply what appear as the wide horizontal stripes—here red—as an overall background color from the reverse side of the paper. The background colors appear muted under the areas where the pattern has been applied and brightest where it shows through the white of the paper. If a more saturated color is required a second layer can be added from the front. Colored pencil should then be used again to redefine the pattern and to add shading in the folds.

NOTE: With plaids and stripes the widest or most prominent stripe falls on the center-front of the garment (or center-front of each pant leg). This prominent stripe is also placed on the edges of cuffs, collars, hems, pockets or other design details.

Cotton. Cotton is shown by filling in the silhouette of the garment with a flat application of the color of the garment and applying shadows with a slightly darker blended color to the insides of the folds. This is a soft cotton and as a result there are many folds. With pants the folds usually fall towards the knee. In this case the pants are drawn as if the fabric were gathered at the inside seam so the folds are more horizontal than usual.

fabrics/three-dimensional rendering

faux crocodile/embossed leather

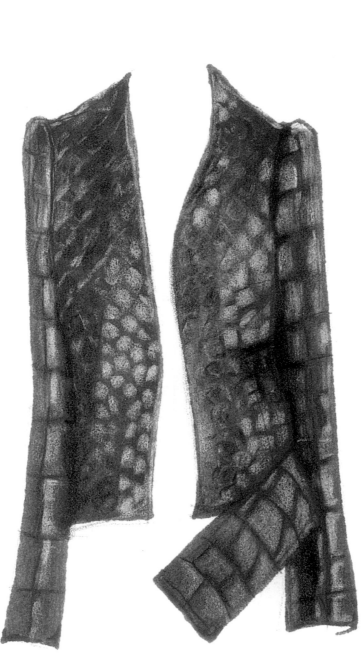

For fake crocodile, other reptilian or embossed leathers, first apply the base color with an even stroke then define pattern using a lighter colored pencil. Shadow is added with black pencil in the areas between the scales. The overall textural quality of the hard leather or skin is then indicated by making an application over the whole surface with the side of a brown pencil to soften and even out the surface. Note that this is a stiffer fabric and the silhouette should reflect its rigidity; with little or no drape, lines are more angular than with softer fabrics.

fabrics/three-dimensional rendering

variations of wool patterns

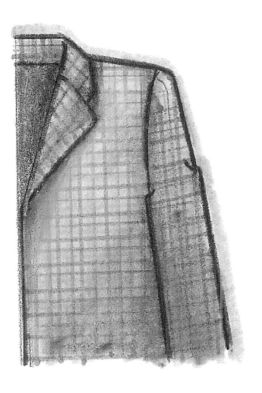

A plaid pattern drawn using mauve and green colored pencils and blended pink shading.

Striped jacket drawn with black and white pencil on a red-brown background.

Striped jacket drawn with white pencil on a blue marker background.

Tweed jacket drawn with white and black pencils over a warm-brown marker background.

orange and yellow colored pencils.

figure and garment/three-dimensional rendering

tailored jacket/fitted evening gown

Tailored jacket. The color of the garment is filled in and the shadows and drape are defined with a colored pencil.

Fitted evening gown. The gown is drawn in back view to show how ,with a fitted garment, the bottom is drawn as two spheres. Slightly darker shadows form under the bottom and a white core-light runs along the back of the left leg. Shadows fill in the drape of the train.

fabrics/details

magnified details (for reference)

Fur

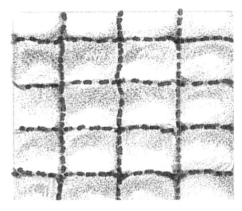

Quilting

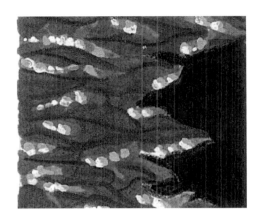

Shiny

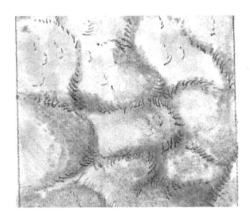

Shearling

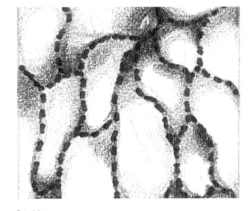

Stitching

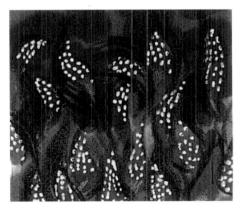

Feathers

Lace

Snakeskin

Velvet

fabrics/details

magnified details (for reference)

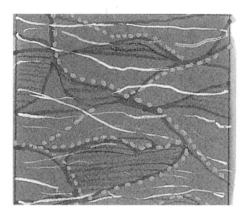

Beading

Plaid

Paillettes on chiffon

Lace

Plaid

Tweed plaid

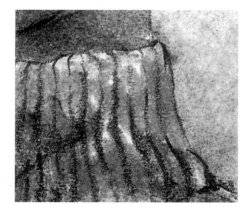

Cotton ribbing

Plaid

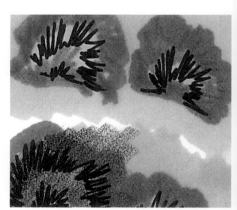

Floral Print

flowers

BODY AND HEAD

choices—face/makeup/hair/skin tone

basic croquis

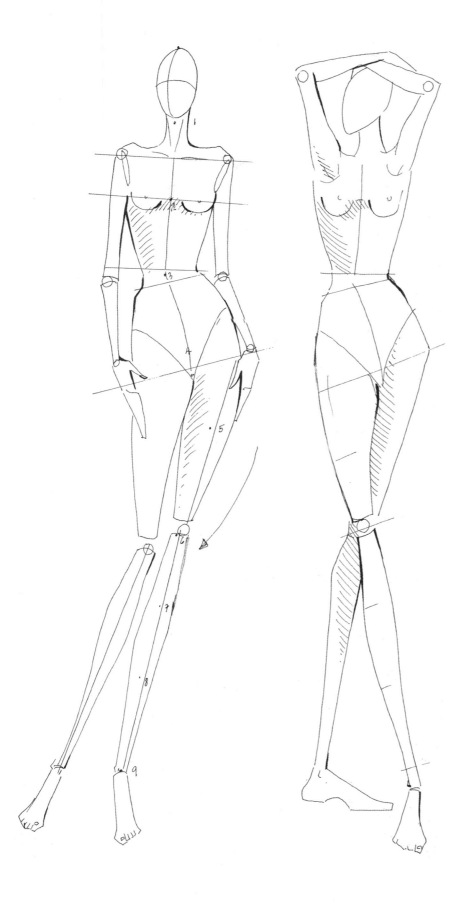

MAKING CHOICES FOR THE FACE, MAKEUP, HAIR AND SKIN TONE.

The choices made in fashion drawing on makeup and hair are similar to personal decisions made for make-up and hair to complement the clothes worn everyday, or the decisions made by the designer and stylist on styling a model for the runway. The treatment chosen for makeup and hair gives a drawing style and individuality: the face can be used as a canvas to extend or contrast with the overall effect of the garments.

The basic rule underlying choices for hair and makeup are the same as for most decisions on the content of a fashion drawing: the best choice is whatever makes the clothes look best. The same observation is usually true for decisions about skin tone on the body, though if a natural look is required it is necessary to ensure skin tone is as realistic as possible.

When drawing skin tone, as in fact with all drawing, it is important always to make the intent of the drawing clear. If the intent is that the skin tone look natural, it should be carefully drawn to look natural; if skin tone is a fantasy color chosen to fit with the garments and the overall composition of the drawing, it should be clear that this is the intention, that it is not intended to be a realistic color and the reason for the decision should be clear.

In general, if the intrinsic colors of a garment are important and feature prominently in a drawing, then making the skin tone/makeup subtly reflect the colors of the garments can be an effective option. This can usually be achieved using a blended version of the garment color to create tints and tones on the face and make-up.

If the color of the garments is not so important, a more natural treatment might be used. If clothes are dramatic, such as daring evening wear, a dramatic skin tone/makeup treatment will be needed to balance the ensemble: contrasting lights and darks, rich saturated colors and heavy lines will echo the features of the garment. Accompanying a dramatic garment with a dull hair/makeup treatment would most likely appear odd and unappealing.

Decisions about hair involve shape as well as color, and in the fashion drawing hair is an important compositional element of balance and/or emphasis. The shape, type and color of the hair should be chosen to balance the shapes and colors of the garments. Hair can be used as an accent to the color scheme of the garments or to fit into the overall color scheme in some other way.

The basic nine-head croquis, front view. These are the two-dimensional contour drawings onto which simple shading is applied to give the figure a more realistic three-dimensional appearance.

base skin tone technique

flat application of color

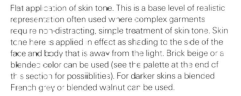

Flat application of skin tone. This is a base level of realistic representation often used where complex garments require non-distracting, simple treatment of skin tone. Skin tone here is applied in effect as shading to the side of the face and body that is away from the light. Brick beige or a blended color can be used (see the palette at the end of this section for possibilities). For darker skins a blended French grey or blended walnut can be used.

Variation of a flat application of skin tone. A small amount of shading is added to give a more realistic three-dimensional feel to the figure. Shading is applied under the hair, along the face, under the chin and around neck, at the collar bones, around the shoulders, under the bust (chest in male), along the side of the rib-cage and hip, in the crotch area, along the edge of the leg and knee, along the arm and around the foot.

base skin tone technique

flat application of color/variation

BASE TECHNIQUE FOR ALL SKIN TONE APPLICATIONS

FLAT APPLICATION OF COLOR

If time is limited, or clothes are so complex that a simpler treatment is called for in other parts of the composition, a simple, flat application of skin tone can be made.

The aim in applying skin tone is to end up with a smooth and even application of color with no streaking or blotching. It is easier to achieve this by applying marker from the reverse side of the paper, as the texture of the paper evens out some of the inconsistencies. If, for the sake of example, a nude figure is being drawn, after drawing the croquis figure with a light value colored pencil (light blue, pink, beige, grey or turquoise for example) the paper is turned over and the marker then applied.

Marker is best applied in sections, moving from the top to bottom of the figure—the head, the neck, the upper and lower torso, each leg and foot, each arm and hand. For the broader sections of the body marker is applied using the broad tip with a scrubbing motion. For the narrower sections, such as the arms and hands and legs and feet, marker is applied using the beveled edge with a vertical stroke extending from the shoulder to the elbow and then from the elbow to the wrist, from the hip to the knee and then from the knee to the ankle. The figure is filled in up to its outline; it does not matter if the marker goes slightly beyond the edge as that color can be incorporated into background shading.

After applying a base coat of marker from the reverse side, additional detail such as further shading to define the areas of the body that are more in shadow can be applied from the front.

Flat application of skin-tone with an alternative color. Here a French grey is used. French grey can be effective to show the shading of darker-colored skins.

base skin tone technique

flat application of color/gradated skin tone

Flat application of skin tone to the center axis. A variation of a flat application of skin tone where color is applied on half the figure to the central axis. Limited shading is applied to the whole figure.

Flat application of skin tone to the center axis. A variation of a flat application of skin tone where color is applied on half the figure to the central axis. Limited shading is applied to the whole figure.

Gradated skin tone, lit evenly from the front. Most of the skin area is rendered. Three layers of color are applied—light, medium and dark.

base skin tone technique

gradated skin tone

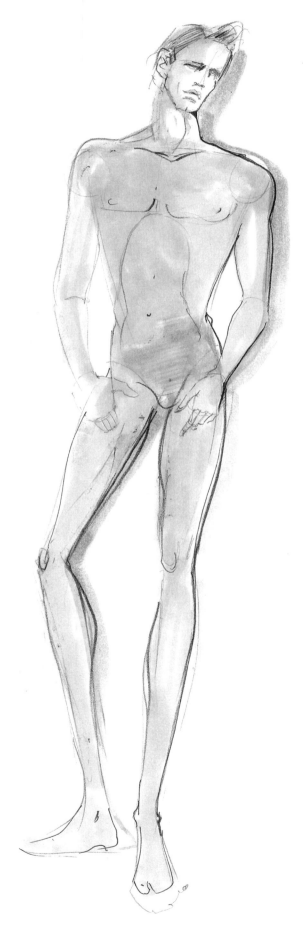

Front and front/three-quarter view male figures with gradated skin tone, lit from front.

base skin tone technique

gradated skin tone/reflected color

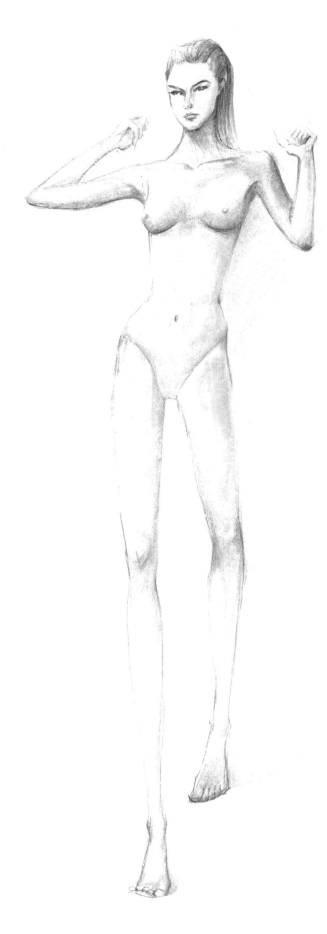

Colors of garments accented in skin tone. With colored garments the colors of the garments can be effectively used as accents in the skin tone, appearing as reflected colors. Colors are applied in layers from light to dark with the white of paper showing through for highlights.

Natural skin tone with reflected color from garment

base skin tone technique

three-dimensional skin tone/gradation of tone

Lightly rendered gradated skin tone. Three colors are used: light, medium and dark, with the darkest at the edge of the figure. The skin tone here carries over anthropomorphically to the dog.

RENDERING SKIN TONE THREE-DIMENSIONALLY USING GRADATION OF TONE

To give the body a realistic three-dimensional appearance, even though the base color can vary, the skin has to be shaded to resemble the way it appears in reality, with areas in light and areas in shadow. Although in actual light conditions there is a continuous gradation of shading on the skin from light to dark, in fashion drawing the convention is, in the interests of speed and simplicity, to reduce this gradation to three values—light, medium and dark (if time permits, however, as seen in many of the drawings in this book, many more levels of gradation can be added). Using markers, the light value is created by leaving the white surface of the paper unmarked, the medium value is the marker color chosen for the skin tone and the dark value is the marker color chosen for shading.

When drawing three-dimensional skin tone, the first decision to be made concerns the direction of the light source—whether it will appear from the front or side. If a decision is made to light the figure from the front, the sides of the figure will be in shadow; if from the side the shadows will appear on the opposite side from the light source.

If lit from the front a narrow strip of light appears down the center of the torso, legs and arms, which is shown by leaving a narrow strip of paper unmarked. The rest of the figure receives an application of skin tone color. On the upper body this is applied on either side of the strip of light using a careful vertical up-and-down stroke On the legs and arms, application is made with long, vertical strokes from the hips to the knees and knees to feet, and shoulders to elbows and elbows to wrists, running the marker along the contours of the figure, allowing a thin vertical strip of light, about an eighth of an inch wide, to remain in the center of the legs.

Streaking can occur in skin tone color if it is applied with short, jerky strokes. To avoid this it is best to apply the marker with smooth, continuous strokes, and not removing it from the surface of the paper in mid-action. This is a technique that has to be mastered, and it is useful to practice making long, continuous strokes on a separate piece of paper before beginning the drawing.

base skin tone technique

three-dimensional skin tone/gradation of tone

Gradated skin tone with full range of values—dark skin.

Application of skin tone on frontal figure, lit from left side
—light skin.

base skin tone technique

three-dimensional skin tone/gradation of tone/lighting variations

Gradated skin tone, side view figure lit from right.

Gradated skin tone, side view figure lit from left.

base skin tone technique

three-dimensional skin tone/gradation of tone/lighting variations

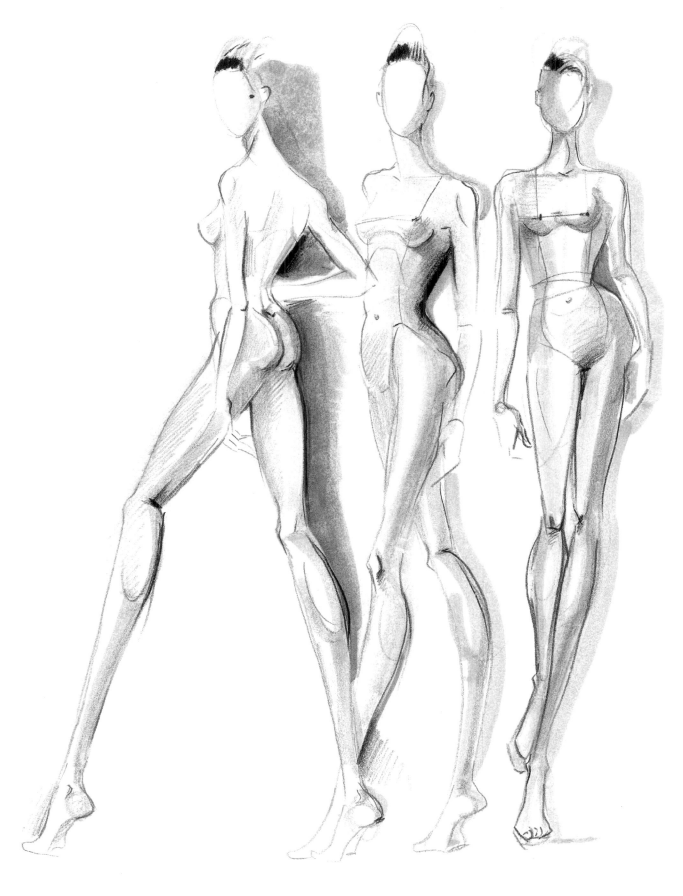

Gradated skin tone on, left, three-quarter back view, center, three-quarter front view and right, front view figure.

base skin tone technique

three-dimensional skin tone/gradation of tone/shading

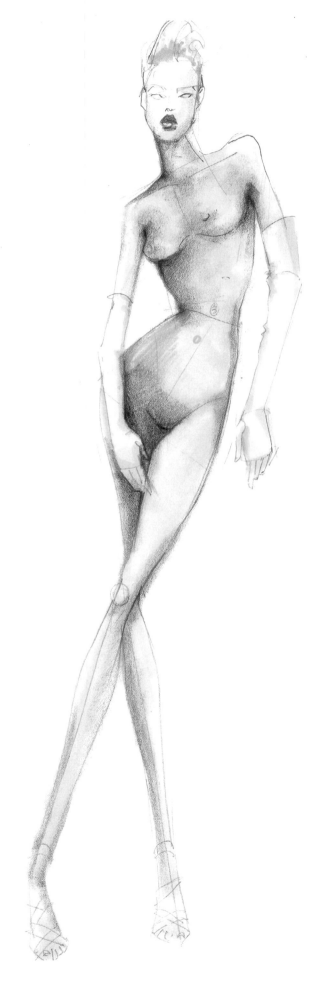

Front view figure lit from front.

Side view figure lit from front.

base skir tone technique

three-dimensional skin tone/gradation of tone

Front view figure with artificial skin tone color and butterflies in hair.

SHADING

Once the base skin tone application is complete, shading is applied. Shading can be applied with another coat of the same color used for skin tone, or a darker color may be chosen for more contrast. The most realistic effects are achieved if the value of the shading color is kept close to that of the skin tone.

Often a second coat of the same color is all that is needed to indicate the subtle shift of value. If a darker color is chosen then it should be fairly close in value, or it will give the appearance of a strip of paint on the leg. The easiest way, in fact. to create a suitable color for shading is to apply a blended version, either marker or colored pencil, of the skin tone color on top of the skin tone.

Shading is applied in areas of the body that recede from the light: the sides of the face, the sides of the neck, under the collar bone, at the shoulder muscles, under the bust, along the arms and hands, around the sides of the upper torso, around the sides of the hip, at the crotch, the sides of the thighs, around the knees, at the sides of the calf and lower legs and around the feet.

face

three-quarter view

Three-quarter face.

THE FACE

The physical appearance of the face communicates more about the moods, feelings and inner thoughts of an individual than any other part of the body. The expression of the eyes and the set of the other features—the mouth, eyebrows, forehead, jaw and nose can be configured in a million different ways to convey every conceivable shade of feeling and emotion. The face is the focus of all human communication and the part of the body the eye immediately seeks out.

In fashion drawing this expressiveness of the face can sometimes pose a problem, as the focus should be on the clothing above all else. The dilemma is solved in a number of ways, either by (i) downplaying the face, omitting or abstracting some of its details or perhaps rendering only a part of the face, (ii) omitting the features of the face completely (and in some cases even omitting the head completely) or (iii) using the face as a billboard to communicate information about the garments and the person wearing the garments (if so desired a wealth of information can be communicated with the face, including age, race, attitude and social status). Before beginnng to draw the face a decision should be made as to which of the three approaches is to be employed and the execution of the drawing planned accordingly.

The following pages contain a number of drawings reviewing the features, proportions and principal planes of the face. These drawings are included for easy reference when planning drawings of the three-dimensional face in color. In order to draw fashion well, though, it is essential to know how to make accurate *contour* drawings of the face (and indeed the rest of the figure). If possible this should be learned before beginning to draw with color. A full treatment of drawing the face and head (and the rest of the figure) can be found in *9 Heads* by the author or other guides to drawing.

face

three-quarter view

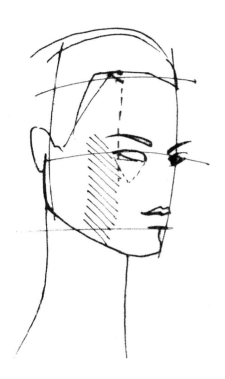

Three-quarter face showing position of eyes, nose, mouth and chin.

Three-quarter face showing the planes of the forehead and the side of the head.

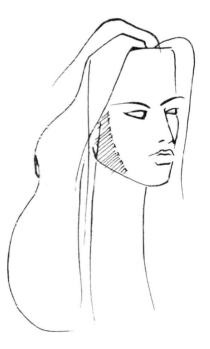

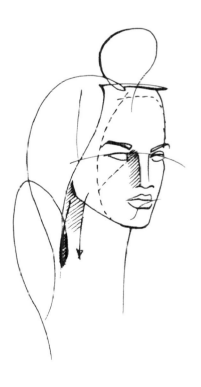

Three-quarter face showing shadows at the side of the face—a softer-looking face.

Three-quarter face showing the shadows around the forehead, the side of the face and the side of the nose—a more chiseled look.

face

three-quarter/front view

Three–quarter face showing shadows under the nose and around the lower lip to emphasize those features, giving a sensuous, pouty look. .

Front view face showing shadows on the right side of the face.

Three-quarter face turned up showing shadow under the chin to elongate the neck and dramatize the face.

Front view face, smiling, with subtle shading in the eye socket and under the jawline. This shading of the eye (and sometimes the cheekbones) is often used when drawing faces of races with strong features as the features are dramatized and made more prominent.

face

three-quarter/side view

Three-quarter face showing the position of shadows in the hair—under the hair, close to the face, neck and jawline.

Side view face showing the proportions of the features. The eyes are positioned half-way down the head.

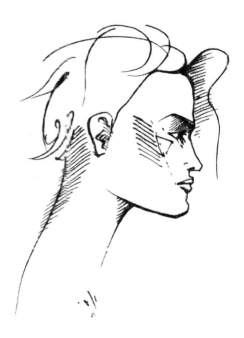

Side view face showing shading around the cheekbone, eye-socket, hair and chin for a more chiseled look.

Side view face showing shadows under the chin, hair, eye-socket and nape of the neck, for a softer look.

face

children/baby

Baby girl—front view face.

Small girl—front view face with shading.

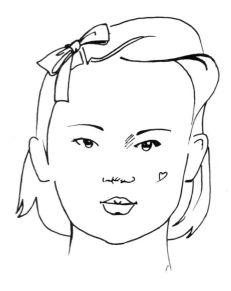

Girl—front view face with shading.

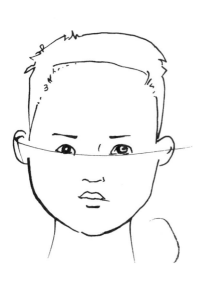

Boy toddler—front view face with shading.

face

boy/young men

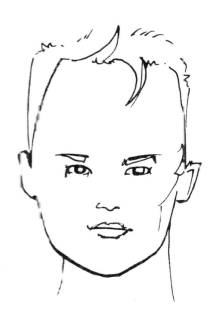

Boy—front view face.

Man—front view face.

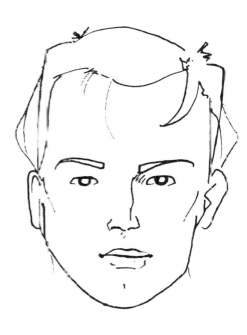

Boy—front view face.

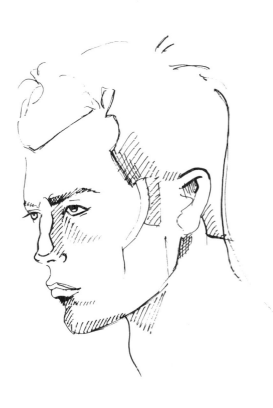

Man—three-quarter face.

face

drawing the face in color

Blended rose and beige skin tone.

Three-dimensional rendering of the face.
Color is applied to define the features and planes of the
face, giving a three-dimensional appearance. The face is
filled in with walnut skin tone with further applications of
color on the forehead and the left side of the face, and
around the eyes.

DRAWING THE FACE IN COLOR

Drawing the face, particularly when drawing it in
color, requires a delicate touch and a sensitivity to
the subtle, tiny shifts in the features which can
result in dramatic changes in expression. In general
the marker should be held close to the tip to exert a
greater degree of control with shorter strokes.

It is easy to make mistakes when drawing the face,
as it contains a large amount of information in a
small area: for example, an eye placed an eighth of
an inch above the other will make the face appear
hopelessly asymmetrical and impossible to look at.
Practice makes perfect, but if experiencing difficulty
drawing the face, it is advisable to switch to colored
pencil to draw the features, as it can be easily
erased and corrected. Keep in mind that all the
main features of the face—the width of the eye, the
length of the nose and the width of the mouth—are
about the same size: a common error, for example,
is to draw the mouth too low on the face; the mouth
should be kept close to the nose, and as a result the
face will look younger and more natural. The chin
should always be included in the drawing—it is the
same size as the mouth!

There are two methods for drawing the face in
color, similar to the two approaches for showing
body skin tone: One way is to show the skin tone of
the face with a flat, even application of a single
color, giving a flat, two-dimensional appearance to
the face. This method might be used where a drawing requires the addition of some strong facial emotion—perhaps in drawing extreme sportswear for
example—but only a limited amount of subtlety and
detail. The other method involves depicting the various planes of the face by indicating areas of light
and shade, resulting in a more realistic, three-
dimensional appearance. This method is used
when a naturalistic treatment of the face is indicated, and to express more subtle detail. If the clothing
itself is relatively simple a finely rendered face can
add to the overall impact of the drawing.

face

drawing the face in color/skin tone colors

Light beige skin tone with highlights at forehead, bridge of nose, chin and under the eye. Soft, blended rose is applied as shading under nose, on cheek, on chin and in the right eye socket.

Natural cinammon color skin tone with theatrical-colored light eye makeup and lipstick, applied with light-blue blended marker. Shading is indicated by a second application of color in areas away from the light. Note that the color cinammon is created by adding a small amount of green pencil into beige marker.

Warm brown saturated skin tone with a white highlight on the bridge of nose and soft lavender pencil shading around the side of face and under eyes. Black pencil is used to enhance the depth of eye socket, under the nose and around the chin. Dark-skinned races often have deep-set eyes that can be indicated with shading.

DO NOT DO. A face drawn without clear definition of the features, resulting from insufficient use of contrasting values.

face

drawing the face in color/flat application/naturalistic rendering

The planes of the face are defined by shadows drawn in with flat, almost graphic applications of blended color.

FLAT APPLICATION OF COLOR

To draw the face using the first method referred to above, with a flat, even application of color, first the outline of the head is drawn with a light-colored pencil— grey, pink or blue. Color is then applied from the reverse side of the paper, preferably leaving *small* slivers of unmarked paper for the eyes (it is a common mistake to leave too much white of the paper for the eyes as this encourages making the eyes too large—it is preferable, if anything, to leave too small a space; if necessary, it is relatively easy to draw the eye on top of skin tone) .Turning the paper back over, the features are drawn in with colored pencil, keeping the point very sharp.

When drawing the face using the second method, using shading to give a three-dimensional appearance, there are two ways to proceed. The first involves defining the full range of values that make up the planes of the face; the second defines only the shaded areas of the face.

For the first method use a blended color to fill in the face in all areas except those where highlights usually appear, i.e., the bridge and tip of the nose, the cheekbones, the point of the chin and the line of the jaw. A second layer of color, slightly darker than the first, is then applied in the areas of the face that are in shadow: the eye sockets, along the side of the nose, under the nose, in the middle of the mouth, under the lips, along the side of the face and under the jaw-line. Blended color can be applied on the cheeks or along the side of the face to show reflected light and perhaps, particularly if a blended rose color is used, a healthy, vibrant skin (especially with children).

When drawing the skin tones of darker skinned races the highlights are applied afterwards using a white pencil.

With the second method of drawing the face naturalistically, the features of the face are first drawn in with a light-colored pencil and skin tone is applied only to the areas where shadows form, using blended color. Variations in value can be achieved by applying a second layer in areas where shadows are deeper.

Color choices can be used, of course, to represent natural skin color, but also as effective devices to create value contrast and dynamism in a drawing. As with the makeup used in fashion shows, license can also be taken when drawing fashion and colors chosen that, though not naturalistic, dramatize and enhance the presentation of the garments.

The drawings on the following pages show a wide range of skin colors and shading techniques, drawn on three-quarter faces. The three-quarter face shows the planes of the face more dramatically so the dark and light areas can be clearly perceived.

face

drawing the face in color/skin tone colors

Light application of beige marker leaving highlights on forehead, bridge of nose and chin.

Beige skin tone with subtle lavender shading at eye, bridge of nose, chin, under jaw and neck. This skin tone is suitable for combining with lightweight fabrics of warm hues.

Dark brown skin tone built up in three layers with white and lavender shading. This dark-race skin tone is suitable for combining with warm neutral or stark white fabrics.

Blended walnut skin tone with second application around side of face. Suitable for a wide variety of lightweight fabrics with warm colors.

face

drawing the face in color/skin tone colors

Theatrical application of cool grey (10%) skin tone for high fashion.

Blended beige skin tone with blended rose around cheek bone. An excellent accent for any soft, lightweight fabric.

Blended beige skin tone leaving highlights on forehead and nose. Can be used in almost any application.

Blended brown applied over blended walnut. Excellent tone for a dramatic evening look for dark-race skin. White pencil is used to bring out highlights around the eyelid on the bridge of the nose, and on the lips.. Black pencil is used to define the eyebrows and eyeliner.

face

drawing the face in color/skin-tone colors

Peach skin-tone with highlights at jaw line and chin. This skin tone can be used with shiny fabrics: the contrast of values in the face echoes that which is present on shiny surfaces.

10% grey skin tone with blue highlights. This skin tone color will enhance any—but especially high fashion—cool-colored garments

Blended blue colored pencil shading applied over 10% grey skin-tone. Excellent with cool-colored lightweight fabrics.

Blended beige skin tone with warm-brown and lavender-colored pencil shading and chartreuse shading at eye and chin. Can be used widely, especially where color is a dominant theme in the design.

face

drawing the face in color/skin tone colors

Blended walnut skin tone with second layer applied to increase contrast of value with the white of the cheekbone. Effective with shiny fabrics such as leather or velvet.

Single application of blended French grey leaving highlights at eye, cheekbone, nose and chin. Suitable for evening looks and soft lightweight fabrics.

Two applications of blended beige with highlight at cheekbone and blended brown colored pencil shading at eyesocket and around cheekbone. Excellent accent for Fall fabrics.

Dramatic makeup with strong contrast of values between skin tone, lips and eyes.

make-up

eyes/eye makeup

EYES AND EYE MAKEUP

As in real life, make-up dramatizes the face and adds accents to the clothing

When drawing eyes, note that they are always lower on the inside and higher on the outside. The line at the top of the eye is the eyelashes viewed from the front and is darker than the line under the eye. Makeup is drawn in with blended color

Dramatic tattooed eyebrow for the catwalk.

Grey marker used as a halo around the eye has a softening effect.

Sexy, sleepy eye with extended mascara.

Warm color broadening the eye gives it a more sophisticated look.

Using grey in eyelid and inner eye gives depth to eye socket. Useful for showing strong bone structure.

Cool shadows add depth to eyelid.

Warm, rose colors give a healthy appearance.

Heavier use of rose colors for more dramatic effect.

Strong eyebrow and eyeliner give dramatic look for evening wear.

Warm and cool colors —modern eye make-up.

Shiny eye shadow shown by leaving white area of paper over the eyeball.

Fashionable smoky look.

50's inspired make-up.

Eye shadow reflecting an autumn or winter palette.

Grey shadow enhancing natural eye color.

Adding color (here blue pencil) to eyebrow and around the eye gives a dramatic effect.

makeup

lips/lipstick

LIPS AND LIPSTICK

The base color of the lipstick is applied with blended marker and accents are added at the curve between the lips with colored pencils. Highlights are created in the center of the lips either by leaving the white of the paper unmarked or drawing in with white pencil (or, with dark lips, white gel pen).

Soft colors.

Medium-intense colors.

Intense colors.

hair

exotic

HAIR

In fashion drawing hair frames the face, making it prettier, and accessorizes the garments. Hair can be treated in a number of ways, ranging from a natural lock to highly artificial colors and shapes.

Accessories can be added to the hair—bows, clips, tiaras, feathers, hair extensions for example—and designers increasingly abandon natural styling on the catwalk in favor of a wholly artificial look, using bright-colored wigs.

In drawing, the hair should be thought of as a series of shapes, sometimes simple, sometimes more complex. For beginners it is easiest to draw the outline of the hair and to fill it in with the desired color. The edges of the hair can then be broken up in a second easy step, using curved lines for wavy hair and straight lines for straight hair. Remember, hair frames the face, falling in at an angle towards the jaw-line. It does not, unless you happen to closely resemble Cleopatra or are wearing her wig, end in a horizontal line!

In more advanced treatments of hair, to add depth and realism to the drawing, the more complex shapes that lie within the simple outline shapes each have to be identified and shaded from dark to light. Darker shadows often appear close to the face and under the chin, and hair further away from the face appears progressively lighter. It is best to avoid using too many lines to express hair: most of the detail should be added only at the outer edges of the silhouette so the drawing does not end up with the look of a bird's nest. Make sure the lines of the hair are parallel and drawn in the direction in which the hair falls. Use a photo of a face for reference and trace in the curve of the hair with a finger, for guidance. Note that with blonde hair, shadows appear darker than the shadows around red or dark hair as the value contrast is greater.

Highlights can be added to hair in one of two ways, either by allowing the white of the paper to show through the hair or by adding highlights with white pencil after the hair has been filled in. Light layers of color built up in the hair can give it a richness and beauty beyond a single application of color.

This exotic hair style is drawn by applying seven layers of blended color, starting with the lightest color, light beige. Blended light brown is added as a second layer close to the face and further layers added as accents.

hair

highlights/voluminous hair

Highlights. Step 1.
Simple application of color allowing white of paper to show through for highlights. Marker is applied where the hairstyle originates at the crown and at the edges of the hair.

Highlights. Step 2.
To complete, yellow and ochre are added over the first application.

Voluminous hair. Step 1.
Outline the shape of the hair and indicate the direction of the styling with beige and pink marker.

Voluminous hair. Step 2.
Fill in the hair with brown and orange marker to add depth and shading and finish off with violet and red pencil for nuance and detail.

hair

straight hair

Short, straight hair. Step 1.
Outline hair and fill in with marker (here, orange, pink and beige). Indicate some shadow at the edge of the hair.

Short, straight hair. Step 2.
Define shadows around the edge of face and sheen on side of hair with black and white pencil.

Long, straight hair. Step 1.
Define shape of hair with beige marker, and break up with black pencil.

Long, straight hair. Step 2.
Add shadows to interior of hair shape close to the skull.

hair

streaked/theatrical

Streaked hair. Step 1.
For streaked hair first define shape with soft shading and
add streaks with light-colored marker.

Streaked hair. Step 2.
Fill in rest of hair with brown- and black–colored pencil.

Theatrical hair. Step 1.
For theatrical hair, define the direction with marker.

Theatrical hair. Step 2.
Add additional layers of marker to give more saturated
color and define shadows and highlights within the shapes
of the hair using black- and white-colored pencils.

hair

curly

Curly hair. Step 1.
Define shape of hair with light grey marker. Add lavender and black marker for shading. Leave the white of the paper to show through to indicate a broad highlight on the crown of the head.

Curly hair. Step 2.
Darken the areas of the hair close to the face and on top of the head with black marker to increase the contrast with the white of the face and the white highlight of the hair, so accentuating the appearance of shine. Break up the edges of the hair with stippling strokes of the marker and indicate curls with half circles.

Long curly hair. Step 1.
Define shape of hair with black marker and break up edges using a curled black line and thinner grey line.

Long curly hair. Step 2.
Add white highlights and finish filling in the main body of the hair with black marker.

hair

straight with complex highlights/tousled look

Straight hair with complex highlights. Step 1.
Draw outline of hair and fill in sheen and shadows with
beige marker and brown pencil where the hair bends
slightly away from the light.

Straight hair with complex highlights. Step 2.
Add more brown marker and pencil for greater shading
and depth.

Tousled-look hair. Step 1.
Define swirl of hair using grey pencil. Add cream marker.

Tousled-look hair. Step 2.
Add darker colored pencil close to eye level. Add more
swirls with cream marker and make hair lighter at edges.

hair

black/blonde/braids

Black hair. Step 1.
Define simple cap shape of hair closest to head with broad edge of a black marker. Break up hair into strands with medium tip of marker starting from the part of the hair at the crown and pulling lines around to neck, and again starting at jaw, moving away from the face.

Black hair. Step 2.
Add further complexity to strands of hair and add white highlights with pencil.

Long blonde hair with pink highlights.
Keep hair close to head until it reaches eye level, then open up to give volume. To show waves, turn wrist to both right and left. The interior of hair is defined with pink and brown shadows to add depth

Braids
Braids are drawn with shapes like almonds or grapes using a light-colored marker. Fill in individual shapes from top and bottom using a beige marker and add layer of darker marker or blended colored pencil for more depth and shading at the points where the hair twists.

hair

wavy hair/do not do's

Wavy hair.
Fill in the shape of the hair with beige marker using a scrubbing motion, allowing the individual strokes to show through to simulate the appearance of curly hair. Add a second application of brown marker and indicate ringlets at the edge of the hair with a twirling motion of the wrist. Colored pencil is used in some areas to show details of wisps of hair.

DO NOT DO. Do not attempt to draw each strand of hair individually– it takes too long and usually ends in a mess.

Wavy hair in extended bun. Shadows fall in the waves and are darkest in the deepest recesses of the hair. Draw the silhouette of the hair so the line expresses the waves of the hair. Fill in the interior parts of the waves where the hair bends away from the light with blended color slightly darker than the main hair color.

DO NOT DO. Do not randomly overlap the lines of the hair or it will begin to resemble a bird's nest.

the completed face

skin tone palette

Skin tone palette. All these colors can be used for body and facial skin tone.

the completed face

women

Pale skin tone, theatrical makeup, icy blonde hair.

Natural-look skin tone, freckles, simple auburn hair.

Simple shading with straight, brown hair.

Simple theatrical makeup with only partly-rendered wavy brown hair.

the completed face

men

Young black with black hair, chiseled features and side-burns.

Young man with white hair.

Boy with straight hair. Softer shadows around the cheeks make the cheekbones appear softer and more rounded.

Straight, black, shiny hair with minimal shading, falling over face. The strong planes of the face in shadow are created with walnut marker applied from the reverse side and a second layer applied from the front of the paper.

the completed face

women/men

Light-colored skin tone with soft shadows.

Black hair with strong highlights, light skin tone and red reflected light.

Bald, dark-skinned man. Multiple layers of shading are applied to create the strong skin tone effects. The white of the paper is left to show through at the cheek bone, nose, chin and top of the head.

Young man with chiseled features, extensively shaded.

the completed face

men/women/fantasy makeup

Artificial skin tone, grey and brown hair.

Young man with cap, shades and goatee.

Traditional good looks with natural skin tone color.

Fantasy makeup face showing strong shadow and saturated lipstick.

the completed face

dark skin tone

African woman. This color skin tone can be highly effective for contrasting with light garments irrespective of the actual race of the figure.

African man. Strong highlights have to be carefully placed high on the cheekbones for a natural expression. If placed too low the skin looks sickly—a mistake that is particularly noticeable with dark skin as the contrast of values is greater.

the completed face

fair skin tone/saturated red lips

A flat application of skin tone made with markers, and shading indicated with colored pencil around eyes and nose and on the lips, showing the areas of the face receding from the light source on the right. The saturated red of the lips was achieved by applying color from both sides of the paper.

beginning to draw/learning markers/short cuts

learning about fashion

BEGINNING TO DRAW/LEARNING MARK-ERS/SHORT CUTS

This chapter is designed to be useful to more than one type of reader. First, as the title suggests, the chapter is principally for those who are new, or relatively new, to the fashion drawing in color and who wish quickly to master the basic concepts of the subject and techniques for using colored markers. Acquiring these basic skills creates a strong foundation and allows readers to move on with confidence to the later chapters of the book that involve more advanced techniques.

Second, this chapter is designed for those who have some experience in drawing fashion, both line drawing and color, but whose experience with color is with watercolors or other media and not with colored markers. The techniques for using markers to draw fashion are not difficult but there are some significant differences in how they are applied when compared with other media. Revewing this section as well as Chapter One: Materials and Technique, will allow the already-experienced reader quickly to attain competency in the new medium.

Third, the chapter is also relevant for those readers with more experience in fashion drawing, and who have quite possibly been using markers for some time but wish either to learn how to draw more quickly, or to improve the quality of work produced under conditions where time is limited (all too frequent in the fashion industry). In these situations, when a deadline is looming, often all that is required is a basic representation of a garment, one that can be fleshed out later if required. This basic representation should, however, be fully recognizable, accurate and attractive. Drawing quickly while making sure the drawing still meets those criteria involves developing the ability to identify the essential elements to be included in the drawing as well as those elements that are not essential and can be excluded. This process quickly becomes intuitive, but this chapter is designed to help to learn and speed up this process.

Those beginning to draw should keep in mind two points: first, that drawing with markers requires practice and study, like any other acquired skill, and the quality of the results depends, to a large extent, on the time and effort that is invested. Second, that fashion drawing is *technical* drawing, intended to convey detailed information about the appearance and construction of garments.

Fashion drawing is a wonderful instrument for expressing ideas about fashion, but those ideas are best expressed (and the resulting drawings will be most effective) if they are coherent, that the garments drawn "make sense" from a constructional point of view and that, if so desired, they could be actually fabricated from the drawings. Fashion drawing is a powerful *language* for communicating ideas about fashion, but, although it assists greatly in learning about fashion, it is important separately to build up a knowledge of fashion and garments so the ideas that are expressed are interesting and logical.

beginning to draw

four basic steps of fashion drawing

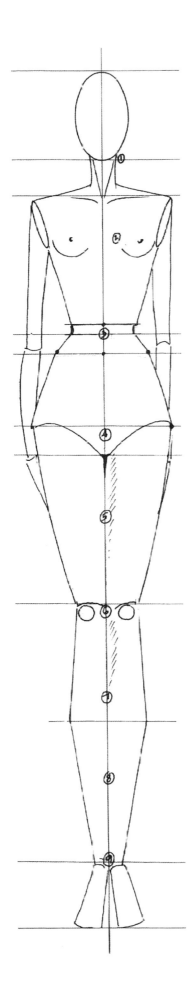

The nine-head croquis.

Knowledge of garments and their constructional details—learning how fabric drapes and falls and about the properties of different fabrics—comes from continual observation and immersion in fashion and fashion images. To begin developing a deeper knowledge of fashion, take out favorite clothes from the closet and inspect closely how they are made; examine garments in the pages of fashion magazines and pull out the pictures that inspire most and keep them in a scrapbook. To be able to draw fashion well and to use it to design new garments it is necessary to build up a rich store of ideas about fashion itself so that the elements included in drawings have a basis in reality.

It must be stressed here that this is the chapter where most of the hard work is to be done; this is the chapter where basic skills are learned and developed and where, the more time and effort is invested, the more the results will be apparent. With practice, drawing will become quicker and more accurate, and with practice, drawings will become beautiful and will call attention to the ideas they contain. Drawing quickly becomes a source of pleasure and satisfaction. Hard work will bring abundant rewards!

BEGINNING TO DRAW FASHION—THE FOUR BASIC STEPS

There are four basic steps that form the foundation of good fashion drawing. In order to develop the skills necessary to draw fashion well time should be devoted to developing proficiency in each of these steps. These four steps are as follows :

STEP ONE: Understanding the proportions of the figure—the nine-head croquis.
STEP TWO: Learning to perceive and draw the basic shapes of garments—the silhouette.
STEP THREE: Showing the constructional details of garments.
STEP FOUR: Shading.

Each of the drawings in this chapter is broken down into the different intermediate parts the four steps refer to. Sometimes more than one intermediate drawing relates to the same single step for example when extra detailing requires more explanation. The reader can make practice drawings for each of the four steps by reviewing the corresponding break-down drawing and either copying it, using tracing paper, or using it as a reference to make a new drawing.

For beginners it is best to focus on each step in the drawings in turn and repeat each of them several times until satisfied with the result, and then to move on to the next step. This will not only give an understanding of the distinct steps involved in completing the final drawings but will also help develop the basic hand/eye coordination and detailed observational skills necessary for good fashion drawing. For those more experienced and interested in learning to draw more quickly the series of drawings for the basic garment silhouettes of interest can be referred to for guidance on how to improve speed and accuracy.

the four basic steps of fashion drawing

step four: shading/shading the unclothed figure

STEP FOUR: SHADING
The final step in drawing the fashion figure and garment is the application of shading. Shading is the depiction of shadow on the surface of a garment and the simultaneous depiction of light where shading is not present (generally speaking, areas that are closer to a light source will have no shadows and areas further away will appear darker and will be shaded). The accurate representation of light and shadow in a drawing is what makes a garment appear real and three-dimensional. Without a realistic application of shading, drawings will appear flat and two-dimensional.

At an advanced level shading techniques can be, if so desired, used to give near-photographic representation of the surface qualities of different fabrics, as is covered in Chapter Four: Fabrics. At this more elementary level, however, the focus is on learning the general rules for how to shade drape as fabric bends around and falls from the figure. These techniques are illustrated with reference to different garments of non-specified fabrics. Shading of different specific fabrics is not yet attempted in this chapter but features in detail in the next chapter, on women's fashion.

Each of the drawings in this chapter shows how basic shading is applied to figure and garments. Note that as a rule shading is added as a final step to accentuate the shape and surface appearance of the fabrics and to help differentiate separate garments where they are layered over each other. When working with lighter fabrics, however, it is quite common to make an initial outline application of marker to represent shading before applying the main colors of the garments: Adding the shading first indicates where the highlights will appear in the final drawing, and with light-colored garments highlights are shown by leaving the white of the paper unmarked. It is easier to tell where these highlights formed by unmarked paper will fall if the position of the darker, shaded, parts is known—if the main color of the garment is filled before indicating shading it is easy to apply erroneously over areas that should be left white.

PREPARING TO DRAW
Before beginning to draw a number of preparatory tasks should be performed. These are listed on page 26 in Chapter One.

Shading. The drawing shows where shading is applied to indicate where shadows form on the unclothed figure, here lit from center-left.

the four basic steps of fashion drawing

step four: shading/shading the clothed figure

Shading. The drawings show where shading is applied to indicate where shadows form on the clothed figure.

basic garments

simple dress

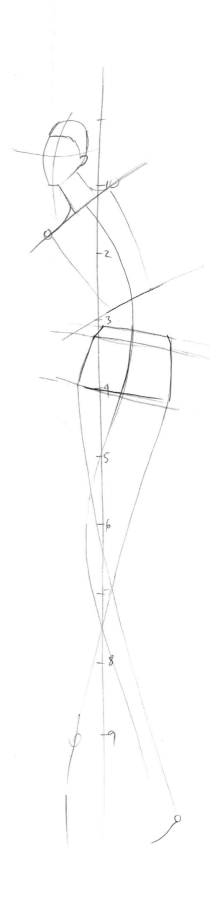

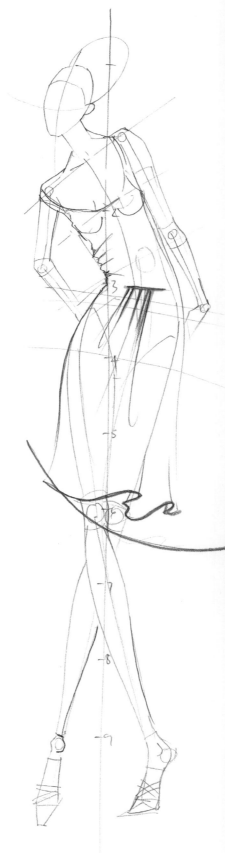

Step 1. Draw the croquis.
In this croquis the weight is on the left side of the figure, the shoulders slope down to the left and the hips pivot up on the left. Remember when the weight is on one leg the hip on that side pivots up and the leg returns to the axis line at the ankle for balance. Draw the axis line extending almost to the top and bottom of the page and divide into nine equal sections (starting with zero!). This is a front-view figure with three-quarter-view head. Draw the curve-of-the-body line (S curve) showing the way the body bends when the shoulders are tilted down and the hip pivots up. Sketch in the line of the shoulders and hips (shown in green). Sketch in the head, in three-quarter view.

Step 2. Complete and add detail to the croquis.
Add the shape of the upper torso and the shape of the hip or lower torso (shown in yellow). Indicate the positioning of the legs by drawing straight lines showing where the middle of the legs will be (shown in purple). Note that although the weight of the figure shifts to one side or the other, the axis line from the head to the feet is always vertical, and the body's center of gravity is always located somewhere on that line. Flesh out the legs and feet and note that the foot on the right side is a three-quarter position. Note the bust is at 2, the waist at 3, hips at 4, knees at 6 and ankles at 9 on the croquis. These positions are the same for all croquis.

Step 3. Draw the silhouette of each garment.
Draw in the silhouette of the dress making sure all lines bend around the figure. Note that the left strap here is positioned low on the shoulder to give the figure a sexy look. The fabric forms folds at the waist that curve around the figure and is gathered at a seam at the waistline (shown in orange). The fabric falls from the seam in the direction of the body. Note the fabric falls softly, following the curve of the body. Draw the hem around the figure at a diagonal (shown in orange) and break up into folds. Do not draw straight lines!

basic garments

simple dress

Step 4. Add color to the upper part of the garment. Fill in the shape of the upper part of the dress with light grey. Add a second layer around the bust-line and around the right side of the body to indicate shading.

Step 5. Fill in the remainder of the garment. Fill in the skirt of the dress with yellow, leaving the white of the paper to show through on the top of the drape of the folds. Add another layer of yellow as shading to indicate the edge of the right leg under the dress. Remember that in order to avoid streaking a circular scrubbing motion should be used when applying marker.

Step 6. To finish off the drawing, add the details of the face and hair with the fine point of a colored pencil.

basic garments

jacket/blouse/skirt

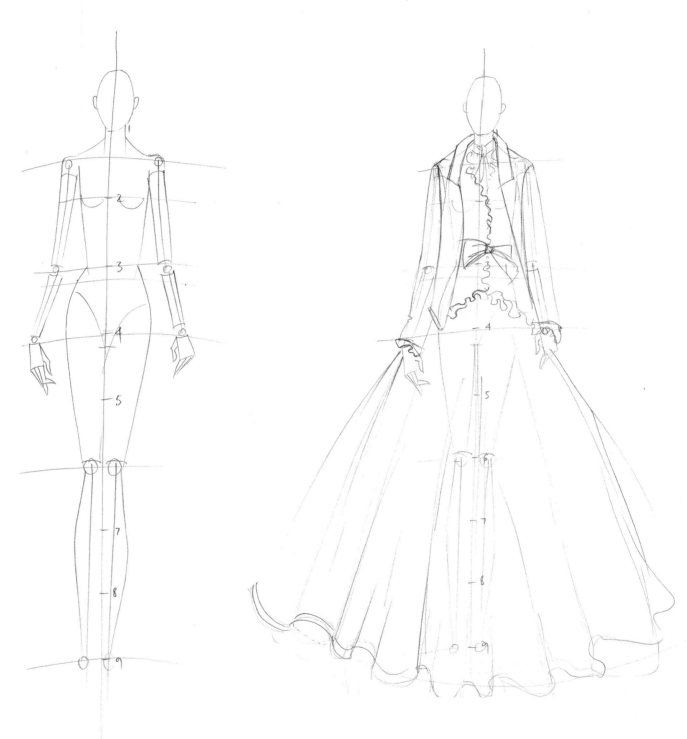

Step 1. Draw the croquis.
Draw the axis line. As this is a front-view croquis the body is not bent and there is no curve-of-the-body line. Draw in the figure, which is symmetrical, adding the details of the hands.

Step 2. Draw the silhouette of the garments.
Draw in the silhouette of the different garments in the outfit. Note that the blouse and collar bend around and cover the neck and the edge of the blouse extends over the center axis to the right. Add a ruffle to the edge of the blouse. The skirt is very full, with the hem indicated as the arc of a wide circle. The fabric drapes from the center of the skirt into cylindrical folds.

basic garments

jacket/blouse/skirt

Step 3. Fill in the color of the garments
Fill in the skirt and bow with yellow and the jacket with
blended turquoise marker. Leave the white of the paper to
show through where highlights will appear in the final
drawing. Add shading in the shirring at the waist with a
second layer of yellow.

Step 4. Add shading.
Fill in the shadows of the jacket and skirt with blended
turquoise. Show trim along the inside edge of the blouse
and pattern in the skirt with turquoise-colored pencil.
Further shading is added to the shirring at the waist with
blended turquoise marker, reflecting the color of the jacket.

basic garments

halter dress

Step 3. Fill in the shadows.
Fill in the dress with a light green marker. Add a second layer of shadows under the dress with yellow marker.

Step 4. Add details.
Indicate drape and folds along the seam at the waist of the dress using a second layer of green marker.

basic garments

halter dress

Step 5. To finish off the drawing add the details of the face, hair and accessories.

basic garments

gathered, fitted dress/coat

Step 1. Draw the croquis.
Front view croquis is drawn with weight on right side of figure, forcing the right hip up and right shoulder down. Left leg is bent at knee, head is three quarter view.

Step 2. Draw in the details of the croquis.
Draw in details of croquis—bust, arms, legs and feet.

Step 3. Draw in the silhouette of the dress and coat.
The center seam is drawn following the curve of the body. Lines of shirring extend out from the center seam so that the upper shirring extends up, the shirring at the hip is horizontal and the shirring over the leg extends down. The hem is draped at a diagonal.

basic garments

gathered, fitted dress/coat

Step 4. Add shadows to the gathers.
As these are light-colored garments, shadows are added at this stage, inside the gathers of the garment, using a dark-grey marker. The white of the paper is left unmarked down the front of the garment.

Step 5. Deepen the shadows.
Add a second layer of color with a light grey marker filling all areas of the outfit to deepen the shadows, leaving the white of the paper to show through along the ridges of the folds.

Step 6. Finish off the drawing.
Redefine the silhouette of the dress to show the separation from the jacket and to reemphasize the details of gathers and folds. Add details to the face and hair.

basic garments

jacket/skirt/party dress/jacket/skirt/hat

Step 1. Draw the croquis.
The figure on the left is a front-view croquis; the figure in the middle has its weight on the left side, forcing the torso up on the left side; the figure on the right has the same pose as the middle figure.

Step 2. Draw the silhouettes of the garments.
Draw in the silhouettes of the garments taking care to indicate where the skirts fall and drape around the body underneath and where the excess fabric of the skirts drapes away from the body.

basic garments

jacket/skirt/party dress/ jacket/skirt/hat

Step 3. Fill in the shadows of the garments.
Add shadows to the skirt in the figure on the left using a warm (French) grey and fill in the base color of the skirt with a warm brown. Fill in the jacket with black marker. In the middle figure, add shadows around the dress with a blended green and beige; this is a light-colored garment so the shadows are added at this stage. Note that the stripes fall diagonally across the folds of the skirt. In the figure on the right add shadows to the fur of the jacket, along the sleeve of the jacket, around the collar of the t-shirt and along the ribs of the t-shirt with a warm grey. Fill in the skirt with a light application of warm brown.

Step 4. Add detailing
Define the seams of the jacket on the left with white colored pencil and the trim with purple marker. In the figure in the middle start to fill in the color, adding light-yellow marker along the sides of the crape. Note that this dress is more structured than previous examples and as a result its folds hang straighter and wider. A second layer of brown marker is added in the fur and the skirt in the figure on the right.

basic garments

jacket/skirt/party dress/jacket/skirt/hat

Step 5. Draw in the details.
Use a .005 pen to draw in the details for all the figures.

basic garments

jacket/skirt/party dress/jacket/skirt/hat

Step 6. To finish off the drawing add the details of the face, hair and accessories.

basic garments

short evening dress

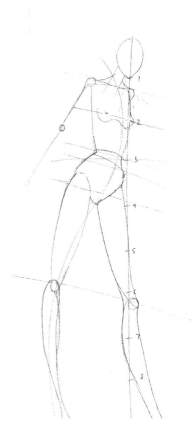

Step 1. Draw the croquis.
This is a three-quarter croquis with the weight on the left leg. The head is in profile.

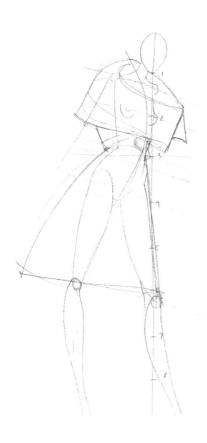

Step 2. Draw the silhouette of the garment. Note that the collar bends around the figure, forming an ellipse, and that the hem is on a diagonal.

Step 3. Begin to indicate the texture and shading in the uneven surface of the fabric using a magenta marker. This also indicates shading, and the white of the paper should be left to show through where the light strikes the fabric.

Step 4. Fill in fabric color and add shadows.
Add a layer of color on the left side of the dress using a medium cool-grey marker. Add shadows under flowers using the thin point of a black marker.

basic garments

short evening dress

Step 5. Add remaining shadows with the thin point of a black marker.

Step 6. Finish off the drawing by adding the details of the face and hair.

basic garments

dress/coat

Step 1. Draw the croquis.
Front-view croquis has weight on left side of figure in walking position, shoulders down and hip up on left side.

Step 2. Draw the silhouettes of the garments.
Draw the silhouette of the coat and dress, noting that the silhouette of the collar reaches half way up the neckline and the cap of the sleeves bends around the arm-hole, defining the tailored shape of the coat. Attention should be paid to the shape of hem of the coat—because it is tailored it has straight lines.

Step 3. Define the shadows of the garments.
Skin tone is added at this point as it is made using the same beige marker as is used in the dress. It is applied along the sides of the leg leaving a white core-light down the middle of the left leg, and to the chest above the dress. This is a light-colored garment so shadows are applied at this stage, using a beige marker in the light areas of the pattern and under the lapel, along the skirt and along the sides of the coat. Define the tucks of the dress using a light peach-colored marker.

basic garments

dress/coat

Step 4. Add further shadows.
Using blended turquoise-blue and lavender add shadows along the outside silhouette and the rear inner part of the coat.

Step 5. Refine the silhouette and add more shadows.
The hanckerchief hem is made of lightweight fabric and is defined with the thin point of a black marker. The silhouette of the coat, including the double-stitching at the hem, is also indicated using a black pencil with a sharp point. Add details to the buttons.

Step 6. To finish off the drawing, the shadows of the buttons, embroidery and tucks are indicated with a fine micron pen or the thin point of a black marker. Add the details of the face and hair.

basic garments

sweater/pants/coat/cable-knit sweater

Step 1. Draw the croquis.
The croquis is a symmetrical front view.

Step 2. Draw the silhouette of the garments.
Draw in the silhouette of the sweater, coat and pants, paying special attention to the exaggerated width of the armhole, the wide collar, the fullness of the sweater and the drape of the pants from the crotch to the knee.

Step 3. Add shadows and texture.
The coat is a light-colored fabric, so its shadows are drawn in first, using beige marker, leaving the white of the paper to show through where the highlights will appear in the final drawing. An initial application of light red marker is made to the sweater to start building up the texture. A little of the red marker is mixed with beige and used to indicate shading at the side of the leg and coat.

basic garments

sweater/pants/coat/cable-knit sweater

Step 4. Add further shadows.
Add an additional layer of shadows to the sweater with a brown marker and to the coat with a grey marker. Fill in the pants with a grey marker.

Step 5. Add texture and shape in the sweater.
Define the texture and shape of the cable knit in the sweater using a black pencil. Add shadows and highlights to the ribs of the sweater using black and white pencils. Define the silhouette of the coat using the fine point of a black marker. Add light brown and light red shadows to the drape of the pants. Add drape from the crotch to the knee and from the knee to the inside ankle on both legs using grey colored pencil. Add also the crease of the pant and some texture on the right leg with the same pencil.

Step 6. Finish off the drawing by adding the details of the face and accessories.

basic garments

shirt/pants

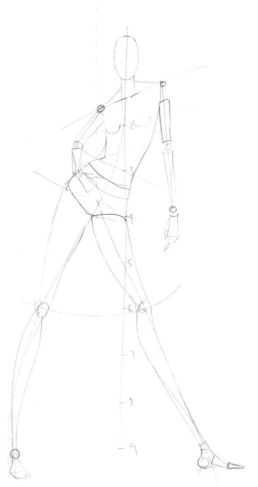

Step 1. Draw the croquis.
The weight is on the left side of the body, shoulders are down and hips up on the left side.

Step 2. Draw the silhouette of the garments.
Draw the silhouette of the blouse and pants paying careful attention to the drape on the left side of the blouse, the foreshortening of the arm on the left side of the figure, the drape of the sleeve around the wrist and the drape of the pants at the knee.

Step 3. Add the stripes.
Add the stripes of the blouse, making sure that the stripes curve around the bust-line, break up at the drape and follow the upward slant of the hip on the left side of the body. Shadows are added to the pants with a light blue marker.

basic garments

shirt/pants

Stripes follow the curves
of the figure

Step 5. To finish off the drawing add hair and a second
layer of shading for greater depth.

Step 4. Add shadows to the body and sleeve of the blouse
on the left side using blended purple and blue marker.

basic garments

suit

Step 1. Draw the croquis.
A three-quarter view croquis with the weight on the right side of the figure, shoulders down and hip up on the right side and three-quarter view face.

Step 2. Draw the silhouette of the garments.
Draw the silhouette of the shirt, tailored jacket and pants paying attention to the closure of t' jacket, that the button lies on the center axis and the jacket overlaps on the right side. The cc turns around the back of the neck at the level of the jaw line, the lapels are symmetrical, the c of the sleeve is indicated bending around the armhole and the waistband of the pants bends low on the hip. Add shadows under the lapel, center-front and sleeve of the jacket using a me um-grey marker. Pay close attention to the positioning of the collar, the jewelry, the tie and th lapels of the jacket so that it is clear which garment sits on top and which sits underneath.

basic garments

suit

Step 3. Add additional shadows.
Fill in the jacket and pants using a light grey marker leaving some of the white of the paper showing along the top of the sleeve, on the button, at the drape of the crotch and the seams of the welt pocket. This is essentially a white garment so a cool-grey (10%) is used for the shading.

Step 4.
Add definition to the silhouette and style-lines of the garment with the fine point of a black marker. To finish off the drawing add the details of the face and accessories.

basic garments

leather jacket/pants

Step 1. Draw the croquis.
The weight is on the right side of the body, shoulders are-down and hip up on the right side.

Step 2. Draw the silhouette of the garments.
Draw the silhouette of the jacket and pants noting that the collar reaches high around the back of the head, the cuffs of the jacket bend around the arms and the trim at the waist around the torso. Clearly indicate the shape of the pockets and the drape at the crotch and knee.

Step 3. Fill in the shadows/base colors of the garments.
The jacket is shiny and there should be a strong contrast between the white of the shine and the dark color of the body of the garment. To make the black as saturated as possible a number of applications of marker are needed. A first application is made at this stage leaving the white of the paper to show through where highlights will appear. The pants are light-colored and so the shadows are filled in first with a light-grey marker.

basic garments

leather jacket/pants

Step 4. Add further shadows and draw in stripes. Add an application of grey marker to the jacket, especially next to where the white highlights will appear—the darkest darks must appear next to the white highlights—and draw on the stripes of the pants with a grey pencil, indicating where they break up in the folds.

Step 5. Define shearling and styling details/define crape. For the jacket, styling details appear at the zipper, snaps and seams with the thin point of a black marker. Using the side of a brown pencil define the shadows in the drape of the wool pants. Using the side of the pencil gives the appearance of a soft, subtle sheen to the fabric.

Step 6. To finish off the drawing add the details of the face, hair and shoes. Add pencil to deepen the value of the shading under the lapel and along the sleeve, and bring out the highlight down the sleeve with white gel pen.

practice and exercises

BEGINNERS

1. Take any of the series of drawings of basic garments and copy every drawing in the series using black, white and greys rather than colored markers.

2. Repeat exercise 1. in color.

3. Draw a croquis, front view. Add the silhouette of a blouse and skirt. Fill in with blended color and shade in the folds of the drape. Take the same croquis with the silhouette of the blouse but replace the silhouette of the skirt with pants.

4. Draw a croquis. Add the silhouette of a coat and dress. Add a floral pattern to the coat and a plaid to the dress.

5. Draw the croquis and silhouette of each outfit in the chapter.

6. Draw a pleated skirt with a lace trim.

7. Draw a leather jacket with a satin trim.

8. Draw a jacket with a print—it can be floral, geometric, ethnic, plaid or some other—and add sequin detailing at the collar, cuffs or spread over the garment.

9. Draw a striped blouse and pants. Make sure the stripes follow the curves of the body underneath.

10. Draw (i) a jacket made of lightweight fabric such as wool challis or silk, (ii) a coat using a medium to heavy-weight fabric such as leather or corduroy.

11. Draw three garments made from transparent fabrics.

12. Draw white t-shirts of different styles—sleeveless, long-sleeved and so on—and add graphic images to each.

practice and exercises

ADVANCED.

13. Copy any of the final outfits in this chapter changing the colors.

14. Copy any of the final outfits changing accessories.

15. Copy two of the finished drawings in this chapter, changing the color of the fabrics.

16. Copy the croquis with the fur on the opposite page and add (i) a straight skirt, (ii) ankle-length pants and (iii) a chiffon full skirt.

17. Copy the figure on this page and change the color.

18. Draw a six-layered skirt using a different print pattern on each layer.

19. Draw two evening gowns, the first made of silk, the second of velvet (refer to the chapter on fabrics for how to draw silk and velvet).

20. Draw a group of three croquis with one of the croquis wearing one of the garments from this chapter and the other two with variations of the same garment. Make the figures overlap at at least one point.

21. Draw a croquis wearing a blouse, skirt and jacket and accessorize using the drawings of accessories in this chapter as references.

22. Take one of the figures in this book, changing it slightly to personalize it, and draw it in twenty minutes.

WOMEN'S FASHION

drawing women's fashion

organization of the chapter

DRAWING WOMENS FASHION

The preceding chapters of this book have covered the principles of design and color theory as they relate to fashion drawing, and the techniques required for drawing different types of fabric and skin tone. Chapter Five: Beginning to Draw explained the processes for making three-dimensional drawings of basic garments quickly and easily. The level of drawing shown in that chapter will be sufficient for the majority of cases where a fashion drawing is required; those drawings do not, however, contain a high degree of detailing, and are not compositionally complex. In this chapter we arrive at the point where all the elements of the first four chapters are drawn upon in order to produce advanced drawings of a wide range of garments constructed of all types of fabrics and often with highly complex detailing. The fashion drawings shown in this chapter are examples of the most advanced type of fashion drawing, of sophisticated composition, often using advanced poses. They are intended to serve as models for the level of clarity and detail to which drawings intended for inclusion in portfolios, for design presentations or for advertising or editorial purposes should aspire.

In this chapter and those that follow—Wardrobe Basics, Men's Fashion and Children's Fashion— all the information needed for the reader to be able to reproduce the final drawings of different garments made of different fabrics is provided. For the simpler drawings, the process itself is sufficiently transparent that only the final drawing is included. For more complex drawings, one or more intermediate-stage drawings and sometimes the initial croquis sketch are included (particularly if a pose is difficult or the garment complex and it is not immediately apparent where the body lies underneath). This allows the step-by-step evolution of the drawing to its final form to be clearly perceived.

The drawings are accompanied, in most cases, by a detailed textual description of the drawing process, indicating also materials and techniques used and compositional and technical fashion considerations. The visual representations and textual descriptions are intended to complement and reinforce each other in order to achieve as clear and full an explanation as possible of how to execute the drawing and drawings of similar garments or similar fabrics. Different people learn to draw in different ways: while some learn almost completely from visual cues, others require the reinforcement of a clear textual explanation, and yet others depend largely on the text. Studying and copying the drawings, or using them as starting points for new designs, will serve as excellent practice, helping to absorb the information they contain and aiding the learning process.

If, even after studying the text and drawing breakdowns, difficulty in understanding part of an explanation is still encountered, whether it is for a cro-

quis, silhouette, application of color, shading, skin tone or hair, reference should be made to the corresponding sections in the Beginning to Draw chapter and the earlier chapters dedicated to those topics. The tasks to be completed before starting a drawing are listed on page twenty six of Chapter One: Materials and Technique and are the same for all drawings.

The drawings in this chapter are designed to help develop advanced skills. They range in difficulty from a medium to an advanced level. Many of the drawings will appear complicated and sometimes daunting to those relatively new to the field, but in fact they are all based on the techniques explained in the earlier chapters of this book: no technique is used that has not already been explained elsewhere. Once the drawings are studied in conjunction with the explanations of how they are made they will soon become clear and less complicated. The main differences between these drawings and those of the earlier chapters are that here more shading is used, more layers of color are applied (resulting in the appearance of greater depth and wider range of colors) and the clothes themselves are more complex and with more design details.

Very often, as has been mentioned, in real life situations in fashion design time constraints will not allow for drawings to be made that are as complex as many of those included here. The best preparation for being able to draw well when working under strict time constraints, however, is to learn to draw to a higher level than will normally be required. If one learns to draw well then the short-cuts and simplifications that have to be made when drawing under time pressure will come quickly and naturally. This chapter provides the elements necessary for learning to draw fashion garments to the level of the drawings provided as examples, and with motivation, practice and application almost anyone can learn to draw to these standards.

HOW THIS CHAPTER IS ORGANIZED

This chapter is organized in a similar way to an advanced course in fashion drawing with markers: it is divided into sections corresponding to garments made of different fabrics. The reason for this ordering is that one of the key elements in successful, advanced fashion drawing is being able to render garments in different fabrics to a degree of realism such that the fabric is immediately identifiable (this is unfortunately frequently overlooked in courses and textbooks with the result that it is often difficult to tell from a drawing what fabric a garment is made from). Fabric defines the garment, and how a fabric looks when made into a garment—the drape, the texture, thickness, the way it holds its shape and the surface appearance—is a vital part of a drawing, and usually more difficult to execute than the drawing of the silhouette and details.

drawing women's fashion

choice of garments/useful tips

The first types of fabric to be covered are patterned prints, both simple, two-dimensional graphic prints and more complex, three-dimensional prints where there is layering and gradation of colors, requiring mixing and blending techniques. These are followed by lightweight fabrics, heavier fabrics and then more specialized fabrics such as transparent fabrics, shiny fabrics, leather, and white, black and grey fabrics. This progression reflects the increasing difficulty of rendering these different fabrics: two-dimensional patterns require the simplest application of flat color; textured fabrics are drawn employing more than one technique and often with several layers of color; shiny fabrics are the most difficult to draw as they include a wide range of values, and how the garment drapes and fits the body must be fully comprehended in order to map these onto the garment. Black, white and grey fabrics have been covered in a final section. Fabrics of these colors are of most of the fabric types covered in the earlier sections but drawing them involves a particular understanding of the distribution of subtle variations in value and an ability to control markers sufficient to produce those variations.

Each fabric section contains a cross-section of garments, ranging from simple to elaborate, with a wide variety of shapes and textures. The drawings parallel the garments in their range of complexity and difficulty, though it is not always the case that the most complex garments are the most difficult to draw, and vice-versa.

A separate section on accessories has been included as these (as they always have) play a vital role in women's fashion and continue to grow in relative importance.

THE CHOICE OF GARMENTS SHOWN IN THE DRAWINGS/USEFUL TIPS

The most important criterion in choosing the garments illustrated in the drawings included in this chapter was—as the title of the book suggests—that they should be modern. As of the date of publication of this book all the garments are contemporary, and in some cases even perhaps a little ahead of trends. It is important that the silhouettes and details of modern fashion are used as examples when learning to draw fashion, because these are the forms that most resemble what will actually be drawn: there is little call or reason for drawing clothes that are twenty years out of date.

As distinct from the subject garments, however, the *techniques* explained for drawing them are timeless, and learning them will equip the reader to draw the most modern and up-to-date garments as fashion changes in the coming years.

Besides being modern, the garments in this chapter were chosen for a number of other reasons. One important reason is the need to include a wide range of garments in order to demonstrate all the techniques required for making the different effects used in drawing fashion garments: if a designer, or aspiring designer, has in mind to design a particular type of garment in a particular fabric, then most likely, examples of similar garments in the desired fabrics can be found here, or if not, then something fairly close will be encountered.

Most of the garments included in this chapter are by well-known designers. The drawings are, as well as aids for learning how to draw the garments, the author's homage to the remarkable artistry and beauty of modern fashion and the designers who create it.

A number of garments in the drawings were designed by the author, some in collaboration with young assistants, and some are the assistants' own designs. Of the author's designs, many of these were drawn to create the ideal garment to illustrate a particular drawing technique or effect: many of the fashion design elements in such cases were taken from other designers and adapted to the needs of the book. This process of designing new garments is great fun, and is how much of modern design actually takes place: design ideas blow in the air and are quickly caught and incorporated into new designs. Readers who aspire to become fashion designers should experiment as much as possible (this is also the best way to practice the techniques for making excellent fashion drawings) and should not hesitate in seeking inspiration wherever it can be found, putting their own personal imprint on ideas that have often been around for a long time and are still vibrant.

Two tips that will often prove useful when drawing complex women's garments: First, when considering how a garment should be shaded—an important part of what makes a garment look realistic and three-dimensional—always remember that the silhouette itself, if drawn correctly, contains key information about how to shade. How the fabric of the garment drapes and where it bends—usually at the elbows, knees, armholes, bust, waist and crotch—give clear pointers as to where shadows will appear and shading should be applied. Second, when a drawing is complex and contains a number of spread-out and differing elements, such as when an outfit is made up of several layered garments, the composition can be unified by introducing a single, subtle color in different areas. Using a blended version of one of the principal colors from the garments and applying it to the hair and skin tone as a reflected color can be an effective way of doing this.

printed/patterned fabrics

stripes

DESIGN: NR

Voluminous striped cotton skirt.

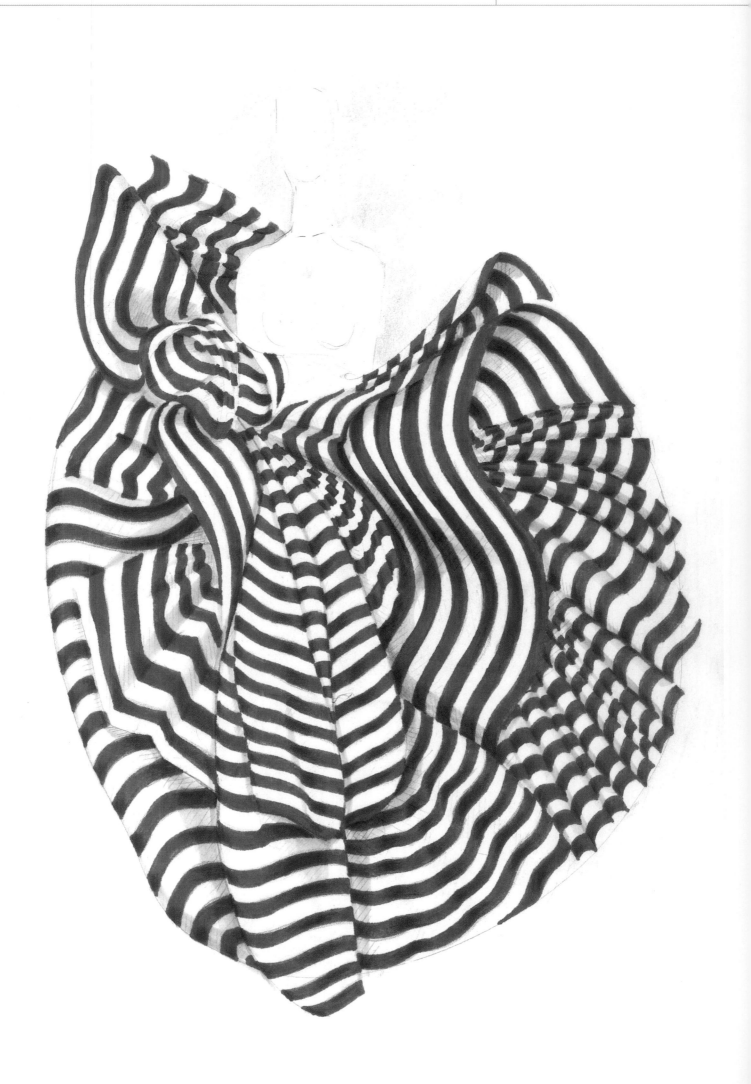

printed/patterned fabrics

DESIGN: NR

stripes

Voluminous striped cotton skirt.

This drawing shows how to draw stripes accurately on complex drape without getting dizzy.

The folds of this fabric are cylindrical and fall in a variety of directions, which is what makes the skirt visually intriguing.

The key to drawing this garment successfully is to plan out each segment of drape as a cylindrical form, with the large primary fold originating at the center of the skirt and secondary folds originating from two other points.

Begin by drawing a simple front-view croquis and add the silhouette of the garment as a wide, almost circular shape around it. Define a point at the waist from which most of the sections of the folds of the dress will radiate. There is a second radiation point to the right of the principal radiation point from which a single section of folds also extend, appearing to originate under the skirt, and a third radiation point originating near the knee. Plan out triangular shapes that define the different sections of folds. In the accompanying drawing these are outlined in different colors for clarity. Divide up each triangle into the folds with a light colored pencil. To plan out the direction of the pattern begin by looking at the direction of the curve at the bottom of the fold and observing if it is convex (bends out) or concave (bends in) (Step 1).

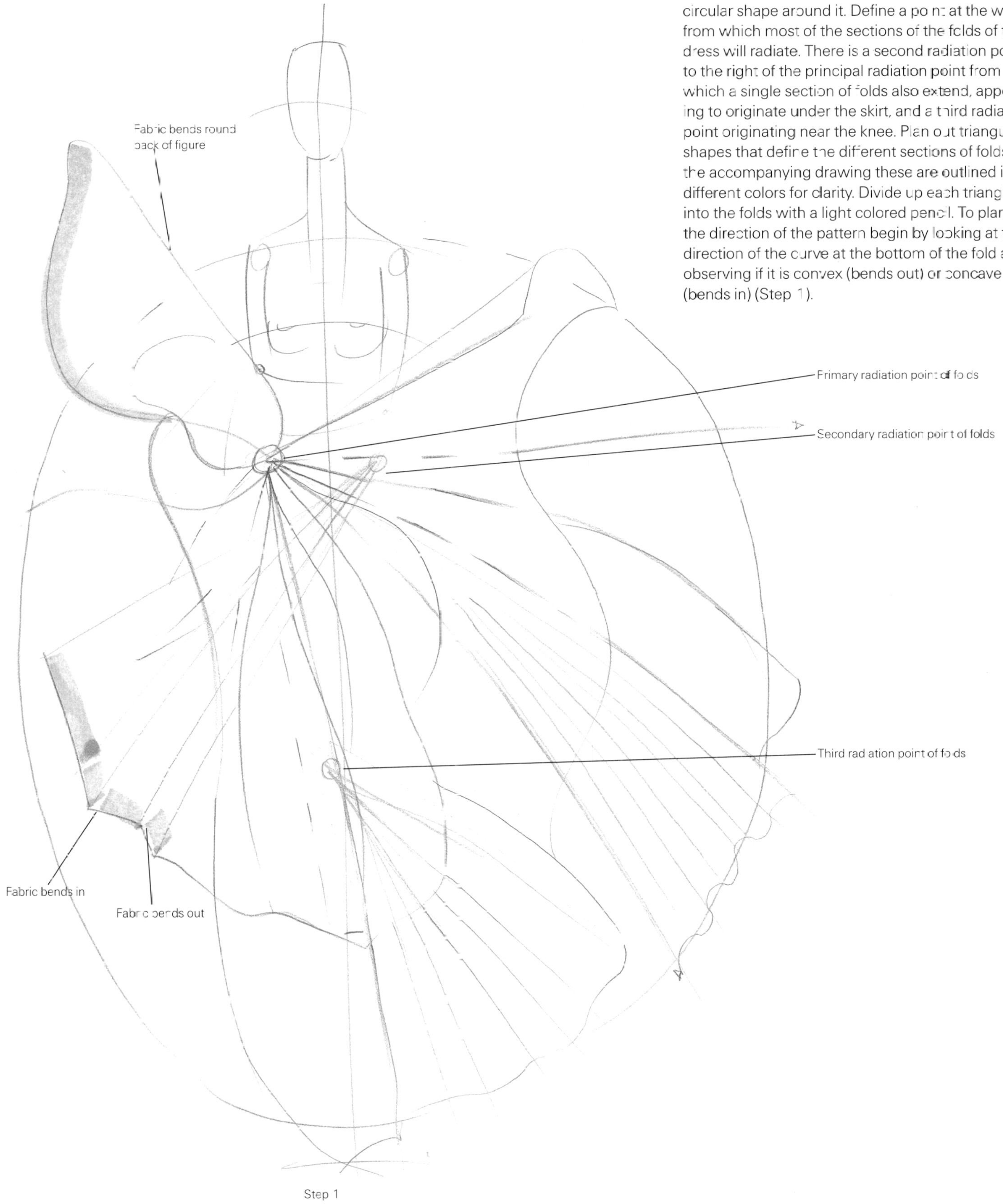

Fabric bends round back of figure

Primary radiation point of folds

Secondary radiation point of folds

Third radiation point of folds

Fabric bends in

Fabric bends out

Step 1

printed/patterned fabrics

DESIGN: NR

stripes

Voluminous striped cotton skirt.

Add shadows using a light-colored marker in the folds of the drape where they recede (Step 2).

The shape of the lines of the stripes in the fold are parallel to the shape at the bottom of the fold. Subtle shadows are added with a blended warm color from the reverse side of the paper at the edges of each fold. The red stripes are drawn using three applications of color to give rich saturation.

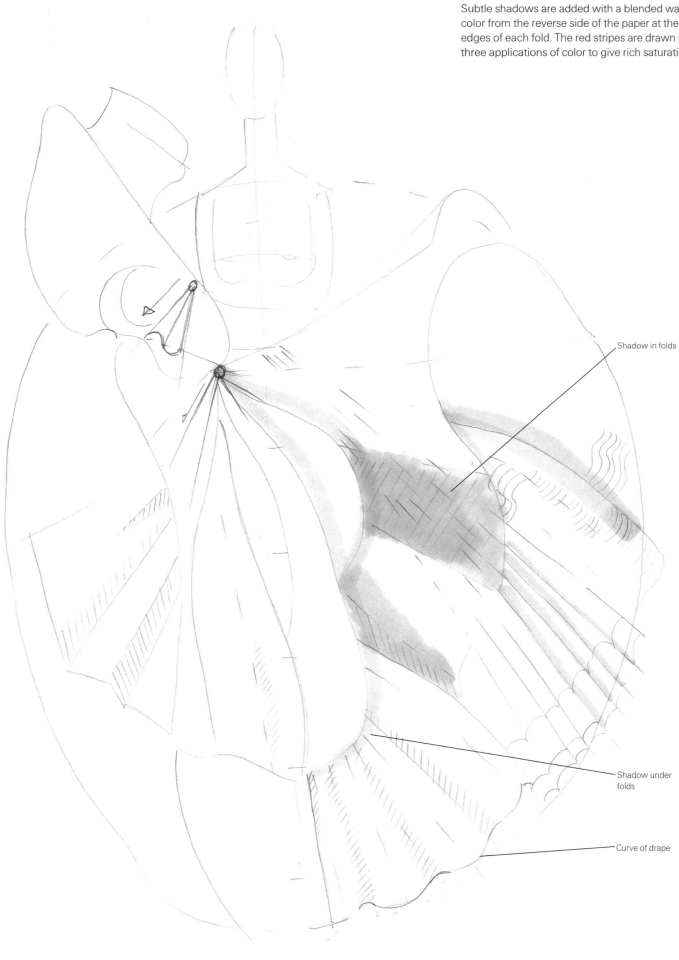

Shadow in folds

Shadow under folds

Curve of drape

Step 2

printed/patterned fabrics

stripes

DESIGN: NR

Striped tailored jacket, stencil-patterned t-shirt, layered skirt with knife pleats, gloves, handbag, necklace, hat, fishnet stockings.

This drawing shows how to draw diagonal stripes as they fall on the flat planes of a tailored jacket and the knife pleats of a skirt. The stripes and patterns are of different scales and fall in different directions. A compositional decision was made to accessorize the garments with fishnet stockings—drawn with open cross-hatched lines—to continue the theme of stripes and echo the angles of the stripes in the skirt. Color is not important in this drawing.

First, draw the silhouette of the jacket with careful emphasis on the angularity of the shoulders and lapels. Draw in stripes diagonally on the lapel, using the upper edge of the silhouette of the lapel as a guide. Beginners may wish to draw the stripes first with a pencil as it is sometimes tricky to keep the spacing between the stripes even (and markers cannot be erased!). Continue the stripes around the torso with the same spacing, bending them around the chest. Remember that stripes break up where fabric folds, such as at the elbows. One way to work out the positioning and sizing of stripes is to divide the garment into sections and then to divide these sections in half, and half again until the desired position and size of stripes is achieved (Step 1).

Shadows are added to the panels of the pleats using a 10% grey marker. Here the skirt is lit from the left side and the right leg from the right side so shadows fall on the left side of the right leg and the right side of the skirt. Showing multiple light sources on a figure can give a vitality to drawings of predominantly black, white and grey and graphic patterns that can otherwise appear two-dimensional.

Diagonal stripes are applied to the flat surface of each knife pleat of the skirt. Note that some pleats may extend at right angles to the body, indicating a swing and lightness to the fabric. It is important to add shadows under each pleat and under the planes of the jacket to show depth (Step 2).

In the final drawing complete the stripes and the mesh of the stocking with the fine point of a black marker and shade the t-shirt. Hat and handbag are of saturated black with white highlights and are strong graphic accents to complement the garments. This figure has soft white hair which acts as a contrast to the graphic stripes of the outfit.

The skin tone is a lightly-blended soft pink which also contrasts with the largely achromatic colors of the garment.

printed/patterned fabrics

DESIGN: NR

stripes

Striped tailored jacket, stencil-patterned t-shirt, layered skirt with knife pleats, gloves, handbag, necklace, hat, fishnet stockings.

Diagonal stripes bend around the bust.

Pleats of skirt flip up.

Step 1

Step 2

printed/patterned fabrics

stripes

DESIGN: JEAN-PAUL GAULTIER

Modified varsity jacket, low cut pants, printed, knit t-shirt.

This drawing shows variations of scale and color saturation in different patterns and trims. The application of color in this drawing is not as difficult as it first appears: once the croquis and silhouette are correctly drawn what remains is a relatively simple process of filling in the shapes with color.

Note when drawing the croquis that the shoulder on the right is leading the shoulder on the left so the shoulder on the left appears compressed. Draw the silhouette of the t-shirt, jacket and pants, paying close attention to the hem of the jacket as it bends around the figure. Remember not to use straight lines to express stripes.

Fill in the entire jacket with light-yellow marker and the stripes with the medium point of a black marker. The orange stripe is made with pencil applied over the yellow, as is the shadow in the interior of the jacket. The pattern of the t-shirt is drawn with blended blue, magenta, yellow, green and orange. A shadow is applied to the right side of the figure under the bust-line at the waist and under the hem, with blended black. The pants are filled in with medium-orange with an application of red-orange at the sides to show depth. White pencil is used for highlights, black pencil is used on the left leg for shading. The shoes and scarf are filled in with yellow marker. Details are drawn in with colored pencil.

Skin tone and hair are blended versions of colors taken from the garments

printed/patterned fabrics

stripes

DESIGN: MISSONI

Left, backless, printed silk dress with reconfigured stripes and train; right, knee-length printed silk dress with train.

printed/patterned fabrics

stripes

Left, backless, printed silk dress with reconfigured stripes and train; right, knee-length printed silk dress with train

This drawing shows how striped silk drapes on the figure. The drawing is composed with overlapping figures, emphasizing proximity and unifying the overall composition. A striking contrast of values is also incorporated into the drawing.

Because of the complexity of the design of the dresses and patterns in the fabric, it is best to draw one figure at a time. Begin by drawing the croquis and silhouette of the figure on the right with a light pencil. When drawing groups of figures first draw the figures in the foreground as they overlap those behind.

Draw in the bodies of the stripes using the lightest color that appears in them, following the curves of the drapes of the fabric. Apply a cool beige skin tone, adding a second application at the knee to indicate shadows (Step 1). Apply the darker colors inside the pattern of the fabric and with a black marker fill in the interior and trim of the train and the scarf that falls behind the figure. Fill in the remaining areas of the scarf and trim with blended black from the palette. Draw in the second figure on the left, which is a back view. Fill in the skin tone and the silhouette of the garment. The skin tone is a saturated flat yellow creating a two-dimensional shape that stands clearly apart from the overlapping sleeve of the other garment (Step 2).

Fill in the fabric in the left hand figure using a bright yellow saturated base color and indicating pattern with black and colored markers. Add a black accent to the trim at the bottom of the dress and at the contour on the left side of the front figure.

Step 2

Step 1

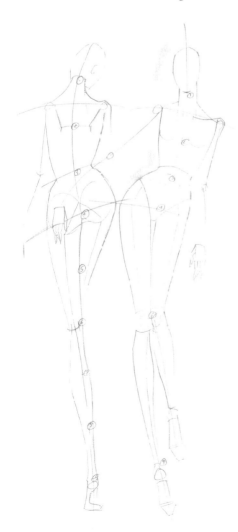

printed/patterned fabrics

stripes

DESIGN: NR

Belted, cut-off denim shorts, t-shirts with striped sleeves, multi-striped thigh-high leggings, sneakers.

These two drawings are color variations of the same garments. In the drawing on the left the three-dimensionality of the figure is shown by the shading and the curvature of the shaped pattern of the leggings and t-shirt. In the drawing on the right the three-dimensionality is further emphasized by the flatness of the background.

Begin both figures by drawing the croquis and silhouette of the clothes. As the clothes are skin-tight the silhouette will follow closely the lines of the croquis underneath. Draw the pattern of the leggings and sleeves of the t-shirt with first an application with the fine point of a marker, and then with colored pencil to heighten the color. The shorts are drawn with layers of blue, and the same blue, blended on a palette, is used for the body of the t-shirt. In the figure on the right a layer of black is directly applied over the blended blue. The lower part of the sleeves of the t-shirt are applied with marker.

The figure on the left has a softer look due to its less contrasted and saturated hues. The figure on the right is drawn using a saturated black, contrasting boldly with the bright colors in the rest of the outfit. A bright yellow background heightens the effect of the contrasting saturated colors. The two drawings show the versatility of markers and the ability to create a different mood by making relatively small changes.

Skin tone is applied with thin layers of color chosen from the colors in the leggings.

printed/patterned fabrics

DESIGN: NR

stripes

Bathing suit bottom, towel, multi-hue striped leggings, booties.

The emphasis in this drawing is on the leggings the other graphic elements are secondary and are included to accentuate the brilliant colors.

The pants and towel are filled in with several layers of blue and magenta. The leggings require several layers of each color, leaving the center part of the leg slightly lighter; color is applied from both sides of the paper. Shadows in the background and hair are layered to give a depth and richness to this drawing. Note that the green background is used as a complement to the magenta and red of the towel, giving a strong contrast. The features of the face are drawn in with colored pencil.

Skin tone is drawn with an even application of beige and a second layer of beige applied to indicate shading under the bust-line, along the right side of the figure and along the sides of the legs.

printed/patterned fabrics

printed silk

DESIGN: CHRISTIAN LACROIX

Full-pleated printed silk dress with wide lace trim, red elbow-length glove.

printed/patterned fabrics

printed silk

DESIGN: CHRISTIAN LACROIX

Full-pleated printed silk dress with wide lace trim, red elbow-length glove.

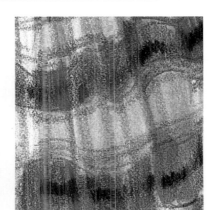

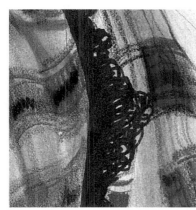

This drawing shows how to render complex plaids on pleated fabric.

Draw the underlying croquis and plan out the radiating tiers of the garment. Define the direction of the pattern as it curves around each tier and breaks up within each pleat.

Observe that the pattern of this garment is essentially a plaid that loops around the full volume of the dress. The plaid pattern is continuous but is broken up due to the numerous pleats and folds of the garment.

First draw in the pleats with colored pencil. Each pleat is drawn as a sharp, straight line beginning at the top of each tier and extending to the hem at the base of the tier. Fill in each section of the garment between the individual pleats with blended red. Add a second layer of the same color at the edge of the pleat and repeat this process with darker red or red pencil. Finally, add black pencil lines to define the plaid. Color is applied so that a tiny bit of the white of the paper remains at the edge of each pleat and fold.

The lace trim is drawn with the medium point of a black marker using a circular motion; closest to the dress it appears black, and away from the dress it retains a small amount of white to indicate the pattern.

Skin tone is an even application of beige to accentuate the warm color of the fabric. A subtle application of red is added to the skin tone as a secondary layer. The glove is saturated red, coordinated with the dress. It is drawn with several layers of color, and white pencil is used to indicate highlights.

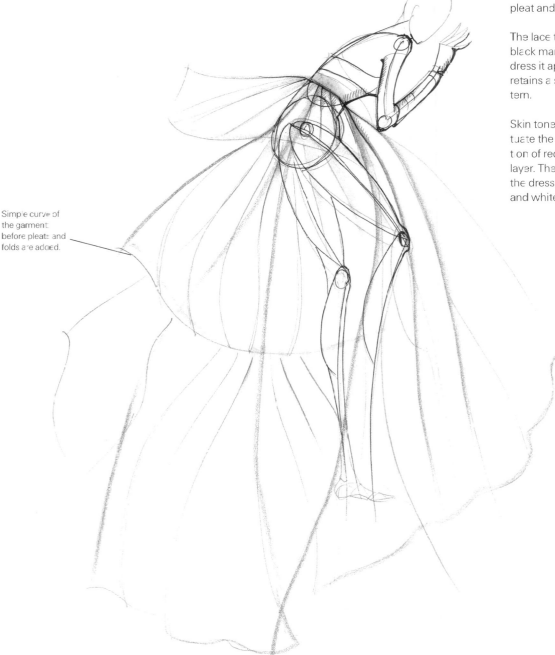

Simple curve of the garment before pleats and folds are added.

printed/patterned fabrics

plaids

DESIGN: SAMANTHA TREACY

Retro plaid cotton suit, flared pants, t-shirt.

This is an unusual three-quarter pose, viewed from below, with the weight on the leg on the right side of the page. With difficult poses it is necessary to draw the croquis accurately, otherwise it is not possible to show the construction and drape of the clothes correctly. The pose, as is often the case, echoes the social statement being made by the garment and its wearer. This is particularly so with fashion associated with a sub-culture such as, for example, hip-hop or extreme sports.

Draw the croquis with the weight on the right side of the figure and the upper torso moving in a diagonal from the upper left to the right side. Because of the perspective the head will appear slightly smaller than in a center-front pose. The silhouette of the clothes is drawn with a light-yellow blended color.

The horizontal stripes are drawn in a spiral around the legs, jacket lapels and sleeves, and the gathered fabric at the waist. Note that the lines of the plaid break up when they come to a fold in the fabric and that the folds follow the line of the torso. Vertical lines are applied with a light yellow marker following the outline of the garment. Shadows are lightly defined with colored pencil under the jacket and in the area where the pant fabric extends beyond the leg. The colored pencil is then softened with an application of colorless blender.

The t-shirt is filled in with an orange marker and the hair is drawn in spirals with the fine point of a black marker, with more visible on the right side because of the three-quarter pose.

The skin tone of the face serves as an accessory to the garment: after each application of blended color to the garment the same color was applied randomly to the face. A small amount of color is applied behind the head to show it is leaning backwards.

printed/patterned fabrics

florals

DESIGN: ALEXANDER McQUEEN

Maxi-coat with floral print fabric lining, layered mini-skirt, high heeled shoes, tiara, skinny extra girl with cotton, sleeveless dress.

These garments are all made from lightweight, soft, patterned fabrics and the drawing is designed to highlight the weightless quality of each of them. To create the desired effect of buoyancy and airiness for this type of fabric and garment it is often best to avoid solid lines when drawing the silhouette of the garments, as solid lines often make for a structured, two-dimensional effect in a drawing. Note that the secondary figure in the background is touching the main figure and directing the eye to the main garments.

Begin by drawing the croquis for each garment with the lightest of lines. Use blended color—either warm or cool pastels—to show the shadows in the crape.

The drape of each garment follows the figure underneath and extends around the outside edge of the garment. Pattern is applied using blended color and breaks up in the folds. A layer of saturated color is added with the fine point of the marker to define the shadows around the parts of the silhouette where the body bends: light cannot bend around a curve so shadows form around the curves of the body. Layers of red and black are applied to the trim of the coat to show the saturated color of this part of the fabric. To give the appearance of dimension to the multiple layers of garments, shadow is applied under the coat, at the center-front, under the layers of the skirt and at the side of the leg. Note the curves of the pretty tiara and curls of the hair accentuate the curves of the trim of the coat.

Skin tone is applied with minimal touches of blended color. The shape of the hair is drawn with colored pencil and filled in with pink marker.

printed/patterned fabrics

complex pattern/florals

DESIGN: CUSTO BARCELONA

Multi-colored, long, draped t-shirt, blocked with contrast fabric, border-print skirt, novelty-printed palazzo pants, scarf, wig.

The complexity of the patterned fabric that is draped and layered around the body makes this a visually stimulating and challenging drawing. Because of the large number of folds it is essential to make a painstakingly accurate rendering of the silhouette of all parts of the garments, paying special attention to the actual size and detailing of the wig and the complex drape at the waist (if the silhouette is not drawn accurately it will not line up with the folds and secctions in the drawing). Note the pants have a heavy lining and so retain a clearly defined silhouette that stands away from the lower leg.

Begin by drawing the silhouette and start to fill in the base colors of the pants and skirt (Step 1). Add base color to each section of the wig, bra, shadows on the right side of the figure, the skirt and the pants. A second layer of color is applied to the far edge of the right side of the draped t-shirt in a deeper maroon to show depth, and some of the pattern is indicated with a tapping motion of the thin point of the marker. A small amount of color is added to the scarf on the right side and a second layer of blue mixed with black is applied to the pants around the silhouette of the leg underneath the garment and the excess fabric where it falls into shadow. Indicate shadows in the folds and gathers using a black pen (Step 2). Note that, in general, a garment appears darker and should receive more shading where no part of the body is directly underneath it.

Pattern is applied to each element of the ensemble using saturated color directly from the marker. Color is enhanced by making a second application from the reverse side of the paper. Care should be taken to break up patterns around folds. Redefine patterns to bring out specific details.using the sharp point of a colored pencil.

Skin tone is applied by layering warm colors to the face, arms and hands. Colored pencil is used in the face to define the delicate features.

printed/patterned fabrics

complex pattern/florals

DESIGN: CUSTO BARCELONA

Multi-colored, long, draped t-shirt, blocked with contrast fabric, border-print skirt, novelty-printed palazzo pants, scarf, wig.

Make sure the edge of the fabric extends up, following the angle of the top.

Stripes bend around the figure

Shadows form in the excess fabric that drapes away from the body underneath.

Step 2

Step 1

printed/patterned fabrics

florals

DESIGN: NR

One-piece slip dress with handkerchief hem, laced shoes.

This garment is made from an extremely light-weight chiffon, and everything about the drawing expresses a breezy and lighter-than-air quality.

To achieve the effect of the lightweight fabric blended pink marker, or alternatively light-pink pencil, is used to show shadow and define the silhouette of the figure and the outfit. Once the silhouette is defined, the shape of the dress on the body is drawn in using light-pink marker to show the shadows around the bustline, leaving a white highlight on the top of the bust, at the drape around the waist, around the curve of the left hip and inside the folds of the drape that falls around the legs under the skirt. Next, the flower design is drawn using green, turquoise and pink pencils. An application of light-pink marker may be used to enhance the petals of the pink flowers. Note that the stems of the flowers break up in the drape, particularly in the folds of the skirt. A small amount of yellow pencil is applied along the seam at hip level, under the thigh, under the left arm and down the outside left leg and along the left side of the face. This leads the eye across the figure to the face, helping to unify the drawing.

The outline of the shoes is drawn in using light-pink pencil and filled in with 10% cool-grey marker allowing for the white of the paper to show through at the highlight on the left toe and along the side of the right shoe. The details of the upper part of the shoe are drawn in with a .005 pen.

Skin tone is created with an application of blended pink marker and a second layer of blended magenta. A core-light formed by the unmarked white of the paper runs down from the forehead to the cleavage. The hair is also applications of blended pink and magenta, with magenta colored pencil applied at the base of the hair, using a circular motion, to represent curls and create more saturated color where the hair is densest.

printed/patternec fabrics

mixed pattern/florals

printed/patterned fabrics

shared silhouettes

DESIGN: NR (SILHOUETTE INSPIRED BY A DESIGN PAUL SMITH)

Man, jacket and pants; woman, stretch wool coat with faux-fur collar.

The drawings on this and the opposite page show two ways to render garments with similar silhouettes.

The drawing on this page shows how the garments can be rendered three-dimensionally, achieved by using a gradation of shades from grey to black to indicate the folds of the fabric. The drawing on the next page is a two-dimensional representation of the garments showing how the design can be extended with the addition of colors and patterns.

Note, particularly when drawing couples like this, that men and women are of different shapes and proportions, even though they might be close in height, and facial features differ markedly. Clearly define the square shoulders on men's garments.

printed/patterned fabrics

shared silhouettes

DESIGN: NR (SILHOUETTE INSPIRED BY A DESIGN BY PAUL SMITH)

Man, jacket and pants; woman, coat with faux fur collar.

printed/patterned fabrics

complex patterns

DESIGN: NR (INFLUENCED BY THE 16TH C. JAPANESE ARTIST SESSHU AND ILLUSTRATION FROM A BOOK OF JAPANESE HAIKU POETRY)

Boxy, cropped jacket, button-front, long-cuffed blouse, soft knife-engineered printed skirt.

printed/patterned fabrics

complex patterns

DESIGN: NR (INFLUENCED BY THE 16TH C. JAPANESE ARTIST SESSHU AND ILLUSTRATION FROM A BOOK OF JAPANESE HAIKU POETRY)

Boxy, cropped jacket, button-front, long-cuffed blouse, soft knife-engineered printed skirt.

This drawing shows garments with patterns drawn with different line weights.

Carefully draw the silhouette of all the garments remembering the jacket is wider than the waistband of the skirt. Using blended colors—cool blue for the skirt and jacket and warm brown for the blouse—fill in the shadows as they fall between the folds of the fabric and draw in an indication of the pattern in the skirt. Plan out the complex pattern in the center of the skirt, breaking it up at the folds, with a .005 pen. The delicate design of the pattern can be defined with colored pencil or the fine point of a black marker (Step 1).

Fill in the blouse completely. Add a second layer of blended brown to bring out the shadow in the blouse and with the fine point of a black marker draw the pattern, breaking up many times in the folds of the skirt and along the right panel of the jacket. Define the contours of the structured, tailored jacket and the pleats of the skirt with the fine point of a black marker (Step 2).

Texture is added to the jacket using a light grey marker with short repeated strokes and an application of dots with a black marker on top to show the tweed-like texture. Black pencil is added for shadows. Further define the silhouette and shadows of the jacket, the shadows in the blouse, the shadows on the left side of the skirt and the patterns in the tights with a black marker. The patterns in the skirt are drawn in with a .005 pen. The shoes are drawn using small curved lines that bend around the leg and foot in dainty shapes; the pattern is drawn in with a .005 pen. The pattern of the tights is drawn with the fine point of a black marker. Note the different line weight between the patterns in the skirt and tights.

Skin tone is added, with the same blended color used in the shadows of the skirt also being used to define the contours of the face. The coloring used on the legs is taken from the color of the blouse.

Pattern breaks up in the folds.

Step 1

Cast shadow is applied to the skin tone under the skirt.

Step 2

271

printed/patterned fabrics

florals

DESIGN: NR

Gathered dress with oversized, inverted pleats.

printed/patterned fabrics

DESIGN: NR

florals

Gathered dress with oversized, inverted pleats.

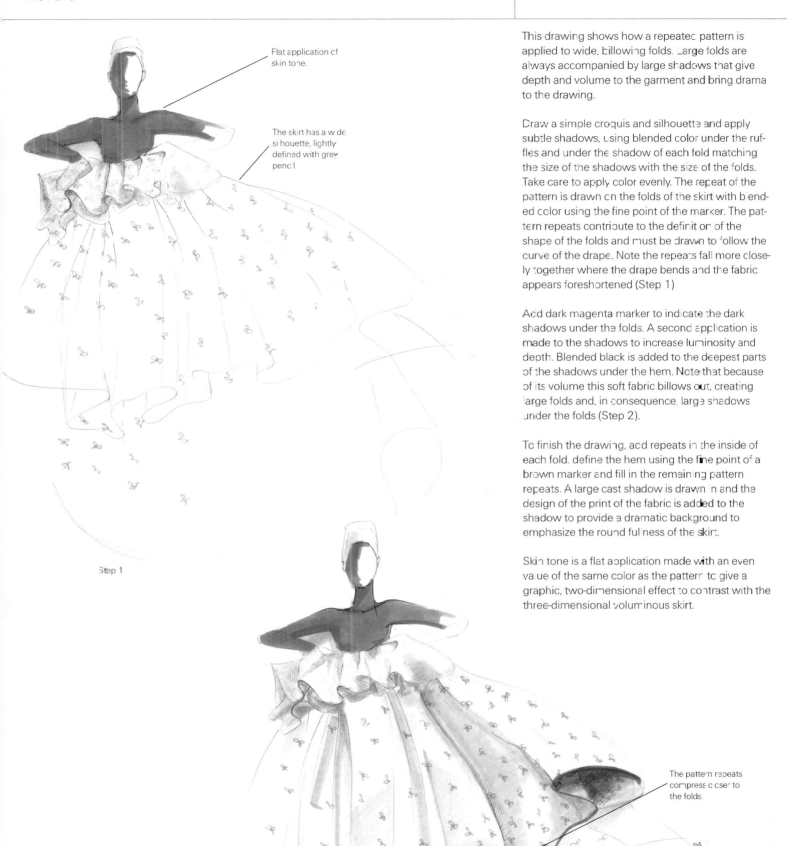

Flat application of skin tone.

The skirt has a wide silhouette, lightly defined with grey pencil.

Step 1

This drawing shows how a repeated pattern is applied to wide, billowing folds. Large folds are always accompanied by large shadows that give depth and volume to the garment and bring drama to the drawing.

Draw a simple croquis and silhouette and apply subtle shadows, using blended color under the ruffles and under the shadow of each fold matching the size of the shadows with the size of the folds. Take care to apply color evenly. The repeat of the pattern is drawn on the folds of the skirt with blended color using the fine point of the marker. The pattern repeats contribute to the definition of the shape of the folds and must be drawn to follow the curve of the drape. Note the repeats fall more closely together where the drape bends and the fabric appears foreshortened (Step 1)

Add dark magenta marker to indicate the dark shadows under the folds. A second application is made to the shadows to increase luminosity and depth. Blended black is added to the deepest parts of the shadows under the hem. Note that because of its volume this soft fabric billows out, creating large folds and, in consequence, large shadows under the folds (Step 2).

To finish the drawing, add repeats in the inside of each fold, define the hem using the fine point of a brown marker and fill in the remaining pattern repeats. A large cast shadow is drawn in and the design of the print of the fabric is added to the shadow to provide a dramatic background to emphasize the round fullness of the skirt.

Skin tone is a flat application made with an even value of the same color as the pattern to give a graphic, two-dimensional effect to contrast with the three-dimensional voluminous skirt.

The pattern repeats compress closer to the folds.

Step 2

273

printed/patterned fabrics

DESIGN: GUCCI, FISICO, ANDREAS SORDA

complex print designs

Art-deco geometric, art-nouveau, floral-printed bathing suits.

These drawings show how the design of printed fabric is depicted both in a draped piece of fabric and when it is tightly fitted around the contours of the body. The process is essentially the same for all three drawings.

Plan the position and direction of the print design on each garment, lightly sketching in with a colored pencil. Fill in the pattern taking great care to indicate the break-up of the pattern inside the folds of the garment. Colors are applied from light to dark. Add a second layer of color from the reverse side of the paper to enhance the brighter, more saturated colors. Use colored pencils to bring out small details. Note particularly how all the contour lines of the garments bend around the curves of the body: to use straight lines would make the figures look like two-dimensional cut-outs.

printed/patterned fabrics	DESIGN: NR
complex print designs	Printed bikini, silk kimono wrap.

This drawing shows a classic garment combination where the outer garment gives a tantalising glimpse of the skimpy garment and figure underneath. The sexy pose also creates ample drape around the sleeves and the hem.

Draw the silhouette of the figure and garment with a light blue pencil and fill in the body of the robe and bikini with magenta marker. Apply shadows, highlights and pattern on top using blue, white, turquoise and green colored pencils. The belt is drawn with the fine tip of a black marker.

Note that the shadows and highlights of the robe are applied using the side of the pencils to make the robe appear soft, and the print design on the bikini is applied with the point to make it appear more graphic and precise.

printed/patterned fabrics

florals

All-over printed, transparent, chiffon sleeveless blouse, transparent gathered mini-skirt, lace-up high heeled shoes.

(The description applies to both the drawing on this page and the page opposite).

These drawings show how to scale down pattern from a fabric sample to a croquis and how to depict lightweight, draped fabric.

The drawing on this and the following page are junior figures, about 19 years old, as indicated in the rounder, softer features of the faces. These girls are almost adults and are drawn with nine-head croquis, but younger juniors can be drawn with underlying croquis of 8½ heads, making the head appear slightly larger and the body slightly less elongated than the normal nine-head figure, giving a younger look to the figures.

These are all lightweight fabrics and are rendered so the patterns bend around the form. and give a three-dimensional appearance. Note the pose of the figure under the garments: in the figure on this page the weight is on the leg on the right side so the hip on that side has shifted out and upwards to the right. In the other figure the weight is on the left side so the hip on that side has shifted out and upwards to the left. The pattern in the hip area accordingly moves to the left in the figure on this page, the right in the other, the vertical elements of the pattern falling parallel to the line of the hip.

In the pants the pattern follows the line of the leg as it returns to the center axis at the ankles (the center axis is that line which runs down the center of the body from the neck to the ankles). In both the blouses, the pattern of the fabric follows the bend in the upper torso as the shoulder bends down on one side and up on the other; the pattern across the torso falls parallel to the line of the shoulders.

printed/patterned fabrics

complex print designs

Chiffon sleeveless blouse, plaid-printed, flared, rayon pants, boots.

(Continued from opposite page)
For both drawings, the silhouette is first drawn with a light blue pencil and filled in with a 10% grey marker. The repeated patterns are rendered over the grey marker with red and green markers and colored pencils, and bend around the body underneath. Shadows are applied on top of the patterns with colored pencil and the facial features and hair are drawn in with blended cool brown pencil. In the figure opposite a blended blue is used to create the transparency of the blouse and mini-skirt, and the pattern is drawn in with a white pencil.

The outline of the shoes in the figure opposite are drawn with a blue colored pencil, the shadows of the laces and the sole of the shoes drawn in with blue marker and the stripe and an additional layer of shadows added in with ochre colored marker.

Both figures show a complex and sophisticated application of skin tone. In the figure on the opposite page, blended colors are used to indicate not only the base color of the skin tone and the shadows that occur around the knees, calves, shoulders and arms, but multiple layers of shading have also been used to indicate shadows from the skirt that fall onto the legs, shadows under the figures that define the palm of the hand and complex shadows in the underarm area. In the figure on this page skin tone is less extensive but is also rendered with several layers of blended colors to create a delicate gradation of tone.

SCALING DOWN FROM A SAMPLE OF A FABRIC WITH A REPEATED PATTERN TO A CROQUIS
To reproduce accurately the scale of a repeated pattern on a fabric sample onto a croquis, hold the fabric sample to the upper body and count the number of repeats of the pattern from the shoulder to center-front and double this number. This is the number of pattern repeats that will appear in the drawing and should be planned carefully with a colored pencil before using markers.

277

lightweight, textured fabrics

DESIGN: JEAN-PAUL GAULTIER

tulle/silk organza

Multi-layered, gathered, silk organza dress, knee-stockings, three-quarter length gloves.

lightweight, textured fabrics

tulle/silk organza

Multi-layered, gathered silk organza dress, knee-stockings, three-quarter length gloves.

This drawing shows how to draw the crisp gathers, tiers and pleats of tulle and the lightness of silk organza.

Begin by defining the simple silhouettes and drawing in the top tier of the dress. Note that each tier is three-dimensional and extends around the back of the garment, so that the underside of the rear part is visible. Each consecutive tier has a fuller expanse of fabric and falls at a lower angle to the tier immediately above.

Shade each individual tier separately using the medium point of the marker. This is one of the rare cases where the individual strokes of the marker are seen in the final drawing—they clearly indicate the pleats and folds of the fabric. Holding the middle of the marker, with a light touch make rapid strokes from the top to the bottom of the pleat using a single action for each pleat (Step 1).

Continue the process of shading each pleat with multiple layers of blended color. More shading is added where the rear interior of the dress is visible near the body. The straps are black ribbons drawn using a black marker with several layers so that the black becomes very saturated. The silk organza of the bodice is built up with multiple layers of blended color. Do not outline the silhouette with heavy lines as it will diminish the appearance of the lightness of the fabric.

To create the shape of the hair use coloring in the same way as when drawing the skirt of the dress, with repeated, overlapping strokes that echo the pleats of the skirt.

The skin tone is taken from the blended yellow colors of the dress. The gloves are drawn with the fine point of a light blue marker to indicate the folds of the three-quarter length gloves.

Shadows appear under each layer of the skirt

Skirt bends around the other layers at the back.

lightweight, textured fabrics

tulle

DESIGN: JEAN-PAUL GAULTIER

Oblique asymmetrical wool top, tulle gathered skirt, knee-high boots.

This drawing shows the juxtaposition of two fabrics of very different weights and textures—wool and tulle.

Draw the croquis and silhouette of the top and draw the silhouette of the gathered skirt as a simple shape. Carefully draw the shape of the boots. Beginning with the skirt (as it is easier to work from light to dark) apply several layers of blended blue with short strokes emanating from the waistline. Remember to leave a little light on the surface of each fold. The layered effect is created by drawing a fine line at the edge of each ruffle.

Fill in the top with a deep saturated mix of brown and burgundy, taking great care not to fill in areas where skin tone shows through the cut-outs of the fabric. Apply a soft sheen of light on the bust-line and over the drape of the top with a white pencil. Note that sheen, as opposed to shine, has a softer, more even reflection over a wider area of the garment—it is drawn with softer, broader strokes than shine and can be best applied using the side of the white pencil.

Skin tone is applied to the hands and upper torso from the reverse side of the paper using a beige marker. Avoid heavy application of skin tone under the tulle skirt in order to retain the quality of lightness. The boots are shaded with a blended dark brown and orange and the contours and details of the shoes defined with colored pencil.

The skin tone of the hands and the sliver of torso that shows above the top are drawn in with brick-beige marker.

lightweight, textured fabrics

lace/patterns

DESIGN: AMY WESSON

Left, floral and leaf printed slip dress with lace trim; right, short white lace slip with butterfly pattern.

These are two variations of patterned lace—the one above with a chantilly trim and below a slightly heavier French lace.

For both garments, carefully draw the silhouette with a sharp pencil, allowing the line to undulate around the many folds of the fabric. Plan out the print pattern, paying close attention to where the repeats bend around the drape of the fabric. Repeats can be blocked out using a simplified geometric version of the pattern for placement—a circle, square or oval—and the detailed design filled in with the fine point of a marker after shadows have been applied.

In the upper garment a little shadow is added along the right edge and bust-line to give a sense of dimension. Because the lace pattern is very fine it is drawn in black ink or with the fine point of a black marker. For especially fine details, enhance the pattern by making little dots using a tapping motion with the marker so only a limited amount of ink saturates the paper. Vary the line weight at the contours and silhouette of the garment so that it appears three-dimensional.

The slip below is cool white and is defined by the shadows applied to indicate the design on the lace where the holes in the lace show the body underneath. The uniform application of light blue emphasizes the idea that the lace is made of cool white thread. A second application of line in a darker blue is made to indicate the pattern of the lace. No head, and only a small amount of shading for the skin was added so that the attention stays on the fabric.

lightweight, textured fabrics

lace/silk charmeuse

DESIGN: NR

Bra and panties, kimono top.

In this coquettish pose the sexiness of the shiny bra and panties contrasts with the soft full drape of the kimono.

First draw the croquis with a light grey pencil and add the contours of the bra, panties and kimono. Add shadows to the bra, panties and robe using a 10% grey marker. Draw in the pattern of the lace using the fine point of a pink marker. Note that it is not necessary to labor to create a photo-realistic representation of lace, as the effect can be quickly created using small scattered half circles that, at a distance, appear as flowers or the pattern of the lace. Fill in the soft folds of the robe using the broad tips of the orange and pink markers.

The skin tone is created with an application of beige from the reverse side of the paper. Cast shadows are applied using blended orange marker. Blended pink is applied to the hair, cheeks and along the torso to give the appearance of a reflected light, serving to add dimension and a luminosity to the drawing. The eyes are outlined with a .005 pen and the beauty spot applied with an orange colored pencil.

lightweight, textured fabrics

cotton eyelet

DESIGN: RUSSELL SAGE

Cotton eyelet skirt and blouse.

Cotton eyelet is a white cotton that has been perforated with many holes that form a delicate repeating pattern, similar to lace.

Define the blouse with a light blue colored pencil indicating soft shadows at drapes and around the bust line where fabric is gathered (this is a *cool* white garment and is therefore shaded with light blue). Add small dots in the same light blue around the arm and across the body to show how the pattern of the fabric forms in drapes and folds (Step 1). Continue this process into the skirt, adding more shadows at the edges between the legs. (Step 2). Add a thin dark line around the belt and neckline to indicate a subtle amount of depth in both places.

Skin tone is not indicated and the shape of the head is defined solely by the silhouette of the hair, which is drawn using black marker and black pencil.

Step 1

Step 2

lightweight, textured fabrics

beading

DESIGN: DOLCE & GABBANA

Shiny, beaded form-fitting dress.

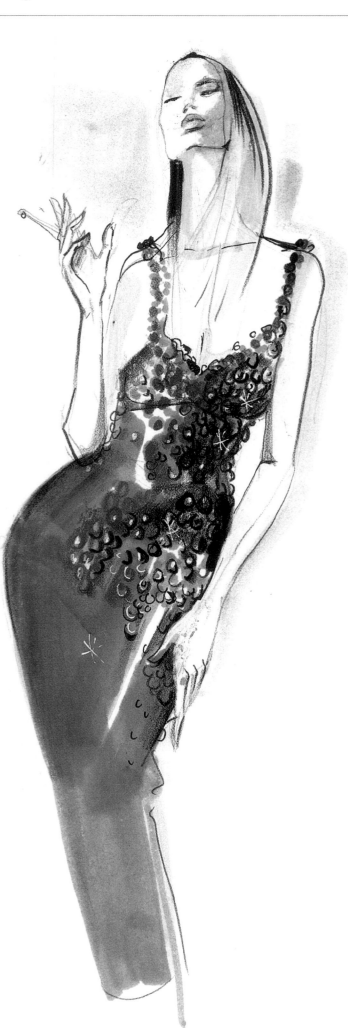

This elegant dress has shine both in the body of the fabric and the beading.

Draw the silhouette of the dress and the figure and fill in the dress with the lightest color of the fabric, leaving the white of the page where there is a highlight over the curve of the bust, around the tummy and over the high part of the thigh. Note that the neck and fingers are elongated to emphasize the length and slimness of the dress (Step 1).

A second and third layer of the color of the fabric is applied, each of a successively darker value, with the darkest color defining the opposite edge of the garment from that where the light falls (Step 2).

Draw the pattern of the beads on top of the folds of the fabric in clusters and scatters, making sure they follow the curves of the body and are seen to extend beyond the silhouette of the garment. Add a highlight to each of the beads in the darkest section of the dress with a white gel pen and draw in a shadow under each with a pencil.

The hair is defined by drawing dark shadows with black marker and applying yellow blended color from the reverse side of the paper. The dark shadows contrast with the light hair, indicating another area of shine and further complementing the shiny dress.

The shadows of the planes of the face are defined by blending the color of the garment until it is transparent and applying on the right side to give the appearance of the reflected color of the garment. This gives the face a three-dimensional appearance. Skin tone is applied with yellow blended color from the reverse side of the paper.

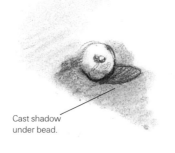

Cast shadow under bead.

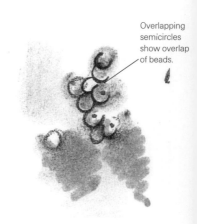

Overlapping semicircles show overlap of beads.

lightweight, textured fabrics

DESIGN: DOLCE & GABBANA

beading

Shiny, beaded, form-fitting dress.

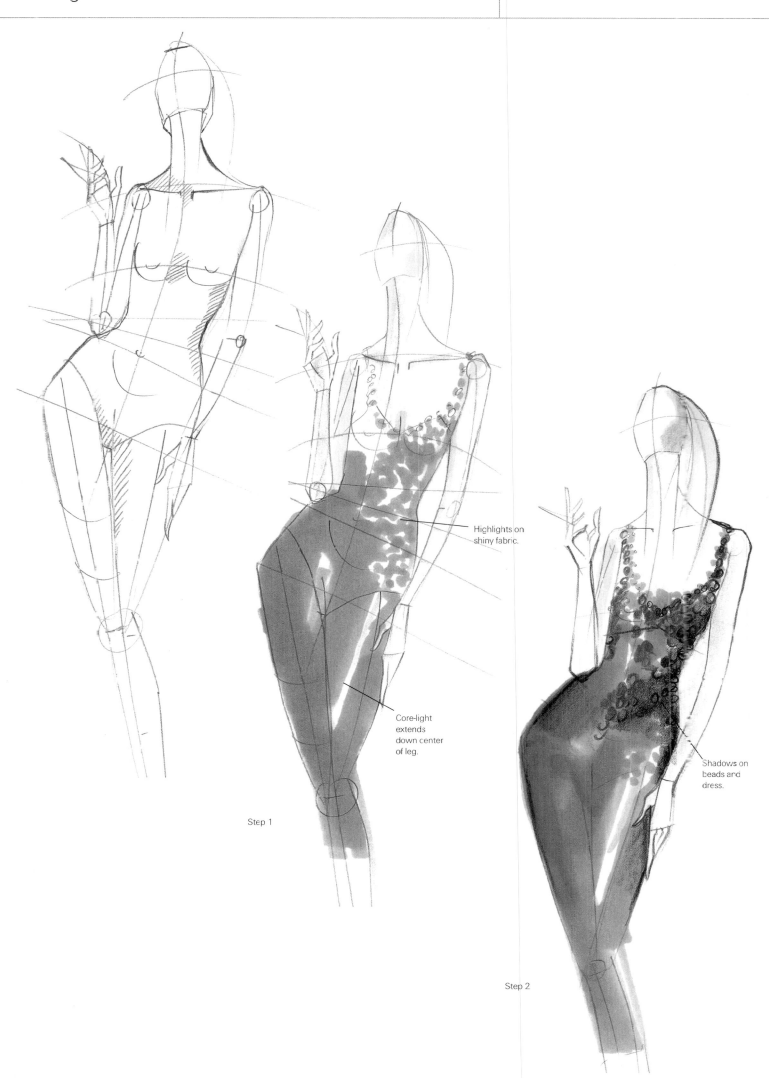

Highlights on
shiny fabric.

Core-light
extends
down center
of leg.

Shadows on
beads and
dress.

Step 1

Step 2

lightweight, textured fabrics

beading/jewel-encrusted fabrics

Silk and jewel-encrusted evening gown.

The fabric of this elegant evening dress is highly reflective, and the glitter and complexity of the beading further adds to its shine. Broad areas of light should be shown in teh fabric and pin-point sharp lights shown in the beading.

First draw the croquis to fix the pose of the figure and indicate the positioning of the garment. Carefully draw the silhouette of this garment as it falls close to the torso, around the bust-line, waist, tummy and hips. Take care to align the center-front of the garment with the center-front of the figure; this is especially important when drawing a three-quarter figure where the center-axis line is off to the side.

Shade around the outside silhouette of the dress with blended color leaving the white of the paper at the bust-line. The bust-line is the part of the figure that protrudes most and so is also the most reflective part of this shiny fabric. Shade also around the hip, and leave the paper white at the highest point where light is reflected. Carry the shading around the left side of the figure to the point where the train of the garment begins to spill onto the floor at a diagonal. Layers of blended color are used to break up the folds in all parts of the garment. Each fold contains about four separate layers of blended blue color.

Beads are indicated on top of the dress by drawing their tiny cast shadow as a semi-circle with the finest point of a marker of .005 pen. The white reflection on the beading is drawn with an almost random application with a white gel pen.

Skin tone is omitted—the white of the paper allows a greater contrast of value with the darker colors, enhancing the shiny effect of the dress.

lightweight, textured fabrics	DESIGN: ROBERTO CAVALLI
beading/chiffon	Corseted, beaded chiffon dress.

This drawing shows strong contrast between the beading on the dress, that reflects light with bright, defined highlights and the soft sheen of the chiffon fabric of the body of the dress that does not reflect as much light.

First, lightly draw the silhouette and figure with a light pencil or blended color using the fine point of the blender. Use shadows at the sides of the figure and in the drape (Step 1). Fill in the main area of the corset with beige from the reverse side of the paper. Using the fine point of the marker add light grey dots to show the shadows of beads in the white collar and skirt. Add more shadow to the left side of the drawing and add semi-circles to indicate the position of each bead in the corset with a white gel pen. Fill in, and add cast shadows to each bead in this corseted area with a .005 pen, with denser cast shadows on the left side. Continue depicting beads in the upper bodice areas by drawing small black semi-circles over the white background.

The skin tone is light blended beige marker. The hair is created in a feminine curve, reflecting the curves of the silhouette; a black is applied on top of the blended color to show the shaded side of the hair and is gradated into the softer brown with a colorless blender. DANGER DO NOT DO: Do not draw an outline around the silhouette of the figure and garment as this will flatten it.

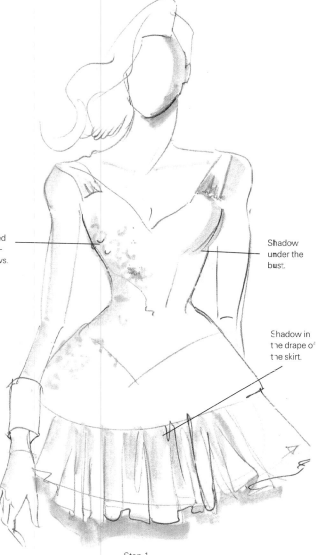

Beads defined with semi-circular shadows.

Shadow under the bust.

Shadow in the drape of the skirt.

Step 1

lightweight, textured fabrics

beading/lace

DESIGN: VALENTINO

Beaded, lace dress, necklace, velvet sash.

lightweight, textured fabrics

beading/lace

DESIGN: VALENTINO

Beaded, lace dress, necklace, velvet sash.

This drawing shows how beading is added to lace.

Draw the crocuis in a walking position. Note the foreshortened rear leg and longer front leg indicating the perspective between foreground and background. The shorter the rear leg is drawn the further it will appear to be behind the front leg.

Draw a simple silhouette of the garment, noting that the sleeves will bend at the elbow (Step 1). Carefully add shadows with blended blue and black to define the body under the dress, i.e. the shadows will define the contour of the hip and legs. Begin to add beads, making them closer together in the shadowed areas. Add an extra layer of blended black shadows to the sleeve on the left side of the figure (Step 2).

Add highlights on top of the beads with a gel pen. Remember to spread the highlights randomly. Indicate the shine on the shoulders of the dress, also with gel pen, and finally add another layer of shadows to define the left side of the figure to give depth, and along the arm to give a rich, saturated color to the fabric. Add extra shadows from the knee downwards and around the drape that falls behind the rear leg to finish off the figure.

A light, blended aubergine is used to subtly indicate African skin tone. African facial features are more pronounced than other races and here the forehead is drawn more rounded and the lips are fuller. The dramatic necklace accents the complex and beautifully crafted gown; the shape of its beading echoes the beading of the dress.

Fabric bends around the shoulder.

Shadows follow the shape of the leg.

Step 1

Step 2

lightweight, textured fabrics

beading/embroidery

Embroidered beaded chiffon dress, floral crown.

lightweight, textured fabrics

beading/embroidery

DESIGN: ALEXANDER MCQUEEN

Embroidered beaded chiffon dress, floral crown.

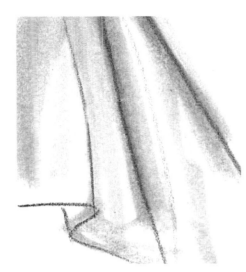

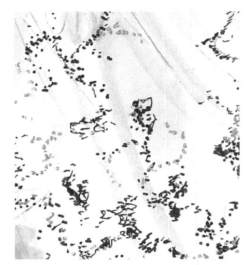

This drawing shows the juxtaposition of fur (or faux fur) silk chiffon and embroidery. The fur and silk are both soft out of different weights and textures; the embroidery adds further textural contrast.

The chiffon dress is created using a light blue color blended on a palette, applied in soft strokes extending out from the bust-line to show the folds of the dress. The blue shadow under the dress is applied using a scrubbing gesture to indicate the underlayer fabrics. The fur is drawn with a blended burgundy applied in four separate layers. A fifth layer is applied from the reverse side of the paper. Using the thin point of a black marker draw the beads on the chiffon with a vertical tapping motion (stippling). Add texture to the burgundy fur using the point of a black pencil and create the soft shadows of the fur using a circular motion with the soft side of the pencil. Add further texture using the point of the pencil.

The burgundy color of the fur is also carried on to the flowers in the hair and green (the complementary color) flowers added for contrast. Yellow and orange colored pencils are used to add details to the flowers and face.

The skin tone of the face is picked up from the blue of the garment and applied to the contour of the eyes and cheeks.

lightweight, textured fabrics

chiffon

DESIGN: UNKNOWN

White wool pants, shiny lurex halter top.

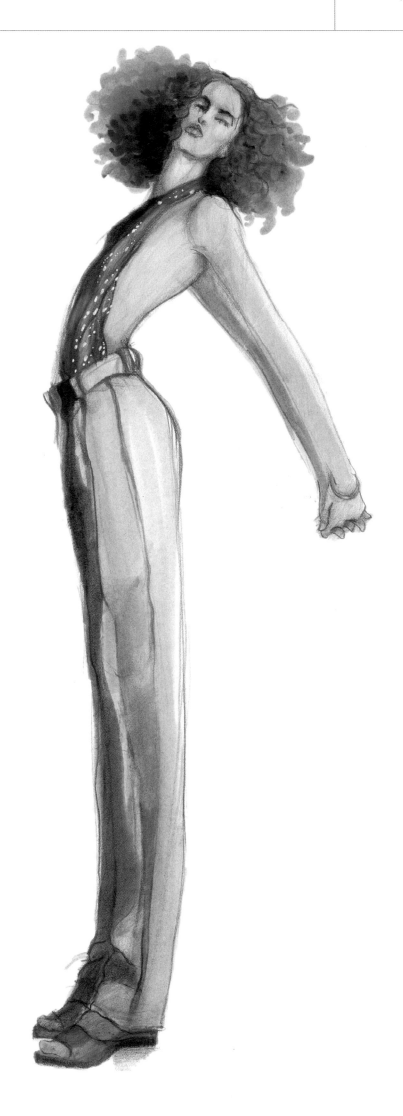

lightweight, textured fabrics

chiffon

DESIGN: UNKNOWN

White wool pants, shiny lurex halter top.

The color white is often mistakenly depicted as flat and without shadows. In reality, a white three-dimensional garment does not reflect all light and does not appear uniformly white. Contrary to what might be expected, white fabric contains many shadows and different tones. Cool whites contain shadows from a cool palette and warm whites shadows from a warm palette. In this drawing the pants are a cool white drawn with blended colored pencils to give subtle and soft tones. Blending colored pencils rather than markers yields the most subtle and transparent tones.

Start by drawing the silhouette of the croquis and the garments. The hair, skin tone, halter top and pants are filled in with blended colored pencil to capture the detailing of the various textures in the drawing. The hair and halter are filled in with rose, the skin tone with beige and the pants with blue. (Step 1).

Add another layer of blended colored pencil to the pants to show drape and a thin black line with a marker to show the folds and contours of the halter top. Add blended dark brown pencil in the hair, features of the face, shadows of the top and pants from the reverse side of the paper. Note that the silhouette of the pants is not outlined so as to enhance the impression of the softness of the fabric. Add detailing to the halter top with a white gel pen to show reflections and brown pencil to show shading. Add deeper shadows to the pants with blended blue colored pencil. (Step 2).

The shoes are drawn with blended colored pencil and a thin black line added to show the contours.

Step 1

Step 2

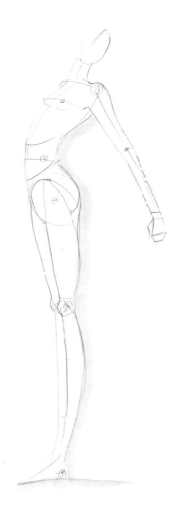

textured fabrics

silk/silk lycra/leather

DESIGN: JEAN-PAUL GAULTIER

Printed t-shirt, pants, underwear, knee-high soft suede boots, hat, headband, scarf, bag.

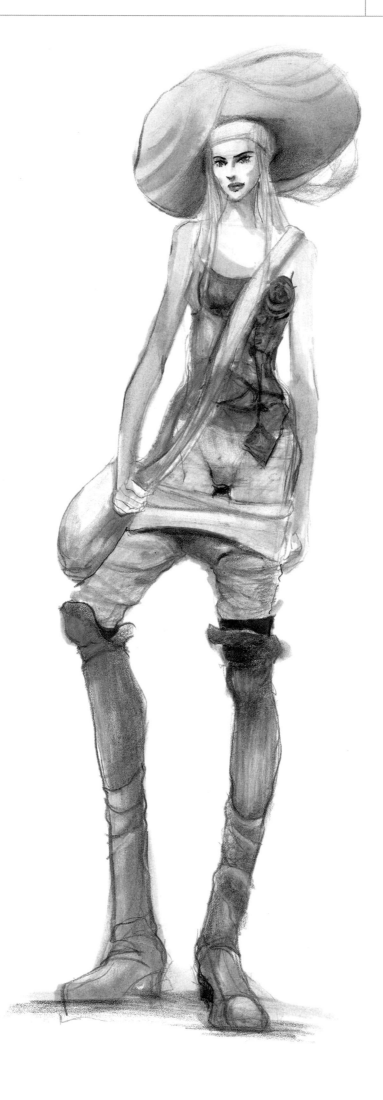

textured fabrics

silk/silk lycra/leather

DESIGN: JEAN-PAUL GAULTIER

T-shirt, pants, underwear, knee-high soft suede boots, hat, headband, scarf, bag.

This drawing shows complex draping and gathering of multiple layers of silk.

Soft tones are chosen to emphasize the softness of the drape and the malleability of the fabric—its ability to hold a drape and cling to a body. Shadows are applied around the hat, across the crotch, in the drape of the pant legs and on the boot on the left side (Step 1). A second layer of shadows is applied leaving some areas white, to become the highlights on the finished garment. Darker shading is applied with blender under the folds to add depth (Step 2).

Using the fine tip of the marker, with a light touch add details of the pattern in the top construction details (the boot straps), details of the face, and nuanced black shadows at the hat, elbows, handbag, pants and shoes. Shadows are placed where the figure bends or areas of the garment recede.

These garments have many folds and gathers and these can be emphasized by applying colored marker and blended colored pencil to accent the shadows in the folds. The highlights are added at the final stage with white pencil.

Skin tone is an even application of blended color taken from the dominant color in the hat, clothes and accessories.

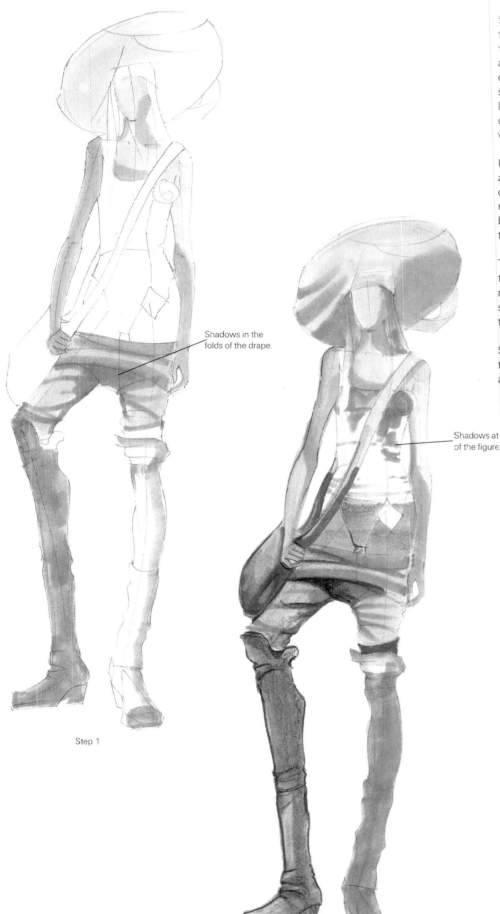

Shadows in the folds of the drape.

Shadows at the side of the figure.

Step 1

Step 2

heavyweight, textured fabrics

wool

DESIGN: YOHJI YAMAMOTO

Wool houndstooth suit with gathered skirt, patterned tights with Japanese motif, gloves, men's shoes.

heavyweight, textured fabrics

wool

Wool houndstooth suit with gathered skirt, patterned tights with Japanese motif, gloves, men's shoes.

Tailored collar bends around shoulder.

Sleeve bends around arm.

Step 1

Folds bend around figure.

Pattern appears on the diagonal.

Step 2

Pattern breaks up in folds.

The workmanship of this garment, both the detailing and construction, is that of a master designer. This suit is constructed from medium- to heavyweight wool tweed fabric, the skirt of which would normally drape close to the body due to its weight. Here, however, the heavy fabric of the skirt has been worked so its drape resembles that of a much lighter fabric. This surprising effect is achieved through a combination of elaborate gathering of the fabric and by placing it over a multi-layered tulle underskirt which creates an armature for the overskirt.

For this garment—as for any garment where the final appearance depends on another supporting garment—it is useful to illustrate both the supporting garment and the final garment. Here, the first group of drawings relate to the final over-garments; the second group on the following pages relate to the under-garments.

With garments of this complexity it is best to employ a simple underlying croquis, choosing a simple pose and leaving out details of the face and hair and the skin tone. Draw the croquis, adding minimal shading to begin the silhouette of the garment and proceed to draw a simplified silhouette, showing the outer edge of the boxy jacket with the wide collar and the multi-layered drapes of the skirt. Note it is essential to extend the folds of the skirt as far as possible on the page so as to give a faithful representation of the skirt (Step 1).

Plan the scale and positioning of the pattern as it bends around the curve of the figure. If a picture of the garment is unavailable and a swatch of fabric is the only reference for the design drawing, hold the fabric to the body and count the number of repeats of the pattern from the shoulder line to the center-front. Double this number to indicate the number of repeats of the houndstooth pattern to go on the drawing. Practice using the pointed edge of the marker to create the shapes of the pattern. Draw in the pattern bending around the shapes of the garment and breaking up in the folds. Add shadows to define the shapes of the folds in the skirt and jacket. Note the pattern is drawn on the diagonal of the fabric. Refer to Chapter Four: Fabrics for a step-by-step breakdown of drawing stripes on the diagonal (Step 2).

To complete the drawing add both saturated and blended black to indicate the interior of the skirt and add final details of the pattern onto the tights with a white gel pen. The shoes are drawn in with a black marker leaving a highlight on the center of the shoe.

heavyweight, textured fabrics

wool/fringe

DESIGN: NR

Left, t-shirt, box-pleated mini-skirt, leggings, boots; right, tailored jacket, box-pleated mini-skirt, leggings, boots.

This drawing shows rich-colored woolen garments with a young attitude. These are stylish young ladies whose bend of the knees, akimbo pose and playful tilt of the head give them a coquettish air.

The croquis are drawn with light blue or pink pencil and the silhouettes of the garments drawn on top, taking care that the lapels of the jacket are lined up and the collar bends around the back of the neck. For the figure on the left, fill in the t-shirt and green mini-skirt with green marker applied both from the front and the reverse sides of the paper to ensure the color is fully saturated. The leggings are drawn in the same way with a grey marker. A sheen is applied to the bust-line and inside the folds under the bust using the side of a white pencil. Depth is added to the shadows under the bust with a black and dark blue pencil. Highlights are applied to the waistband and the edges of the pleats also with a white pencil to indicate the sheen of the wool fabric. Black marker is used to show the depth of the shadows in each pleat. The pattern on the leggings is drawn in with brown and white colored pencils.

The figure on the right is drawn in similar fashion with the jacket, skirt and boots in blue and the leggings filled in with several layers of blue and magenta markers applied from both the front and reverse sides of the paper to achieve the saturated colors. The shadows of the jacket are indicated with a soft application of blue pencil under the lapel, pocket, sleeves, sides and princess line of the jacket. White pencil is applied to the edges and black marker is used in the insides of the shadows of the pleats. White pencil is also used to show sheen on the leg on the left side, indicating the direction of the light source. Pattern is added to the leggings with dark-blue colored pencil.

The boots on the figure on the left are filled in with blended brown marker and the fringe applied using the fine point of the unblended marker. The details of the boots on the right—seams, heel and shading— are drawn in with a dark-blue pencil and the cap is filled in with blended violet.

Skin tone is deco-peach marker applied directly from the reverse side of the paper; the figure on the right has a very light application. The make-up of the figure on the left is drawn in with pink pencil and the hair is drawn in with blended pink marker, leaving some white highlights to show through. The features of the figure on the right are drawn in with a .005 pen and the braid is made with the fine point of a black marker.

medium–heavyweight fabrics

wool

DESIGN: STELLA McCARTNEY

Soft tailored jacket with below-the-knee pencil skirt.

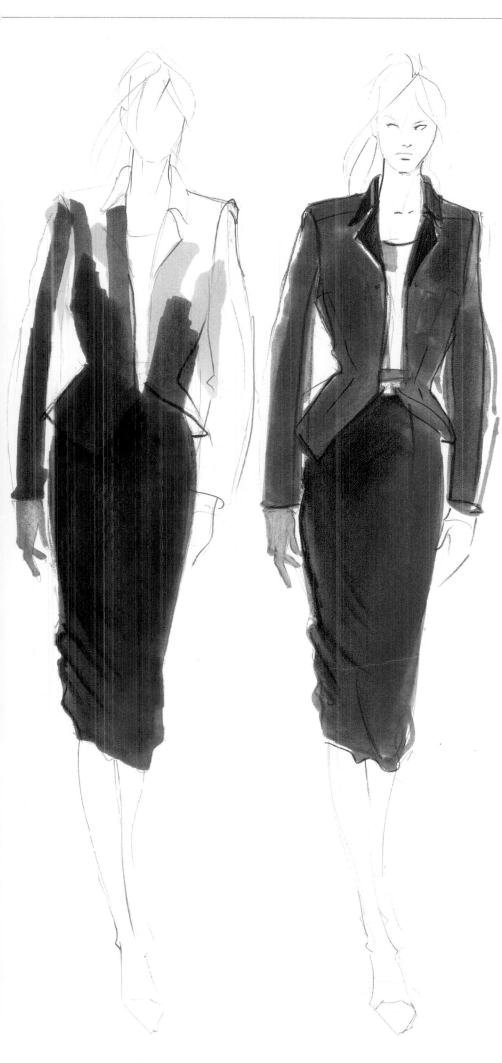

This drawing shows how the appearance of wool fabric is achieved through a flat application of color and how to shade a dark-value fabric.

Draw the silhouette of the garment with special attention to the folds of the fabric, which is softer than a more structured tailored garment—folds appear at the waist, elbow and above the knee. Fill in the skirt and jacket, working carefully and slowly at the edges with the medium point of the marker and in the interior of the garment with a more rapid, circular stirring motion so that the marker fully saturates the paper. Do this first on the front of the paper and then repeat on the reverse side to maximize the saturated rich color of the garment (Step 1).

Complete the process by adding a white line to define the lapel. Add shadows with the side of a black pencil under the lapel, at the top of skirt under the shadow of the jacket (note the shadow here is wide as the flap of the jacket casts a wide shadow) and in the gathers of the drape as they fall from the hip towards the knee. The small amounts of orange at the trim of the blouse, the belt and hand, add a graphic—almost abstract—complement to the garment.

No skin tone is applied here and just the barest outline of the hair and facial features are shown in pencil for maximum value contrast and to lend an edgy feel to the drawing.

Step 1

heavyweight, textured fabrics

DESIGN: JEAN-PAUL GAULTIER

fur

Sheepskin and fur coat, jersey top, mini-skirt, fur leggings, colored tights, sheepskin boots, leather purse.

heavyweight, textured fabrics

DESIGN: JEAN-PAUL GAULTIER

fur

Sheepskin and fur coat, jersey top, mini-skirt, fur leggings, colored tights, sheepskin boots, leather purse.

This drawing shows how soft blended color is layered to create the effect of soft texture and supple, draped fabric.

Draw the silhouette of the coat, top and skirt with a colored pencil. Mix four or five variations of red on the palette, being sure to make sufficient quantities to cover all the areas of the garment. Start applying layers of rose or magenta blended color to indicate the gathers of the top and skirt and fill in the garments with blended colors. Each layer will appear transparent, but the application of four or five additional layers of similar and darker hues will result in a soft and luminous opaque color, with darker areas in the interiors of folds and drapes. The tights are drawn in using orange marker allowing the white of the page to show through for the core light running down the center of the leg (Step 1)

A final application of a darker red than the original rose or magenta is made to fill in the skirt, working from the reverse side of the paper. Add a blended red (less saturated than the skirt) to the top, also from the reverse side of the paper. Apply the same colors used in the skirt and top to the coat, adding a brown blended color to indicate the edge of each pelt of the fur. The same blended brown is used to draw the shadows of the inside of the coat. A blended rose color is used to fill in the lining of the coat and the lighter shadows of the sheepskin. The same process is used to express the fur over the tights. Note that almost everything has been drawn using blended color (Step 2).

Eyes, mouth and hair are drawn in with the fine point of a marker. The shadows behind the head and on the face are drawn in with blended pink. The overall effect of the drawing of the face is to create a translucent effect, contrasting with the rich layers of texture in the garments.

Skin tone is an application of blended red reflecting the color of the garment.

nitial three layers of blended color in folds.

Step 1

Sleeve bends around bottom of arm.

Step 2

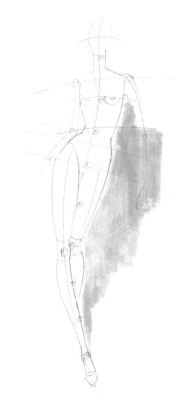

heavyweight, textured fabrics

fur/pleated silk/tulle

DESIGN: JOHN GALLIANO

Fox-fur coat, voluminous crystal pleated dress with knitted arm-band, knitted hat.

heavyweight, textured fabrics

fur/pleated-silk/tulle

DESIGN: JOHN GALLIANO

Fox-fur coat, voluminous crystal pleated dress with knitted arm-band, knitted hat.

This drawing shows how markers and pencils are used in combination to create textures with strong linear elements—here the individual fibers of fur, the pleats of the silk and the lines of the tulle. Note the silhouette of each garment contains diagonals that help the eye to move continuously around the ensemble.

Draw the croquis of the figure and first indicate the positions of the main sections of the dress and coat using simplified shapes. Make sure the silhouette of each shape bends around the body and avoid using straight lines. Next, add the shadows that fall in the tiny folds of the gathers of the dress emanating out from the center of the dress to the sides, with blended pink marker. The edges of the pleats and folds are then defined with a pink colored pencil. There are so many tiny folds and pleats that these steps of adding shadows and defining edges can be repeated several times, each application giving the drawing more depth and texture. Black pencil is used to indicate the bottom of the fan pleats where they cast a shadow over the fabric underneath.

It is important to note that the fur covers the back of the neck and head. It is filled in with a blended warm-brown marker where the fur is closest to the body on the right side, and has most shadow, and on the left side towards the edges, leaving the core of the fur lighter to show sheen. The individual fur fibers are drawn in with many strokes of brown, beige and black colored pencils. The darkest colors are used at the interior and exterior edges of the fur. The cap and armband are filled in with blended warm-brown and the rib knit drawn in with a brown pencil.

The ghostly-white skin tone of the unmarked paper contrasts with the richness and complexity of these extraordinary garments.

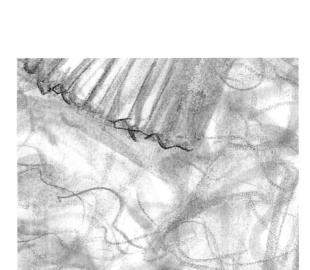

heavyweight, textured fabrics

fur

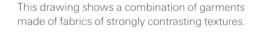

Leopard print, faux fur jacket, shimmering silk tunic, sleek black pants, leather boots.

This drawing shows a combination of garments made of fabrics of strongly contrasting textures.

Draw the silhouette of the jacket taking care to show the shape of the tailored collar, lapel and shoulder construction, which do not follow the contours of the body underneath. Fill in the garment with yellow marker and add a layer of ochre at the sides of the sleeve and under the lapel to show depth.

Draw in the spots of the leopard skin with brown marker taking great care to space them evenly on the flat planes of the garment and closer together where the garment bends around the body. Add another layer of black marker to complete the spots and add the richer dark areas of the fabric using a blended brown applied from the reverse side of the paper; this gives the jacket a softer, more fur-like appearance. Apply white pencil on the upper surfaces of the folds to give a "sheen." Note that the lines used to indicate sheen are not thin, but are broader marks made with the side of the pencil (thin lines are used to indicate the higher degree of contrast associated with "shine"). Fill in the remaining parts of the garment with black marker and bring out the shine on the silk top and jacket collar by applying small dots with a tapping motion of a white gel pen.

The pants are filled in with two applications of brown marker from the front and reverse sides of the paper and the shoes are drawn using an ochre marker and shadows added with a brown marker.

The embroidery on the shoes is drawn in with the fine point of a black marker and the highlight on the left shoe is added with white gel pen.

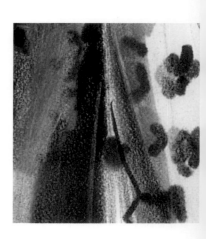

heavyweight, textured fabrics

fur

Fur-trimmed minidress in patterned, wool fabric.

This drawing is of a garment with strong contrasts between the textures of the faux fur trim and the the patterned wool fabric. To create the appearance of texture in a drawing several layers of color have to be applied.

To begin, lightly draw a simple silhouette of the garment. Add a base blended color around the trim at the bustline and the bottom edge of the dress, both of which are of the same faux fur. Add a second layer of blended color over the torso between the bust and legs and a third layer at the sides of the bust and legs to create more depth. Lightly draw in the pattern of the garment, using blended yellow and beige marker applied with the beveled edge. To show the softness of the fabric, avoid using heavy lines to define the edge of the garment: using heavy lines makes the drawing appear more two-dimensional. Add fibers at the edge of the fur using a colored pencil.

A minimal application of skin tone is made around the head, under the chin, around the arms, along the legs and under the fur of the dress with red and brown colored pencil, and a small amount of beige marker is added from the reverse side of the paper under the chin and under the fur to give depth

heavyweight, textured fabrics

fur

Tailored tweed suits with fox and faux fur accents, leather handbag, shoes.

heavyweight, textured fabrics

fur

DESIGN: NR

Tailored tweed suits with fox and faux-fur accents, leather handbag, shoes.

This drawing shows how to render tailored garments made of tweed and fur.

Carefully draw the silhouettes of the garments, bearing in mind that the garments are highly structured and do not directly show the figure underneath. With tailored garments it is important to draw the silhouette accurately. Pay special attention to the angularity of the shoulders, the position of the collar and lapel, the closures slightly to the right of center-front and the detailing of the pockets (Step 1).

Fill in all areas of the garments, leaving thin strips of white at the edges of the lapels, pockets and base of the jacket. This allows the cut of the garments to be clearly seen. Apply a second layer of color from the reverse side of the paper to show shadows under the lapel, under the front of the jacket, pocket, shadows as they fall from the bottom of the jacket onto the skirts and around the sides of the legs. Define with blended color the shape of the fur at the collar and at the edges of the garment on the right. Use a colored pencil to add the texture of the fur, using multiple strokes and working from light to very dark at the edge. A heavy black line is added to the edge of the lighter colored garment on the right to emphasize its tailored structure (Step 2).

Texture is added to both suits. For the suit on the left, dots are applied using a tapping motion with the fine point of a black marker. Additional dots are added with black pencil, and the side of the pencil is used to give more depth to the shadows under the lapel, the bow and hem of the jacket and in the folds of the skirt.

In the figure on the right a further layer of black marker is used to give additional texture to the skirt and jacket. Highlights of blended magenta are added to the fur on both suits. The background is used to add energy to the drawing and to unify the figures.

Skin tone is minimal—a touch of blended color on the legs and faces.

Fur bends around head and neck.

Pocket bends around hip.

Tight-fitting skirt follows line of leg.

Cap of sleeve.

Step 1

Texture breaks up silhouette.

Step 2

| heavyweight, textured fabrics | DESIGN: JOHN GALLIANO FOR CHRISTIAN DIOR |
| fur | Taffeta skirt with extended fur top and long velvet bow. |

heavyweight, textured fabrics

fur

Taffeta skirt with extended fur top and long velvet bow.

This is not a drawing to be attempted by beginners: it is a complex piece requiring time and patience to ensure the colors are applied correctly.

Begin by defining the underlying shadows of the voluminous skirt and the fur. Touches of layered shadow are added to the fur to create a contrast of shadows in the fur. Use a tapping motion with the marker to create the texture of the fur. Build up colors from light to dark with more saturated color at the edge of the fur. Blended colors may be applied from the reverse side of the paper to help indicate the soft body of the fur. (Step 1).

Taffeta requires a sharp edge and highly contrasting shadows. Black is used in the shadows to enhance the contrast with the blue body of the skirt and make it appear shiny. Make sure that shadows fall from a given point on the figure—in this case the hip—and extend out from this point like a flower. Shadows should be drawn in different shapes and sizes, reflecting the uneven way the fabric falls. Light will be reflected from the high points of the ridges of the folds and this is indicated by leaving light blue lines surrounded by deep black shadows to indicate the high sheen of the fabric (Step 2).

Shadows are completed with care, making sure to keep the highlights thin and sharp. White is applied with gel pen or white pencil on the tops of the folds of the light areas to emphasize shine. Note the difference between drawing shiny fabric and fabric with a sheen: shiny fabric reflects light as highlights with sharp edges; fabric with a sheen reflects light more evenly over its surface. A final application of blended cool shadow is added to the fur to express the reflection of the color of the skirt.

Skin tone is created by the lightest application of blended color with colored pencils so as not to distract attention from the garment. The bow also shows minimal application of shadow.

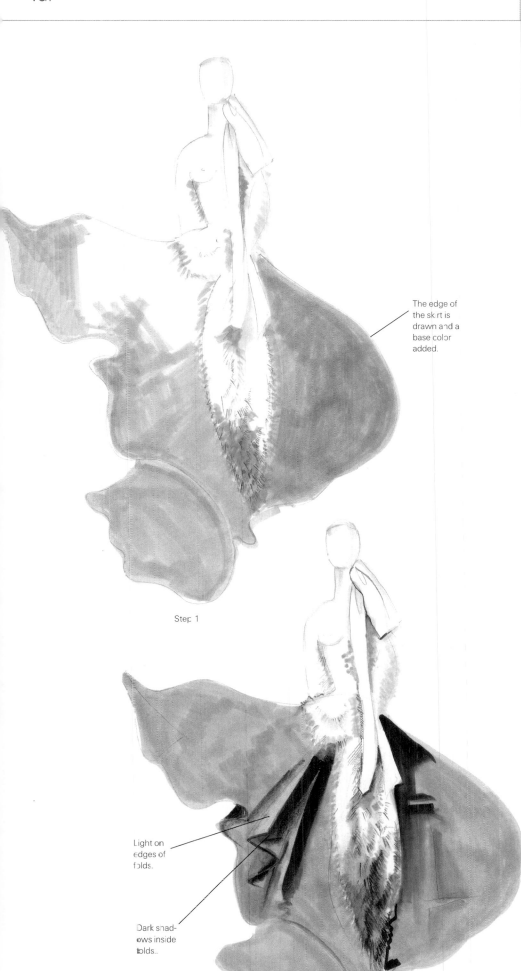

The edge of the skirt is drawn and a base color added.

Step 1

Light on edges of folds.

Dark shadows inside folds..

Step 2

heavyweight, textured fabrics

feathers

DESIGN: JEAN-PAUL GAULTIER

Mini-skirt with strapped bra top, feathered boa, full cape.

This drawing shows the complex textures of layered feathers. It requires a considerable effort of rendering to do justice to the detailing in the feathers, but such an effort can be thought of as a homage to the brilliant and painstaking craftsmanship reflected in the design and construction of the garment.

With such complex detailing it is necessary to begin drawing by defining the underlying shape of the garment with simple shapes. A layer of shadows is then added to give luminosity (Step 1).

Next, a layer of shadow is applied to the feathers and the large area of color of the lower part of the cape, using a scrubbing, circular motion with the marker for the blue of the lower part. Colors are applied from both sides of the paper to achieve dense saturation (Step 2).

Finally, short light strokes with the fine tip of the yellow marker are used to define each feather and final accents are applied with colored pencil. Note that a compositional decision was made to focus detail on one side of the figure. It is not always necessary to render detail uniformly throughout a garment, particularly when it is as complex as this one.

heavyweight, textured fabrics

DESIGN: JEAN-PAUL GAULTIER

feathers

Mini-skirt with strapped bra top, feathered boa, full cape.

Add shadows under feathers.

Shadow and color are added to the feathers.

Step 1

Base color of garment is filled in.

Step 2

heavyweight, textured fabrics	DESIGN: ALEXANDER McQUEEN
heavy silk	Full, layered, multi-colored dress, shawl, stiletto-heeled shoes; man, bare-chested with tattoos, tight-fitting pants.

heavyweight, textured fabrics

heavy silk

Full, layered, multi-colored dress, shawl, stiletto-heeled shoes; man, bare-chested with tattoos, tight-fitting pants.

Simplify the dress by drawing in the different horizontal layers of color and indicating the shadows in the vertical folds of the fabric.

Step 1

Deepen the shadows in the vertical folds.

Step 2

This drawing contrasts intense detailing based on line drawing with intense layering of color and shadow—the skirt requires about six layers of color. Needless to say, the drawing is one of the most complex in the book and is not for beginners!

Given the complexity of the application of color and the detailing in the final drawing, it is essential to begin by outlining the silhouette and the areas where the main underlying colors are to be applied. First fill in each section of colors with rows of horizontal lines, then make a second application of the same color to show the the shadows where each row bends in (Step 1).

Define the shadows that appear in between the deep folds of the fabric of the skirt with blended black, noting that shadows bend in a variety of directions and are deepest on the right side where the skirt is away from the light. Fill in the area for each band of color with a light value of the color to be applied. Begin adding detail to define each segment of the gathered fabric crossing the different bands of color. Use a white pencil to show the highlights on the ridge of each segment. Each segment of the drape will appear as a cylinder, with the lightest part of the shadow in the center of the cylinder, continuing downwards and extending into the deeper parts of the folds. The deepest part of each fold is accented with black pencil. When applying the color the gesture of the wrist should try to follow the trajectory of the shape of the cylindrical fold-the wrist rotates as it moves (Step 2).

A second and third layer of color is applied from the reverse side to deepen the saturation in the color of the dress and white is added to the surface of the folds. The color below the garment is a cast shadow and is drawn with a similar gesture as the folds of the garment as a lyrical accent. The hair is drawn with a .05 pen and blended color is applied from the reverse side of the paper.

The man's contour is defined by the background shadows and reflections from the woman's dress. The tattoos are drawn with a .005 pen, using a magnifying glass. Note the dramatic difference in scale between the man and the woman: he is very much in the background!

Skin tone is applied with the lightest accent of blended green and blended pink to echo the colors of the garment. The white netting of the back of the dress is drawn over the skin tone with a white gel pen.

heavyweight, textured fabrics	DESIGN: ALEXANDER MCQUEEN
heavy silk	Full, layered, multi-colored dress, shawl, stiletto-heeled shoes; man, bare-chested with tattoos, tight-fitting pants.

Note that in a crouched pose the hip is compressed.

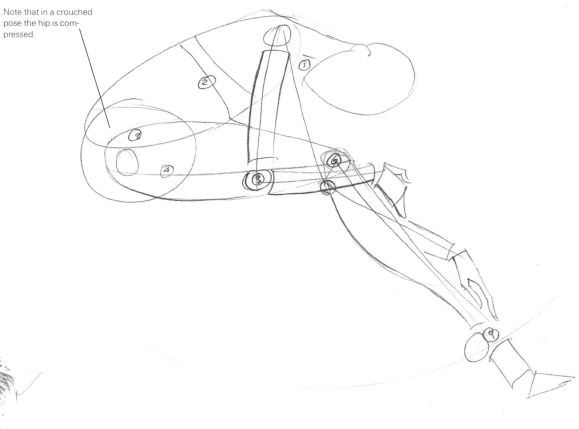

heavyweight, textured fabrics

crochet

DESIGN: UNKNOWN

Long crochet-knit dress.

This drawing shows how the texture of a knit garment is rendered using the fine point of a marker. This is one of the rare occasions when the individual strokes of the marker are seen on the finished drawing.

First draw the croquis and silhouette of the garment with a light grey pencil. Clearly define the undulating drape of the knitted garment with a line that bends in and out. Add the lines of the knit using a short stroke of a brown marker held close to the tip for control (Step 1).

Subtle shadows are applied with a light grey marker along the right side of the figure from the reverse side of the paper. A second layer of color is applied over the knit using the same short stroke, and a fine black line is drawn around the edge of the garment to emphasize the texture and body of the fabric. Brown colored pencil is used to add further color and texture.

Skin tone, hair and the details of the face are drawn with a light grey (10%) marker and thin black lines are applied to show shadows.

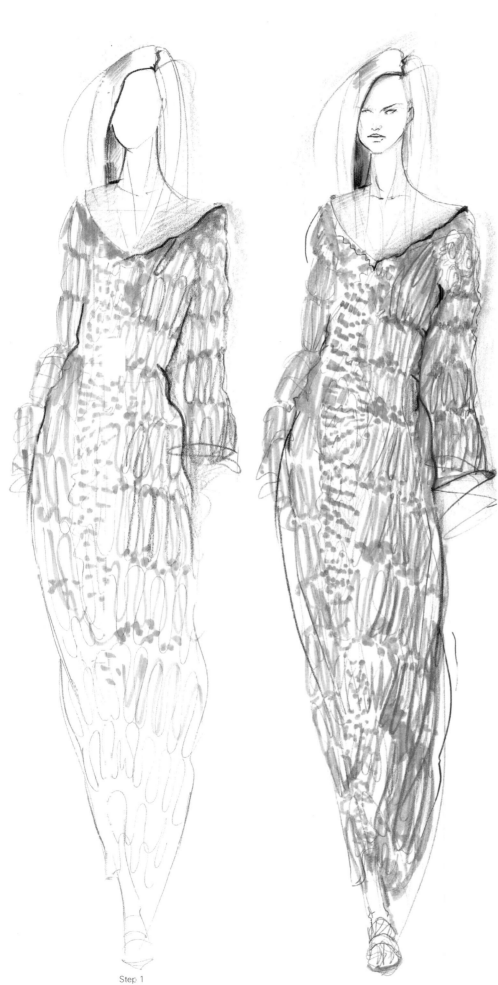

Step 1

heavyweight, textured fabrics

DESIGNER: JEAN-PAUL GAULTIER

denim/beaded chiffon/heavy cotton

Left, asymmetrical top with wide, beaded border and sash, shorts, satchel; right, military-style utility vest, pants, belt, head-band.

These drawings show the juxtaposition of fabrics of sharply different weights, luminosity and densities.

The figure on the left has a simple three-quarter croquis with the weight on the front leg. Draw the outline of all the garments lightly with a colored pencil. The effect of each of the three different fabrics is created with a separate technique: The silk blouse, the lightest weight fabric, is shaded with blended yellow, layering the same color several times with the darkest tone appearing in the interior of each fold; the beads are defined with the fine point of a marker. Notice that the white of the paper was left showing under the edges of this fabric to give the impression of luminosity. The shorts were filled completely with light blue and a darker blue was used to define the folds at the crotch. The shoulder bag is of a heavier fabric and a saturated color is achieved by applying several layers of color.

Note that the sequence in which the garments have been drawn is significant, working from light to dark. If colors were to be applied in the reverse order, from dark to light, then bleeding could occur and the drawing could end up a mess. Hair and features are drawn in with a light blue pencil picking up the color of the shorts.

The rest of the figure on the right is drawn in with the fine point of a dark marker. Blended color is used as shadow to give depth to the pockets, and applied from the reverse side of the paper. The pants are drawn as a silhouette with large folds and filled in with a sequence of light blue, cranberry and dark blue colors. These rich colors and large folds will make the fabric appear more voluminous. The tops of the folds are accented with a light colored pencil. Hair is drawn with a black marker.

Skin tone for both figures is a light application of blended pink.

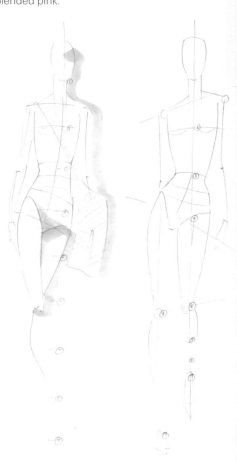

heavyweight, textured fabrics	DESIGN: JEAN-PAUL GAULTIER
denim/lace	Denim overalls with lace hat and top.

Like those on the preceding page, this drawing shows the juxtaposition of fabrics of different weights, luminosity and density.

First the pattern of the lace top and hat are drawn with the fine point of dark brown and red markers, and blended pink and light blue are applied from the reverse side of the paper to represent the body of the lace. The denim overall is drawn with wide folds to show the loose fit and heavy weight of the fabric. It is completely filled in with several layers of blue. White pencil is used to indicate the soft upper surface of folds, top stitching and the twill weave of the denim.

Hair is drawn in with a heavy application of black marker, contrasting with the fine line of the lace of the hat and blouse and accenting the heavier blue of the denim pants.

Skin tone is an application of pink marker made from the reverse side of the paper.

heavyweight, textured fabrics

silk

DESIGN: JOHN GALLIANO

Solid silk tafetta kimono with wide-striped bands.

This drawing shows how the folds and shine of heavy silk are rendered.

A symmetrical, front-view abstract croquis (the face is absent and the parts of the figure are minimall-yarticulated) creates a mannequin on which the clothing is draped. When clothing is voluminous and luxuriant the figure should not draw the attention away from the garments.

Draw the silhouette to represent the kimono with a full skirt. The saturated color of the kimono skirt is created by applying marker from both sides of the paper. Use warm blended color in the sleeves and indicate the pattern of the stripes with the fine point of a marker (Step 1).

Continue filling in the skirt and sleeves and add stripes in all areas of the kimono with warm-brown marker where indicated, following the drape of the skirt as it is seen at the hem and the drape of the sleeve as seen at its edge. White pencil is added to create highlights. Note that the shapes are broken up in folds, shown by using darker tones (Step 2).

Indicate depth in the folds using black pencil and finish filling in the base of the kimono with blended yellow marker applied from the reverse side of the paper. White highlights are added to the tops of the folds with white pencil. A sparkle is added to the interior of the folds with gel pen.

Skin tone is made with a subtle, light application of color with blender and freckles drawn in with colored pencil. The hair is created with the same technique—without freckles!

Step 1

Stripes follow contours of sleeve.

Stripes follow contours of hem.

Step 2

transparent fabrics

vinyl

Transparent plastic raincoat with green trim.

Drawing transparent garments is an oxymoron: what is truly transparent has no appearance! To draw transparent garments is, in fact, to draw the parts that are not transparent—the shadows that form in the fabric folds, where fabrics overlap, where the fabric recedes from the light source and, importantly, the shadows of the figure under the garment.

It is intriguing that with transparent fabrics the shadows are darkest where the body underneath shows through the garment (as opposed to garments made from most other types of fabrics, where the shadows are darker where the fabric falls away from the body). Subtle shadows will also occur in folds throughout the transparent fabric.

To draw this transparent vinyl raincoat, begin by drawing the croquis. In this drawing the figure under the garment is drawn with minimal clothing for dramatic effect. To reproduce this effect, think of how one dresses in the morning, starting with the nude body, adding lingerie and then the outer garment.

Carefully draw the silhouette of the garment using a thin line to indicate crispness. Use blue-green marker to define the trim at the edges of the garment and add outline lines with black pencil. With transparent garments the seams and hems are always visible and should be indicated with thin lines.

Because vinyl (or plastic) is a rigid fabric its drapes appear linear and it is shaded with straight edges. Add light shadows using a 10% cool grey in the drape of the body of the coat, under the belt, under the collar and under the cuffs. Fill in the skin tone of the croquis where it appears under the coat with the same 10% grey marker, applied from the reverse side of the page, and with blended beige where it is seen outside the coat.

transparent fabrics

diaphonous silk

DESIGN: VIVIENNE WESTWOOD

Wrapped tunic dress with contrasting-color hood and trim, belted at waist, shoes.

This drawing shows how to depict garments made of transparent fabric with voluminous drape and where the trim is in a contrasting opaque fabric.

The croquis and outline of the garment are drawn with a light grey pencil. The drape and volume of the fabric are best shown off if the figure is drawn in motion. Here the hip is up on the left side and the fabric bends to the left, following the movement of the figure. Apply a very thin coat of grey marker throughout the garment and a second and third coat of the same color inside the shadows of the folds of the drape. Each consecutive layer is darker as it is applied closer to the edge of the fold. Resist the temptation to define the folds with lines as this will give the fabric a starchy appearance, which is not the desired effect.

Note that the shoes, although minimally indicated, have ruffles that complement the folds of the fabric of the dress.

Define the trim and the inside of the hood with a warm brown marker. The shine on surface of the folds of the trim is drawn in with a white pencil, forming a highlight on the seam as it follows the curve of the hood to the back of the figure.

The skin tone is the subtlest application of beige with a little attention from the reverse side of the paper to show the outline of the bust under the transparent fabric. A small amount of blended green is applied around the figure to reinforce the three-dimensionality of the dress.

shiny fabrics

man-made

A number of fabrics reflect light, but do so in different ways. In this ensemble different fabrics are used in each garment and each fabric reflects light in a different way.

The metallic t-shirt has broad, flat reflective planes. The metallic effect is achieved by applying highly contrasting colors. First, draw the silhouette of the t-shirt using a black pencil, varying the line to indicate the curves and folds. Using 10%, 20% and 40% cool greys, build up shadows from light to dark along the outline of the garment following the shape of the folds. Apply dark back along the outer edge to deepen the shadow and increase the contrast with the shiny white body of the shirt. Use the fine point of a medium-grey marker to indicate the shadows within the light areas and to define the beads. DANGER DO NOT DO: Do not make shadows all the same size—shadows are never the same size!

The skirt is made of a fabric with soft sheen so the value contrast between the highlights and the main color of the fabric is not as great as for the shiny t-shirt. The color is filled in with beige marker, layered from both sides of the paper. The highlights are drawn in with the side of a white pencil. The remainder of the skirt is filled in with black marker. The straight hair is created with the same palette as the skin with subtle variations for shadow and shine. The eyeglasses are also an a most graphic application of matt black, with gel pen used for the highlights.

The skin tone is drawn as a pure matt surface in high contrast to the t-shirt, accentuating the illusion of shine with its range of contrasting values.

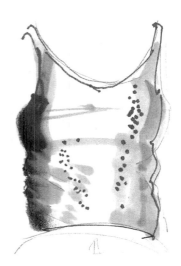

To create the effect of a metallic sheen four or five layers of grey marker of different values are used.

shiny fabrics

silk taffeta

DESIGN: UNKNOWN. SILHOUETTE BASED ON LINES OF DRESS IN A PAINTING BY WATTEAU (1684-1721)

Taffeta evening dress.

shiny fabrics

silk taffeta

DESIGN: UNKNOWN. SILHOUETTE BASED ON LINES OF DRESS IN A PAINTING BY WATTEAU (1684-1721)

Taffeta evening dress.

Taffeta has crisp, sharp edges to each fold and is drawn using a layering of light to dark colors so that the final color is saturated and shows the contrast between the inside edge of the folds and the white reflection on their ridges. With taffeta and other shiny fabrics the darkest parts of the shadows in the folds are generally next to the lightest areas on top of the folds.

The figure is drawn in an unusual and striking pose where the shoulders and hips are folded towards each other, compressing the upper and lower torso. Note that the fabric falls dramatically from the back of the dress and forms a cowl drape where it is gathered in the hands.

The breakdown of this drawing is shown in a different (complementary) color. Although it is not the final drawing, note that juxtaposing complementary colors enhances the intensity of each color. A black line is drawn around the underskirt and the side of the garment to emphasize the crispness of the fabric.

The hair is drawn with short strokes with layered hues of magenta, light and dark brown.

The skin tone of the face and arms is created using layered warm colors with a thin ridge of light on the top-center of the forehead, nose, lips and chin. This gives a high-contrast shine to the face which echoes the shine of the taffeta.

shiny fabrics

leather/lightweight wool

DESIGN: UNKNOWN

Left, leather jacket with soft wool pants; right, alligator jacket.

White core light down center of leg.

Shadow at side of leg.

Step 1

sh ny fabrics

leather/lightweight wool

Left, leather jacket with soft wool pants; right, a li-gator jacket.

These two figures show variations in silhouettes of tailored leather garments, the texture of which is contrasted with soft, unstructured pants.

With any tailored garment the silhouette is of primary importance, as the structure does not depend on the body underneath. Here, the jacket on the left is made of two tones of leather bands sewn together. Leather is a skin, not a fabric, so the width of any single piece is limited and as a result leather garments must often be constructed with seams. To indicate the position and direction of each section of the leather use a blended brown color, noting that the direction of each leather "stripe" runs parallel to the hem. Add shadows under the lapel and center-front edge of the jacket. Draw a silhouette of the pants using a softer line quality to that of the jacket, indicating the less structured, softer drape of lightweight wool. Shade around the thigh with several layers of brown tone (Step 1).

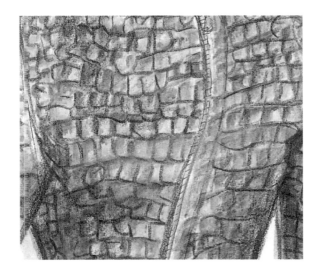

Continue layering shadows along the outside contours of the jacket to give depth and around the knee and other leg of the pant, building up tones in the pants from light to dark. The leather of the jacket in this illustration has been treated with a shiny finish so it is necessary to finish off the drawing by applying white with a white pencil to the ridges of the folds. Using a colored pencil draw in the pattern of the wool pants.

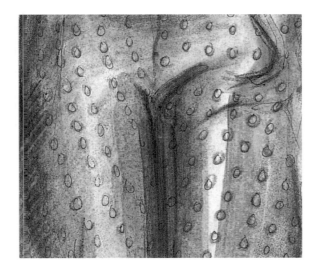

The alligator jacket on the right is made from a skin with a textured pattern that can be drawn with a colored pencil. Shadows can be applied from the reverse side of the page under the bust-line and around the waist, and, from the front, to each of the scales of the skin. Note that alligator skin is slightly more structured than the type of leather used in the other jacket.

In the figure on the left the hairstyle is geometric, contrasting with a softer tailored jacket. The figure on the right has a softer hairstyle, offsetting the more tailored fit of the jacket.

In the figure on the left the skin tone is a flat application of grey marker to give a contrast with the texture of the garments. The figure on the right has a minimal application of reflected light for the skin tone.

shiny fabrics

DESIGN: UNKNOWN

silk

Silk evening gown with full skirt.

shiny fabrics

silk

Silk evening gown with full skirt.

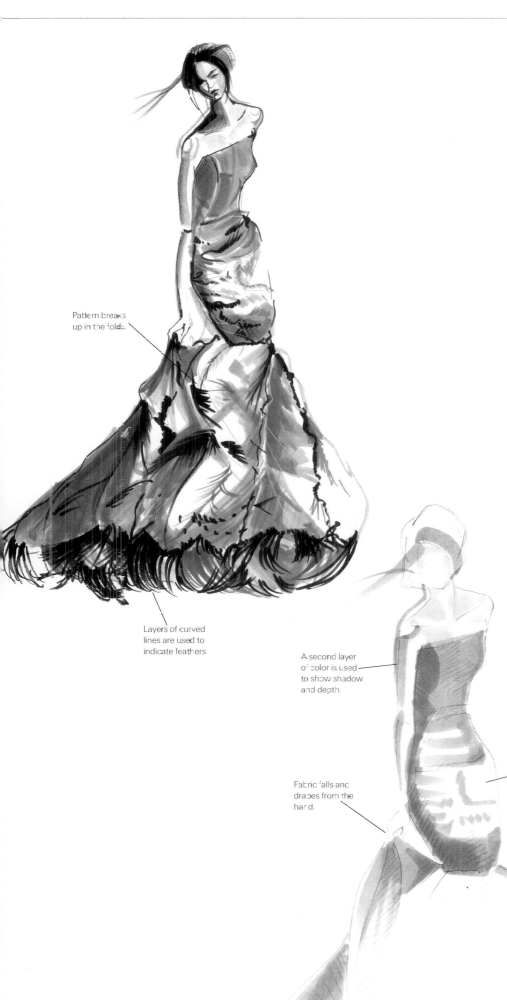

Pattern breaks up in the folds.

Layers of curved lines are used to indicate feathers

A second layer of color is used to show shadow and depth.

Fabric falls and drapes from the hand.

White of the paper is left to show through to indicate shine.

The diagonal pose of the figure from head to feet—slanting from upper left to lower right—causes the fabric to fall in the opposite direction, with dramatic effect, freezing in time a beautiful, momentary gesture. This luxurious, complex garment appears, at first sight, difficult to draw; the task is greatly simplified, though, when the main parts are considered as geometric shapes.

Begin by drawing the underlying croquis noting that the weight of the figure is on the leg on the right and the other leg is flexed. This is a three-quarter figure, with side and front planes visible. First fill in the areas of the garment with blue marker to indicate the folds and drape of the garment. The dress is silk and the light source is intense, so where the light hits the fabric the pattern of the fabric and contour of the garment all but disappear. Indicate these areas by leaving the paper white. A second layer of shadow is applied along the right side of the figure to darken the first layer and further define the side plane of the figure (Step 1).

Continue shading large areas of the drape. Adding layers of the same or similar colors will give the drawing depth and richness. With the thin point of black and magenta markers add the pattern of the fabric and, with a curving motion of the wrist, the feathers of the underskirt (Step 2).

The range of colors in this drawing is achieved by applying many separate layers of color. In the final stage several layers of blended color are applied from the reverse side of the paper to give saturated, luminous color. Finally some of the details can be enhanced using colored pencils—the feathers of the skirt and the position of seam lines.

The skin tone has been created using four or more applications of warm tones. Using a blender, dark shadows are applied around the contours of the face, neck, shoulder and arm using warm black and violet colors. This gives an additional contrast between the dark and the light areas of the figure.

shiny fabrics

silk/silk chiffon

DESIGN: JOHN GALLIANO FOR CHRISTIAN DIOR

Left, silk chiffon shawl, embroidered t-shirt, floral appliqué and iridescent silk miniskirt; right, corseted top, long floral print silk skirt over silk underskirt.

shiny fabrics

silk/silk chiffon

Left, silk chiffon shawl, embroidered t-shirt, floral appliqué and iridescent silk miniskirt; right, corseted top, long floral print silk skirt over silk underskirt.

Just as the garments in fashion shows are often displayed with a theatrical backdrop, this drawing conjures an atmosphere of eroticism and sensuality around the garments. The execution of an advanced drawing such as this takes time, an advanced skill level and much attention to detail.

The drawing shows strong luminous effects, both in the draping of the rich fabrics and in the skin tones, which appear iridescent, with overlaying and interweaving of warm and cool tones. The luminous effects are also echoed in the background, a more transparent version of the textures seen in the clothing. Note that the degree of outlining applied to the garments is limited, enhancing the fluid, ethereal feeling in the drawing.

The figures are symmetrically balanced in an S configuration. The spaces between the figures—the "negative space"—include variations of small, medium and large spaces. Because the clothing is so complex, the hair is indicated as a simplified abstraction. Blended color is used to create the soft gradated tone in the draping of the skirts. At least four or five layers of color are applied, with final touches made with colored pencil.

Begin by drawing the croquis and silhouettes of the figures and garments using a warm colored pencil—perhaps pink or orange—paying close attention to where the fabric drapes in the shawl and miniskirt on the left and the skirt on the right. Apply a very light coat of blended color, warm in the warm areas of the garments and cool in the cool areas to provide a base tone to express the color of the fabric. Add a second layer of blended color, slightly darker than the first, to express shadows in the drapes. A third layer is then added with a complementary color—cool in the warm areas of the garment and warm in the cool—to give the garment its iridescent appearance. A fourth layer of highly-saturated color is applied with colored pencil to areas where the effect of luminosity is most pronounced.

The skin tone is created using the same technique of layering thin layers of color as in the clothing to reinforce the idea of luminosity and dramatic artifice.

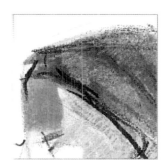
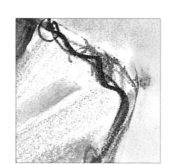
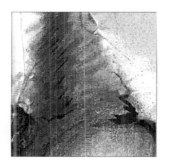

shiny fabrics

leather

DESIGN: NR

Short strapless dress with full flounce, belt and buckle feature and dropped v-shape hip-line, gloves.

This drawing shows the soft shine and sheen of glove leather.

As opposed to heavier leather that has a more rigid drape, this type of leather is extremely supple and drapes almost like a soft fabric, showing many more curves and folds than other leathers. As a result light and shadows appear frequently on the surface.

The simple croquis is sketched with a light grey pencil and the silhouette of the garment drawn on top with bumps and curves to indicate the folds of the fabric along the hem-line and at the waist. Shadows fall in the interior of the folds and will appear narrower at the waist where the fabric has been more compressed.

This leather garment drapes and folds in almost the same way as if it were made of soft fabric, but soft leather is a skin and on the figure behaves almost like a second skin, molding itself to the body's contours. To make a realistic rendering of the pattern of light and shadow on the garment it is necessary first to plan the size and location of the drape (it will be wide if the fabric is thick and narrow if the fabric is thin). The areas that are concave, receding out of the light, will receive shadows and are filled in with blended black right up to the edges where the fabric comes towards the light and turns convex. Filling in the areas of shadow with marker automatically defines the areas of light, which are the parts where the unmarked white of the paper shows through. The diagram below shows how the shading of the garment can be plotted.

The skin tone is applied with light beige marker to lightly define the contours of the face and rest of the skin, and shadows are applied under the chin and on the arms and legs with grey colored pencil.

Silhouette of upper section of dress showing where shadows fall on the surface of the leather.

shiny fabrics

polished cotton/silk

DESIGN: WOMAN, ANN DEMAULE-MEESTER; MAN, UNKNOWN

Shiny t-shirt and shiny, softly draped pants; man, black leather shirt jacket, matching pants.

This drawing shows how to render shine in draped fabric and the spatial relationship between a seated and a standing figure.

When drawing a seated figure the hip area appears smaller due to the foreshortening of the legs. Here, the man's front leg almost completely obscures the hip area and the leg appears to connect at the lower waist line. This effect is not quite as pronounced with the back leg as the foreshortening is not as great.

The man's outfit is filled in with layers of navy blue marker. White pencil is applied to the knee, the side of the leg, the shoulder and the arm to show shine.

On the woman's figure all the emphasis is on shine. Blue and violet blended together are used as an accent along the sides of the legs and around the knee to indicate a contrast between shine and shadow. A secondary color—blue-violet, obtained directly from a marker, and a little more saturated than the original blended color—is used to enhance this contrast of dark and light. Dots are added to the pants to give texture and added contrast to the shine. The top is filled in with green marker, with blended black marker used to indicate shadows and draw the lettering.

Skin tone and hair are applied as extensions of the application of color to the garments so as not to distract attention from the primary focus on the shiny pants.

shiny fabrics

silk

DESIGN: GUCCI

Full-length backless evening dress with sweeping train.

Garments in which some parts that are tightly fitted and other parts are loose and flowing will display a variety of drapes. Each of these types of drape has to be shaded correctly to accurately depict the close fit or flowing train.

A careful drawing of the silhouette is essential to show the soft, contoured draping of this beautiful garment. Once the silhouette is complete, fill in with the desired color—in this case red—with several applications of color from the front and reverse side of the paper. Black pencil is used to define the shadows of the folds and contours of the fabric and white pencil used on the top of the folds.

Skin tone is drawn with an even application of a beige marker from the reverse side of the paper. The highlights on the shoulder blades are drawn in with white pencil.

shiny fabrics

silk/man-made

Left, softly draped silk evening dress with plunging neckline, mid-calf boots; right, bathing suit with pleated bra top, matching bag and bathing cap.

Shiny fabrics are used in a wide range of garments, some examples of which are seen in this drawing. Although the fabrics of the two garments appear similar, that of the dress is a natural fiber while that of the bathing suit is a man-made fiber. The natural fabric of the dress has more drape, while the man-made fabric—which probably includes stretch-lycra—hugs the body, although in other respects the fabrics appear almost identical.

Draw the silhouettes of both garments on the croquis with light blue pencil. The poses are the mirror images of each other, with the weight pushing up the hip on the left side in the left figure and the right side in the right figure

Fill in the garments with a deep olive marker. If this color is not available in a single marker it can be easily produced by mixing red and green markers.

In the dress, define the shine along the ridge of the fold with a white pencil, and in the bikini along the center-front and in the pleats of the top. To increase the contrast in value between the highlights and their adjoining shadows—so enhancing the appearance of shine—add shadows adjacent to the white highlights with a black pencil; the darkest darks sit directly next to the lightest lights. Black marker is used to fill in the sunglasses, around the sides of the cap and to add depth to the pleats of the top and the seam of the bikini bottom.

shiny fabrics

silk

Backless silk evening dress with distinctive low cowl drape.

In this figure the anatomy of the figure is drawn in with more detail than usual to provide an exciting complement to the small garment (the intention of small garments is usually to draw attention to a pretty figure).

This is a simple skirt that fits tightly to the lower torso, and shadows must emphasize the dimensions of the bottom, hips and thighs. Several layers of blended color are applied with strokes that follow the lines of the figure underneath the skirt. A final darker layer is applied to emphasize the outline of the figure at the thighs and calves. Black marker is used to follow the folds of the cowl and a white gel pen is used to indicate sparkles in the skirt and the white at the ridge of the folds. Note that the green version of the dress shows a slightly more flaired skirt and small variation in the shading.

The hair is filled in with black marker for the parts that are close to the head, and , using a blender and colored pencils, is extended away from the head to show the separate sections of the hair.

The back is drawn with layers of blended color to give a high contrast between the light and shaded areas and to appear slim and athletic (using several layers of blended color creates deeper value while at the same time creating a semi-transparent luminosity). Black is applied to create the effect of a very deep shadow under the side of the dress and below the skirt along the line of the thigh and calf.

leather

suede

Soft-tailored suede jacket, blouson blouse, jean-style pants, sunglasses.

Although this jacket is tailored, especially around the shoulders and arms, it is fabricated with soft, medium-weight fabric and very little internal construction, so it drapes more like a sweater than a tailored garment.

To draw this type of softly draped garment the silhouette is drawn with a nuanced line—a line that changes from light to dark as well as from thick to thin. Because the fabric is soft and curves around the contours of the body there will be many areas where the edge of the garment is softer and less defined, and this is represented by a more delicate line. The lapel, shoulder seam, hem and flap do contain structure, however, and require a firm line.

A blended color is applied in layers around the folds of the jacket and to define the soft folds of the blouse. The pants are filled in with a light rose blended color, leaving a white highlight along the center of the leg on the right side. Define the cast shadow on the blouse from the jacket with a beige marker and apply along the side of the pants to give them further dimension. Draw the zipper and j-seam pockets, characteristic of jean styling, with colored pencil.

The skin tone is a continuation of the blended color that is used in the pants. The eyeglasses are drawn using the same color as the skin tone, allowing for reflected light. A second application of light blended blue to the frames echoes the color used in shading the blouse.

white, black and grey

linen

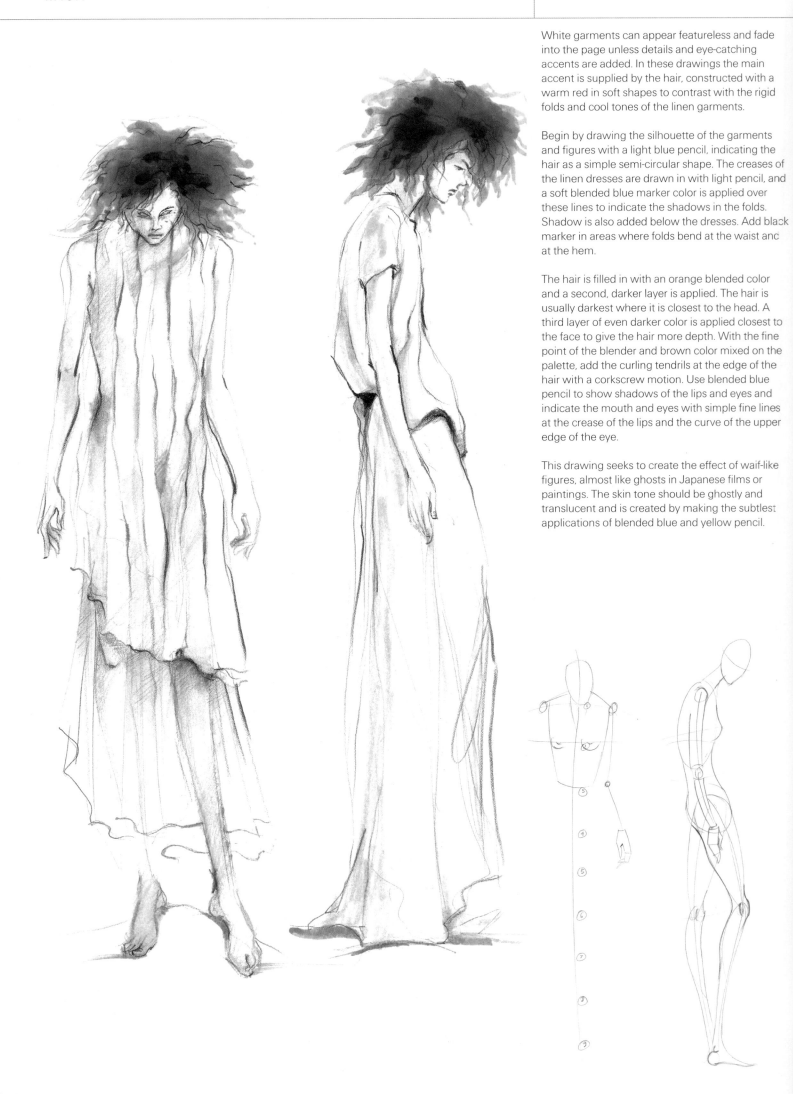

White garments can appear featureless and fade into the page unless details and eye-catching accents are added. In these drawings the main accent is supplied by the hair, constructed with a warm red in soft shapes to contrast with the rigid folds and cool tones of the linen garments.

Begin by drawing the silhouette of the garments and figures with a light blue pencil, indicating the hair as a simple semi-circular shape. The creases of the linen dresses are drawn in with light pencil, and a soft blended blue marker color is applied over these lines to indicate the shadows in the folds. Shadow is also added below the dresses. Add black marker in areas where folds bend at the waist and at the hem.

The hair is filled in with an orange blended color and a second, darker layer is applied. The hair is usually darkest where it is closest to the head. A third layer of even darker color is applied closest to the face to give the hair more depth. With the fine point of the blender and brown color mixed on the palette, add the curling tendrils at the edge of the hair with a corkscrew motion. Use blended blue pencil to show shadows of the lips and eyes and indicate the mouth and eyes with simple fine lines at the crease of the lips and the curve of the upper edge of the eye.

This drawing seeks to create the effect of waif-like figures, almost like ghosts in Japanese films or paintings. The skin tone should be ghostly and translucent and is created by making the subtlest applications of blended blue and yellow pencil.

white, black and grey

silk

DESIGN: ARMANI

Asymmetrical layered silk blouse, classic pants.

This is a deceptively simple drawing: at first sight the blouse and pants appear simple because of the lack of design detail and variation of color. In reality, though, this is one of the most difficult drawings in this book because of the accuracy and delicacy required in the application of the shading and subtlety of the drape.

The fine tailoring and fabric used in this designer garment give a luxurious appearance to the surface drape, with complex patterns of shadows and light. Carefully draw the silhouette of the blouse and pants allowing for the curves of the folds of the fabric along the sleeves and the asymmetrical cut of the blouse. The surface of the fabric of the blouse is depicted by using a number of small applications of light grey and blended violet marker to indicate the subtle sheen of the silk. Black pencil is then used to add nuanced lines to reinforce the beautiful silhouette of the garment in the areas where the body bends most—along the sleeve, hip and drape at the bottom of the pant.

The hair is drawn as a simple blended yellow accent and a further accent of skin tone is seen at the wrist. Note that the angle of the strands of the hair echo the angles of the layers of the blouse.

white, black and grey

silk

DESIGN: ARMANI

Sophisticated, soft-tailored blazer, blouse and pants with elastic casing.

This is a loosely tailored garment made of a fine, soft fabric that drapes away from the body.

The silhouettes of the jacket and pants are drawn on the croquis using a very light touch to avoid a hard edge that would make the fabric look too stiff. Take care to place the collar around the back of the neck, to draw accurately the cap of the sleeves, to drape the fabric at the elbow and to draw the lapels symmetrically. When drawing the pants make sure the waist-band, made of elastic, bends around the torso. The fabric is soft, curving around the contours of the body. A more delicate line is used for the body of the jacket and sleeves than when normally drawing tailored garments because they are not constructed. The lapels, shoulder-seam, hem and front of the jacket are constructed, however, and require a firm line.

The garment is filled in with blended color mixed from the palette. The jacket, blouse and pants are shaded with a second application of blended color and navy blue shadows are applied along the inseam, outside left leg and crotch of the pants and under the lapel and armhole of the jacket. The vest is drawn with a spare application of a brick-colored pencil.

Skin tone is omitted so that the focus is kept on the dynamic movement of the figure and garment.

white, black and grey

cotton

DESIGN: UNKNOWN

Linen, pin-tucked, short, sleeveless dress.

white, black and grey

DESIGN: UNKNOWN

cotton

Linen, pin-tucked short sleeveless dress.

This drawing shows how to draw the knife edges cf pin tucks and complex shading of a sophisticated white dress.

Blended warm grey is used to fill in the shadows of the flat folds of the pleats. Skin tone and hair are indicated with a beige marker.(Step 1).

A thin layer of slightly darker grey is added to areas of the garment where the folds are deeper: in the waist area, inside the tucks, under the dress where it touches the chair and inside the hair where it touches the face (Step 2).

Complete the drawing by adding a contrasting dark grey tone at the edges of pleats and to the chair. Note that the chair complements the geometry of the garment (this is a nine-headed chair for a nine-headed figure!). Note also the foreshortened rear legs of the figure and chair.

Skin tone complements the warm white of the dress. A subtle rose tint is applied with blended colored pencil to the face and figure, over the beige skin tone.

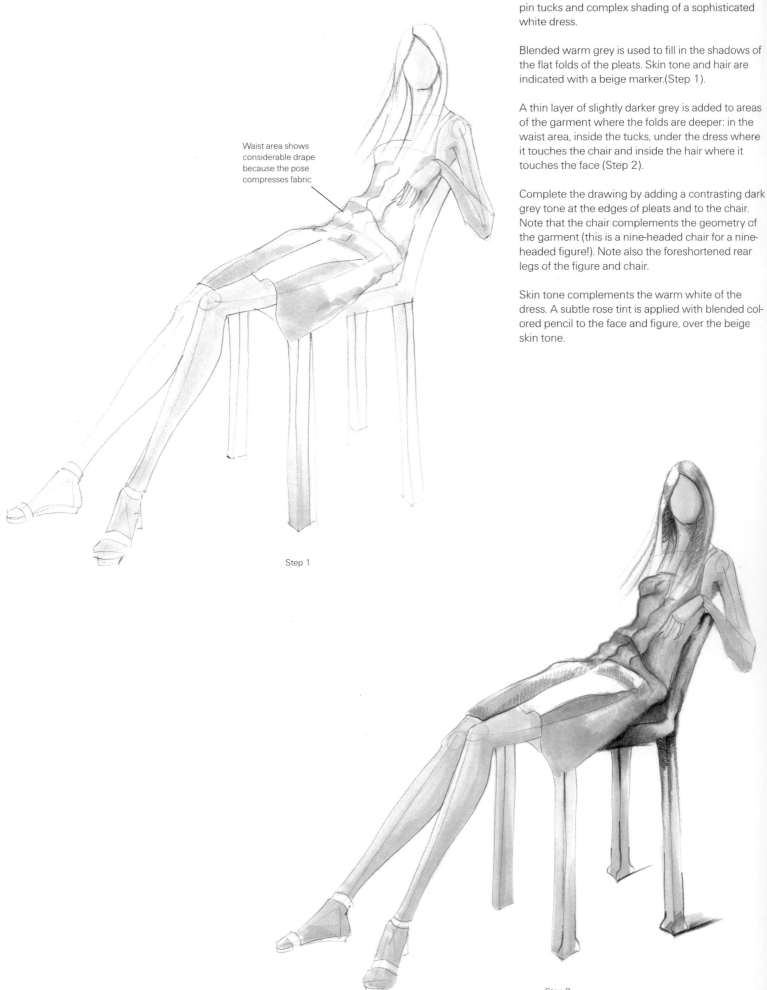

Waist area shows considerable drape because the pose compresses fabric

Step 1

Step 2

378

white, black and grey

cotton

DESIGN: ISTVAN FRASER

Striped blouson dress with gathered, belted detail at dropped hip, smocking detail on top.

This garment is made from lightweight, soft, print fabric and the drawing is designed to highlight its extremely light weight. To create the desired effect of gossamer weightlessness for this type of fabric and garment, it is best to avoid solid lines and complex, detailed figures as they often create a structured, two-dimensional effect. Omitting parts of the figure or features, as in this drawing, can in general be an effective device in reinforcing the appearance of garments that are ethereally light.

Begin by drawing the croquis with the lightest of lines. Use blended color—either warm or cool pastels—to show the shadows in the drape. The drape of the garment emanates from the band at the waist and the belted area under the hips. Very little shadow is required, to avoid a heavy look. Pattern is applied using blended color and is broken up in the folds. Detail is added to the pattern with a .005 pen and delicate shadow is indicated on the right side of the figure, at the shoulder, at the waistband, at the full drape of the skirt and at the shoes with the same pen.

Skin tone is applied with minimal touches of blended color.

white, black and grey

silk chiffon

DESIGN: ALEXANDER McQUEEN

White silk chiffon dress

Any garment can be drawn in an "artistic" manner, where the emphasis is on conveying mood and overall effect rather than detail and construction. Some garments, however, particularly lend themselves to such interpretations, and this is a good example of one with a special, ethereal quality that sets it apart from more functional garments and invites an artistic rendition.

The overall effect of the drawing is very similar to that of a watercolor, but this drawing can be completed much more quickly and easily with marker: when layering with watercolors, every separate layer has to be allowed to dry, taking about fifteen to twenty minutes, whereas markers dry in a few seconds.

There is virtually no silhouette to this garment. The dress is created with subtle applications of blended color using both the broad and the fine points of the marker to define the shadows of the drape of the dress. The same color is used in the background with subtle shifts in value. The hair is drawn with a simple shape, diffused at the edges, accenting the shape of the garment, and a few shadows are indicated using a darker blended brown. Shadows are also indicated under the chin, in the facial features, in the hand and under the hem.

No skin tone is indicated on the body—the white of the skin blends with the lightness of the garment. The skin tone on the face blends into the background.

The silhouette shows considerable drape and bending of the contour line. Shadows fill in the folds.

380

white, black and grey

wool tweeds

DESIGN: UNKNOWN

Wool tweed jackets and pants, knit sweaters, scarves, hats, sunglasses, belt, casual shoes.

Drawing in patterned designs with photographic precision can be time-consuming and inefficient, and sometimes the result can appear too busy and provide more information than is required. This drawing shows how complex patterned designs of different scales can be rendered efficiently and clearly.

Note that these figures are based on the same croquis: the two on the left are almost identical and the one on the right is their mirror image. It is only necessary to draw one of the figures; this is done on a separate piece of paper and then used as the template for all three figures by tracing over directly onto the marker paper and making slight changes to the heads and limbs.

Once the figures are on the paper the silhouettes of the garments are drawn with a light grey pencil. A 10% grey shadow is applied under the collars, jacket front panels, center-front seam of the pants and into the creases and folds at the knees and elbows of all the garments. Because these are three-quarter pose figures, in order to plot the designs of the patterns correctly it is helpful to locate the center axis line of each figure and sketch a grid to indicate where each pattern repeat or element will fall on the foreshortened surface of the figure.

Starting with the figure on the left, draw in with a black pencil the plaid of the jacket collar with diagonal lines. The vertical and horizontal lines of the plaid on the body of the jacket bend around the cylindrical shape of the body of the jacket, breaking up in the folds that appear where it is compressed at the waist. Plotting out the pattern design first with pencil makes it easier to correct mistakes. The design on the pants is drawn in with the same technique as is used for the jacket; close attention should be paid to the direction of the stripes. The design on the sleeve of the jacket is defined using the side of the black pencil to give a soft texture.

The sweater of the figure on the right has a less regular design that can be drawn in with black pencil. Note that the triangles break up inside the folds. The designs on the pants and jacket are created using a tapping motion with a 10% grey marker. In both this figure and the one on the left the print design has been more closely rendered on the left side of each pant leg than on the right. The left side is more in shadow and the eye reads the lack of pattern design detail on the right sides of the garments as due to the effect of the lighting. This is an efficient and effective way to depict patterned designs realistically.

The figure in the center has less detail. The jacket and pants are filled in with grey marker. The trim of the sweater adds a bold graphic balance to the other two figures.

The accessories accent the geometric patterns of the garments and are drawn in with black pencil.

A small amount of skin tone is indicated on the face of the figure on the right using blue blended pencil.

white, black and grey

tulle/silk/beads

DESIGN: JEAN-PAUL GAULTIER

Flowing wedding veil, wedding bonnet, beaded wedding bathing suit.

Olympic swimmers with nuptial plans might give some consideration to this exotic wedding ensemble.

Draw in the croquis and then the bathing suit on top. Draw the outside silhouette of the veil as a triangle extending from the top of the bonnet to the ground. The veil forms cascading, conical drapes. These are drawn, as can be seen in the diagram, by dividing the veil into two triangles and then plotting the line of the folds inside the edges of those triangles.

Add shadows in the curves of each fold of the veil with blended blue marker and under the beads of the bathing suit and bonnet. A second layer of blended pink is used to add luminosity to the shadows, beading and bonnet. More shading is added to the curves of the veil and beads with an .005 pen. The hair is filled in with black marker.

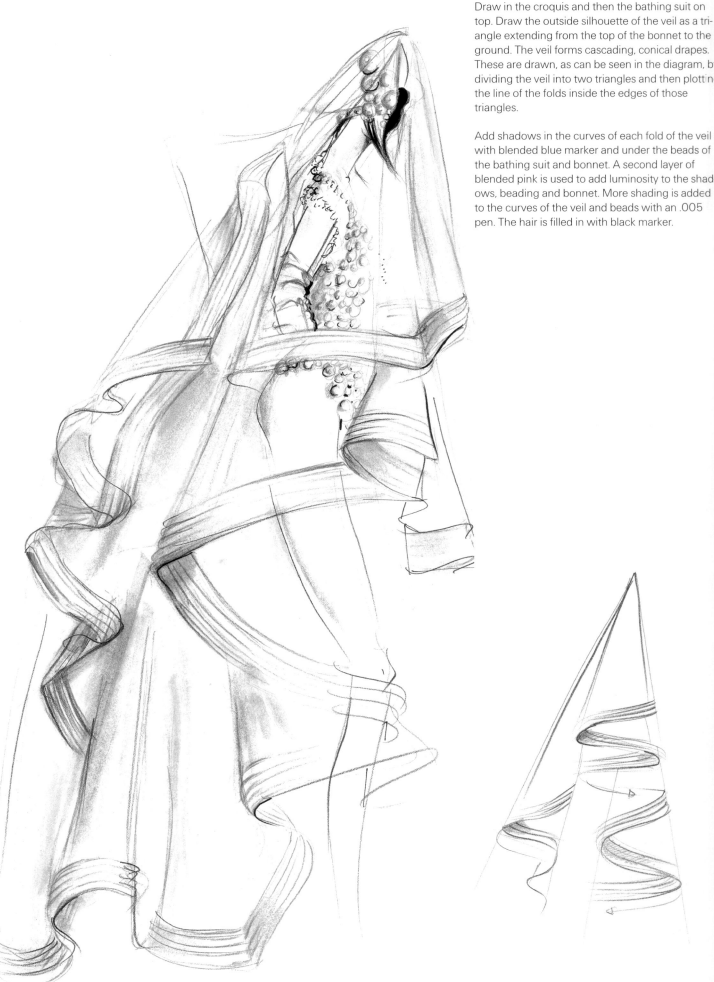

382

white, black and grey

silk

DESIGN: MILA SCHON

Wedding dresses of medium-weight embroidered silk with trains.

If garments are similar, with only subtle differences, they can often be drawn as pairs, mirroring one another and simultaneously highlighting the differences between the garments.

These wedding dresses are almost identical—one is made with a cool white fabric and the other with a warm white fabric. Note the unified composition of the drawing: the figures are placed facing each other, with the leg of the figure on the right extended towards the figure on the left so that the figures are tied together visually.

A blended tone is applied to all the areas around the contours of the torsos and the drapes of the skirts and trains. A second and third layer is applied to give depth and a black colored pencil is blended and applied to areas of shadows to create contrast and shine. The embroidered details are drawn in with colored pencil and appear more defined in the shadows of the crape. The curls of the hair echo the curves of the dress. A cool background color is applied for the cool figure and a warm one for the warm figure.

Skin tone is a minimal application of blended beige with reflected blue and yellow color pencils showing the reflections of the colors of the dresses.

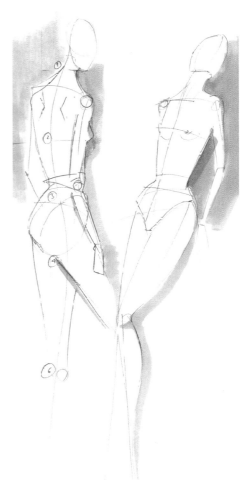

white, black and grey

wool/fur

DESIGN: NR

Left, three-quarter length double-breasted herring-bone tailored coat with fox fur collar, turtle-neck top; right, tailored jacket, softly-draped skirt.

These garments are very different but both have constructed shoulders and soft-drape lapels.

The silhouette for garment on the left has to be carefully drawn to show accurately the structure cf the coat. Special attention must be given to the asymmetrical button closure. Fill in the body of the garment with a saturated navy blue, adding a second application of color from the reverse side to achieve the required saturation. A sheen is applied to the surface of the folds with a white colored pencil. The herringbone pattern is then applied with colored pencil. The complex and detailed pattern would take too long to render in all areas of the garment, so it is applied liberally on the left side and allowed to fade away on the right.

To draw the fur collar, consider it as a three-dimensional cylinder. Fur has a sheen, so some parts of it will reflect light more than others, and should be left free of shadows. First add the darker colors to create the shadowed areas, as stripes that follow the contours of the fur, using a navy blue mixed on the palette and applied with the broad tip of a blender. With a white gel pen add light areas into these dark areas of the fur using small strokes. Add some additional color—here a magenta is used—with colored pencil. To the areas of the collar which have been left as bare white paper build up a texture using dark-blue colored pencil, also adding some magenta and white highlights.

For the garment on the right, the silhouette is drawn with a cool or warm color blended on the palette and larger areas of the same blended colcr are applied to show the drape of the garment in the roll of the collar, under the lapel, in the drape of the sleeves, under the jacket, around the drape of the skirt at the edge of the legs and at the flaring hem. The same blended color is used as minimal accents for hair and skin tone.

white, black and grey	DESIGN: NR
man-made/cotton	Classic long-sleeved t-shirt and black stretch pants.

This drawing shows the juxtaposition of sharp shiny fabrics that hug the contours of the body and the soft drape of a cotton t-shirt.

In this drawing the darker garment is drawn first as some of the color used to draw it will also be used in shading the lighter garment.

Draw the silhouette of the pants, which will be almost identical to that of bare legs, and fill in with black marker from the front and reverse sides of the paper to achieve maximum saturation. Hold a blender to the broad tip of the black marker to pick up some of the color and apply to the edges of the t-shirt to give a soft shadow, and into the body of the shirt to define the drape. Define the highly reflective light on the side of the leg and around the knee using a sharp white pencil. This process should be repeated several times to achieve the opaque white effect. At the top of the leg the shine becomes sheen, and is drawn in using the side of the pencil.

accessories/shoes

above-the-knee boots

When drawing soft leather bear in mind that it drapes, and when fitting close to the leg will drape particularly at the knee and ankle, the parts where the leg bends.

With this in mind, carefully draw the silhouette of the boots and fill in with saturated color. For both pairs of boots the shine on the ridges of the folds is defined with white pencil. On the blue boots black pencil is used to define the shadows in the recessed areas of the folds and along the sides of the legs.

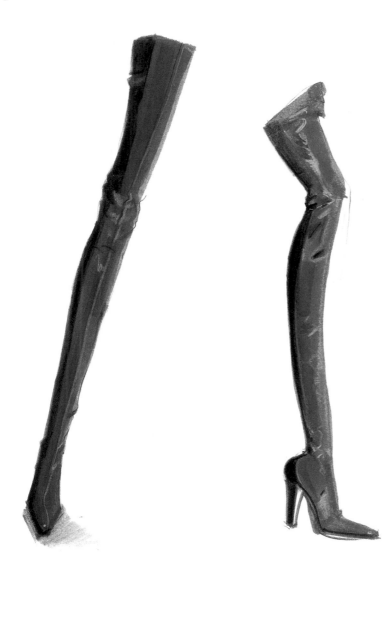

accessories/shoes

sports shoes

Shiny satin.

Sport jogger.

Color stripes.

Elastic lace-up, sporty.

Round, shiny, uniform.

Velcro fastening.

Cha-cha, point form, sporty.

Pointy sneaker with Asian embroicery.

Retro soccer shoe.

Sporty, colored T-boot.

Hiking boot.

Boxer with decoration.

Sneaker, wedge, colorful.

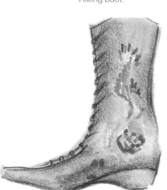

Boxing boot, Asian embroidery.

Pointy boxing boot.

399

accessories/shoes

historical shoes

Although the techniques and principles are the same for drawing any type of shoe, "historical" shoes were often much more sumptuous than shoes of today, with embroidery, lace embellishments, tooled leather, buckles, bows and gold and silver threads. Due attention must be given to these details when drawing this type of shoe.

Shoe belonging to Pope St. Sylvester, Bishop of Rome 4th century.

Ceremonial shoe of Pope John XXIII (20th century).

Shoe worn by the Emperor Charlemagne at his coronation—9th century AD.

16th century shoe.

accessories/shoes

ruben alterio

accessories

handbag

Feather handbag with chain detail.

Handbags are made in an enormous variety of shapes and sizes and from an enormous variety of fabrics and materials. They are made with or without drape and can have buckles, belt-clips and large or small straps or chains.

The shape is the most important feature of a bag, and, when drawn, bags are usually depicted in three-quarter view so the length and width of the bag can be appreciated.

The techniques used in drawing bags are largely the same as those used for depicting different types of fabrics in garments.

accessories

handbags

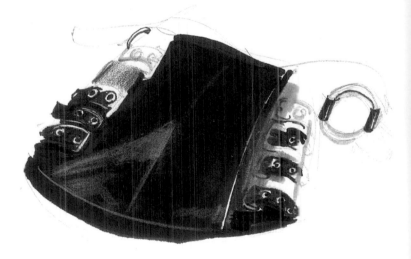

accessories

handbags

accessories

hats

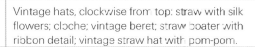
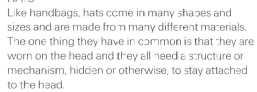

Vintage hats, clockwise from top: straw with silk flowers; cloche; vintage beret; straw boater with ribbon detail; vintage straw hat with pom-pom.

HATS

Like handbags, hats come in many shapes and sizes and are made from many different materials. The one thing they have in common is that they are worn on the head and they all need a structure or mechanism, hidden or otherwise, to stay attached to the head.

A common mistake when drawing hats is to draw them as flat and two-dimensional. This is ironic because the head is the most rounded of the body's forms. Hats—garments for the head—follow these rounded contours and are, in fact, more three-dimensional than other garments.

Because hats have to fit a rounded form, the fabrics they are made of usually have to be soft, flexible and malleable and this should be kept in mind when they are drawn. To indicate the round, three-dimensionality of hats, shadows must be indicated at the sides of the hat, where it bends around the head. Brims must also be seen to bend and are drawn with oval, elliptical shapes.

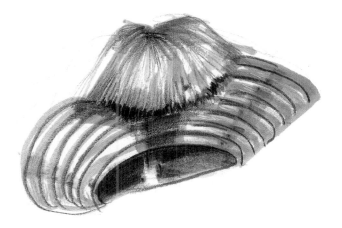

HATS

Like handbags, hats come in many shapes and sizes and are made from many different materials. The one thing they have in common is that they are worn on the head and they all need a structure or mechanism, hidden or otherwise, to stay attached to the head.

accessories

hats

Clockwise from top: vintage turban; canvas hat; boa hat; turban; straw boater with straw flowers.

Although perhaps not as commonly used as in the past, hats are still worn on many formal occasions and their use has grown considerably in casual situations. Casual hats are often derived from sportswear garments—baseball caps for example—and often show the same innovations in construction, including top-stitching, molded or fused seams, rivets, parachute clips and extensive use of ultra-light fabrics. When drawing these types of hats it is important to show these details of construction and indicate the special nature of the materials used. When drawing top-stitching, buckles or construction details it is easiest to work with colored pencils.

The other category of contemporary hats, those worn with a more formal look, emphasize aesthetics more than function. They are usually made from pretty materials and contain purely decorative elements; in drawing them the relative importance of these elements should be clearly indicated.

When drawing hats made of soft fabrics, or when depicting floral designs on hats, layers of blended color are used to show the softness of the materials.

accessories/hats

ruben alterio

accessories

miscellaneous

Classic watches and eyeglasses.

MISCELLANEOUS ACCESSORIES

Most of the objects shown here are made from hard, reflective materials that have very different properties from fabric and as a result must be drawn differently. As opposed to garments, which are often defined by drape and shadows, hard objects are defined by their contours, and it is important to make sure these are clearly defined with crisp, sharp lines.

Begin drawing these objects by defining the edges. Where the accessory has surfaces that will show reflections of light (such as in eyeglasses or watches or the facets of gems) plan out the areas that will appear white and the positions of the different tones and shadows. Fill in working from light to dark. With highly reflective materials, such as glass, shiny metal or gems, in order to give the effect of a high shine it is necessary to juxtapose the lightest light colors with the darkest dark colors.

With cylindrical forms, drawn with a series of ellipses, a dark stripe runs through the core and is framed by light white stripes on either side.

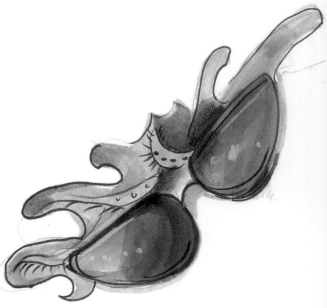

accessories

metal/glass

accessories

jewelry/gems

Jewel-encrusted brassiere.

JEWELRY/GEMS

When drawing gems the shape of the reflections is directly related to the shape of the surface: a rounded gem will have round reflections, a flat-faced gem will have flat reflections.

Show the facets of a gem with clearly drawn edges using colored pencil. Where objects—beads for example—are touching and no light is reflected from the touching surfaces, define this area with a dark semi-circle.

For this jewel-encrusted brassiere note that a grey cast shadow has been added under the whole garment from the reverse side of the page to give the appearance of depth and physicality.

accesso ies

jewels

accessories

jewels

Lady-bug brooch with plaid ribbon, assorted rings.

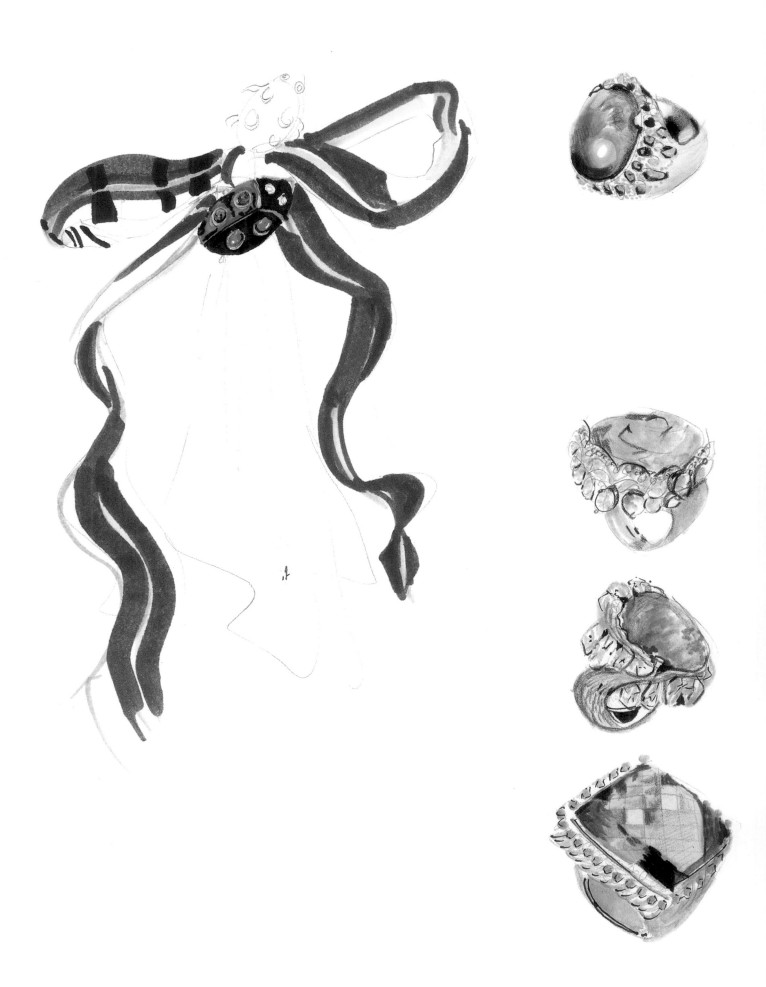

accessories

scarves

Cotton bandana, silk chiffon scarf.

Scarves are made of a variety of fabrics. The bandana here is drawn with red pencil and filled in with two applications of red marker from both sides of the paper to give saturation. The patterns are drawn in with a white gel pen and black .005 pen. Shadows are drawn in with a black pencil.

The silk chiffon scarf below is made of a transparent fabric. The pattern is filled using blended color only, leaving the white of the paper as highlights on the folds.

accessories

fans

Paper fan; feather fan.

The fan on top is drawn with a grey pencil and filled in with marker for the more saturated colors and colored pencil for the lighter colors. A small amount of a deeper red is added for shading.

The fan below is made up of layers of blended blue with blended grey and pink added for the shadows.

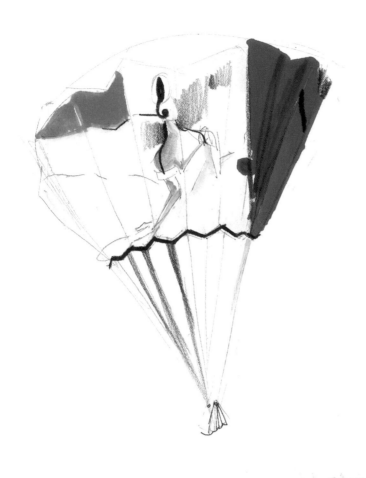

accessories

DES GN: NR

flowers

Chiffon shawl with roses.

To draw flowers the basic shapes are defined with marker and individual petals then drawn in as a series of arcs that overlap and become smaller as they spiral into the center of the flower. Shadow is applied under each petal with a darker value color.

practice and exercises

BEGINNERS

1. (i) Copy a croquis from the Appendix. Add a belt, necklace and shoes. This exercise is to learn that garments fit round the figure. (ii) Copy the same croquis and add the silhouette of a jacket and skirt. (iii) Copy the same croquis, add the silhouette of a jacket and skirt, and add shading. (iv) Copy the same croquis and silhouette, add color, shading and texture (this could be lace, fur, corduroy, beaded paillettes or quilting).

2. (i) Draw the silhouette of any of the garments in this chapter and fill in with markers to create flat colors. (ii) Using the same silhouette, divide into two sections, head and torso and legs. FIll in the head and torso with a floral pattern ignoring the facial and body features. Fill in the legs with a plaid pattern.

3. Take the silhouette of (i) a jacket and pants, (ii) a full skirt, (iii) a party skirt. Fill in the silhouette with one of the following design patterns: (i) stripes, (ii) animals, (iii) musical notes. The silhouette can be two- or three-dimensional, draped or flat. The drawing can be embellished with images of choice as background elements.

4. Draw a lace bathing suit.

5. Draw three jackets on croquis, the first made from corduroy, the second from tweed and the third with a Prince of Wales pattern.

6. Draw an outfit consisting of a hand-knitted sweater and jeans, using cable and popcorn stitching in the sweater (see Chapter Three: Fabrics for references).

7. Draw your wedding dress or outfit then draw your bridesmaids' (or wife-to-be's bridesmaids') dresses.

8. Draw a simple black skirt with a white trim and a white blouse with a black trim.

9. Copy a picture of a hat and add a rose.

10. Copy a picture of a handbag and change the colors.

ADVANCED

11. Draw an outfit with a floral printed blouse and an iridescent silk jacket and pants.

12. Using ten different printed fabrics draw two ensembles (prints may be used in any area of the garments including lining, trims, buttons or accessories).

13. Draw (i) a lace nightgown, (ii) a satin wedding dress, (iii) a quilted jacket and wool pants for a wedding trousseau (the bride's honeymoon wardrobe).

14. Draw three bathing suits with graphic prints using cartoon characters, faces of well-known personalities or exotic animals.

15. Copy the silhouette of the Yohji Yamamoto jacket and full skirt from this chapter and fill in with a different print.

practice and exercises

16. Draw an evening gown encrusted with jewels.

17. Draw two jackets for a cold climate with fur accents.

18. Draw a pant suit made from heavy silk fabric and accessorize with satin items.

19. Using an active pose, draw the silhouettes of (i) blouse and pants on the croquis, and (ii) the silhouettes of active sportswear garments. Fill in both drawings with marker and shade with pencil.

20. Draw a cocktail dress made of (i) a matt fabric, (ii) a fabric with a sheen and (iii) a fabric with shine.

21. Draw night-club outfits showing fabrics with (i) a fringe, and (ii) sequins.

22. Spot a trend in a fashion magazine—it could be patterns, texture, accessories or a silhouette—and tear out the photo. (i) Trace the image to learn the silhouette (ii) Translate the photo into a nine-head drawing, copying the details exactly using markers and colored pencils. (iii) The same as (ii) but changing the details—the buttons, hem, size of sleeves, pockets, trims.

23. Using a croquis from the Appendix draw an outfit inspired by a swatch of fabric

24. Take any garment from this chapter and re-draw in a different fabric (though one still suitble for the garment). Indicate in the drawing where the silhouette, crape and shading are diferent from the original version of the garment.

25. Draw three croquis and design simple outfits. Add a total of 15 accessories to the three figures.

26. Using the section in this chapter on accessories for reference, draw a shoe, a purse and jewelry for (i) a wedding, (ii) the beach, (iii) a nightclub.

27. Draw shoes for (i) a movie star, (ii) a business executive, (iii) an Olympic athlete.

28. Draw a range of accessories for a woman and, keeping the silhouettes the same, change colors, fabric and styling to make them suitable for a child.

everyday garments

Most of the clothes in our closets are not high-fashion designer garments but those we wear every day. While fashion is important and we wish to look chic and smart in our everyday activities, these clothes—referred to as "wardrobe basics" in this chapter—have to be functional—comfortable, durable and easy to care for, as well as stylish.

When drawing these staple favorites of our wardrobes, the same techniques are used as for higher-fashion garments of the women's chapter, even though they tend to be simpler and made from less luxurious materials. The silhouettes of these clothes are usually less extreme—shapes conform more to the natural shape of the body—and detailing is less prominent and less expensive. The presentation of the clothes in the drawings, however, is quite different. Here the emphasis is on the clothes themselves rather than on the figure and the accessories. Although these clothes have been included after the chapter on women's fashion clothes, it is important, in fact, to be able to draw the clothes and the fabrics they are made of alone, without the figure, before progressing to more elaborate compositions featuring the body in different poses. Focusing solely on fabric and silhouette can allow garments to be seen in a fresh way and encourage them to be drawn more accurately when it comes to drawing them on the figure.

Just because the clothes are not expensive designer garments does not mean that they should be drawn with any less care and attention to detail. In fact, if at all, even more attention should be given to ensuring that the silhouette and detailing are correct, as any small error is easily noticed in garments that are so familiar.

The drawings in this chapter are particularly useful to refer to when beginning to learn to draw. A common misconception held by beginners is that fashion drawing is learnt by studying and sketching wedding gowns and evening dresses. In reality, only princesses have more than two evening gowns in their closets, and it is easier to learn how to draw evening gowns by first learning to draw the other more numerous, simpler garments in the closet—even for princesses!

The volume of everyday, staple garments produced throughout the world greatly exceeds that of specialized designer-wear, and the fashion professional will most likely spend more time drawing garments of the types shown in this chapter than other types of garments. As staple garments are usually what determine how we look most of the time, though, they should be drawn to look as attractive as possible, so that this feeds into the design process and the garments that end up forming the majority of the clothes in our closets also look as stylish and attractive as possible. This chapter shows how to draw staples so they look their best, as well as appearing realistic and technically accurate.

black velvet pants/white silk camisole

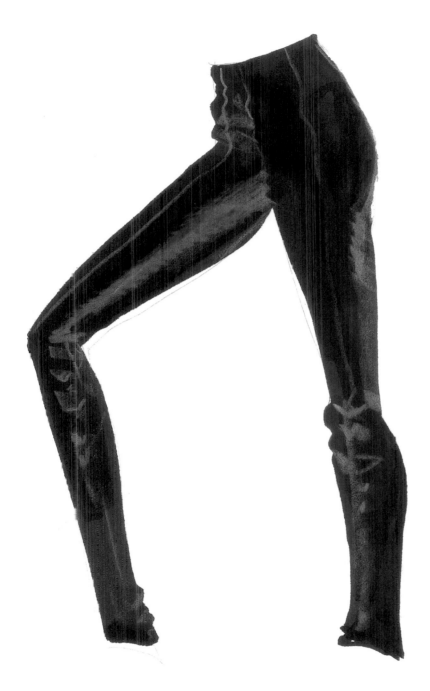

These are two common wardrobe items that are constructed with widely different variations of fabrics with shine—one a heavy velvet and the other a delicate silk.

For the pants, the silhouette can be drawn with either black marker or pencil: skin-tight garments follow the contours of the figure and there is less chance of making errors than when complex draped shapes have to be drawn.

Fill in the garment with several layers of black marker applied from both sides of the paper and allow to dry. When dry, add sheen and highlights along the side of the hip, thigh, calf and on top of the folds with a white pencil. Resharpen the pencil to define the seams and add extra highlights on the tops of the folds.

For the camisole, carefully draw the silhouette with a very light grey marker. When drawing white shiny fabrics, the shading is indicated with cool grey marker and the white shiny parts by leaving the white of the paper to show through. Mix cool grey and black on the palette and apply with blender, using a light touch. Allow for one side of the camisole—here the right— to receive more white reflections than the other.

Define the shadows in the strap, the lace of the collar of the camisole and along one side with the fine point of a black marker.

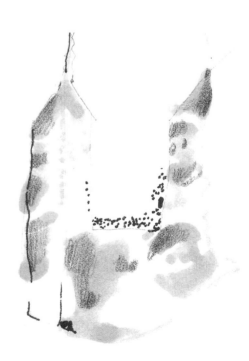

mens t-shirts/classic cotton shirts

Shirts are a staple of every man's wardrobe and must be drawn accurately as their appearance is so familiar.

For the t-shirts, carefully draw the silhouettes with a light grey marker, showing the soft curves of the draped cotton. Add blended grey to define the drape within the shirts and the interiors of the necklines. Note that for warm white garments a beige or warm grey is used for shading; for cool white a cool grey or light blue. A variety of background shadows can be experimented with to separate the white shirts from their white backgrounds.

Both the collared shirts are drawn with blended light-blue marker; for the blue shirt it is used to fill in the whole garment. Accent shadows are applied with the fine point of a blue marker under the collar, under the facing and around the buttons.

short silk beaded dress/rayon printed dress

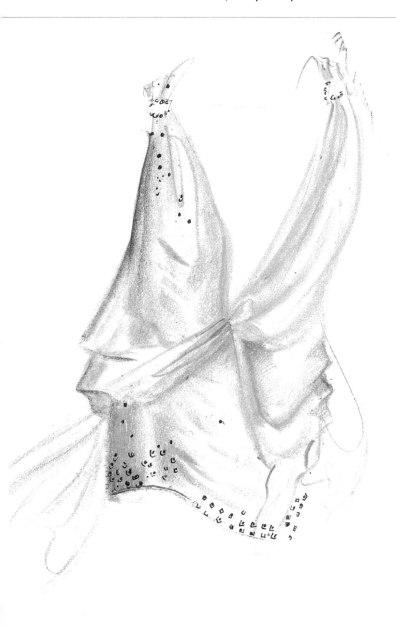

Dresses are fundamental to every female wardrobe. These are two sleeveless dresses of lightweight, feminine fabrics with differing drapes.

The dress on the left is drawn with a light pink pencil, taking care that the silhouette accurately shows the drape of the folds. The shadows are filled in with blended pink. Note that the white of the paper is left to indicate a highlight on the left side where the leg would be under the dress. A second layer of apricot blended color—marker or pencil—is applied for luminosity. The rhinestones are drawn with a .005 pen.

The garment on the right is a simple basic dress silhouette where the drape occurs at the bust-line and from the hip.

The colors used in drawing the print are mixed on a palette with a colorless blender and then applied working from light to dark. A light blue blended color is used as a shadow to show drape. A light application of colored pencil is used to define the silhouette.

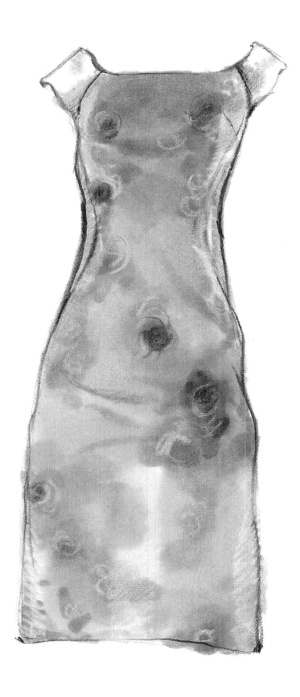

427

crocheted sweater

When drawing knitted or crocheted fabrics extensive use of pencil is made to express the variety of lines, textures and shapes created by the crocheted or knitted yarn.

Draw the silhouette in pencil. Fill in with several layers of red from the front and reverse sides of the paper. Use the fine tip of the marker to fill in the details of the fringe and softly draw the shadows using a black pencil. Add black pencil or marker to define the shapes of the shadows in the crochet.

man's dressing gown

Dressing gowns are designed for comfort, with relaxed fit and long drape. When stripes are involved they must be drawn with care to follow the folds of the fabric.

Draw the silhouette of the gown with a light grey pencil. Remember that men's clothes have closures from the left to the right side, the opposite way to women's clothes. Draw the stripes of the fabric with the fine tip of a black marker following the folds of the garment. Make sure the stripes bend diagonally across the shawl collar, bend and break up in the bends of the sleeves, in the body of the robe and around the knee.

Add shadows from the reverse side of the paper with a 10% cool grey marker.

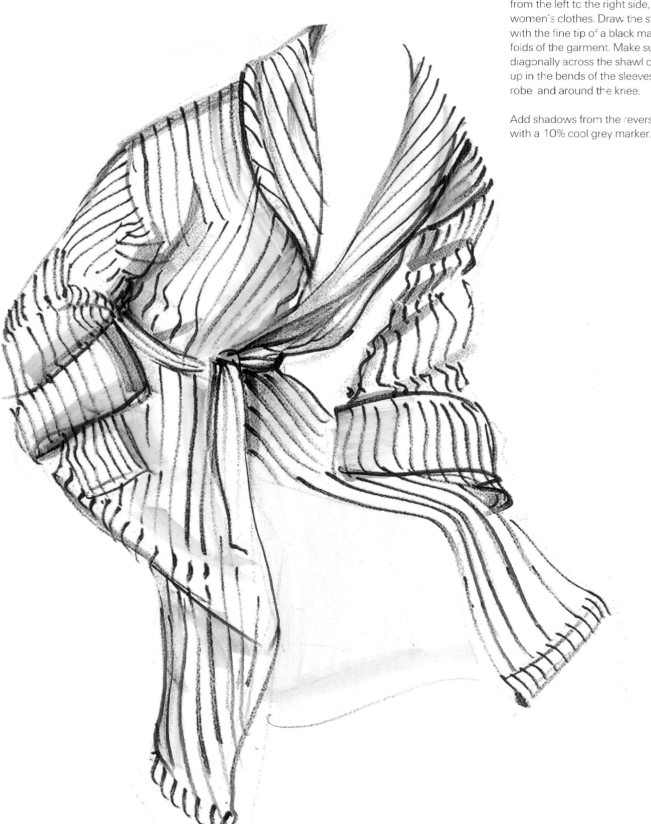

snakeskin pants/corduroy pants

Pants are a common staple in modern wardrobes. When drawing them care must be taken to show how they bend around the body at the waist, cuffs and bottom.

For the snakeskin pants, using a combination of cool grey and light blue blended color, layer shadows at the sides of the thighs and lower leg, leaving a strip of white in the middle. Remember to drape the fabric at the knee, and apply shadows with colored pencil. The snakeskin texture and design is applied last and follows the direction of the leg. It must be drawn with a very sharp pencil to show the intricate and delicate texture and pattern.

For the corduroys, draw the silhouette of the pants with a light grey pencil showing the round, soft drape below the knee. Using a brown marker, fill in the pants with several layers applied from the front and reverse sides of the paper. Apply shadows with a black pencil using the side of the pencil to indicate the softness of the fabric. White highlights are applied on the thigh and on the surface of the folds with a white colored pencil. The ribs of the corduroy are then indicated with the fine point of a black pencil.

hand-knit wool sweater

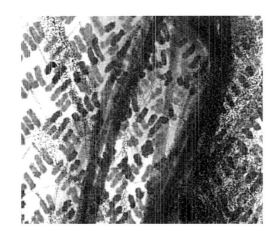

Hand-knit garments tend to be slightly heavier and more textured than machine-knit garments where the stitches are tighter.

To achieve the effect of weight and texture, apply a thin layer of blended color in the shadows of the drape of the sweater, after drawing the silhouette with a very light colored pencil. Two points to be noted: first, the line of the silhouette should not be noticeable in the finished drawing; second, as the garment is thick, shadows tend to be soft and wide, especially under the collar, at the elbows and at the sides of the sweater.

The texture of the garment is created using colored pencils and the pattern drawn in with short strokes. Refer to Chapter Three: Fabrics for different stitches that can be used.

This sweater has a fringe, which is drawn in with colored pencil. When drawing the fringe do so with a movement of the wrist so that it the fringe appears to be moving and not stiff.

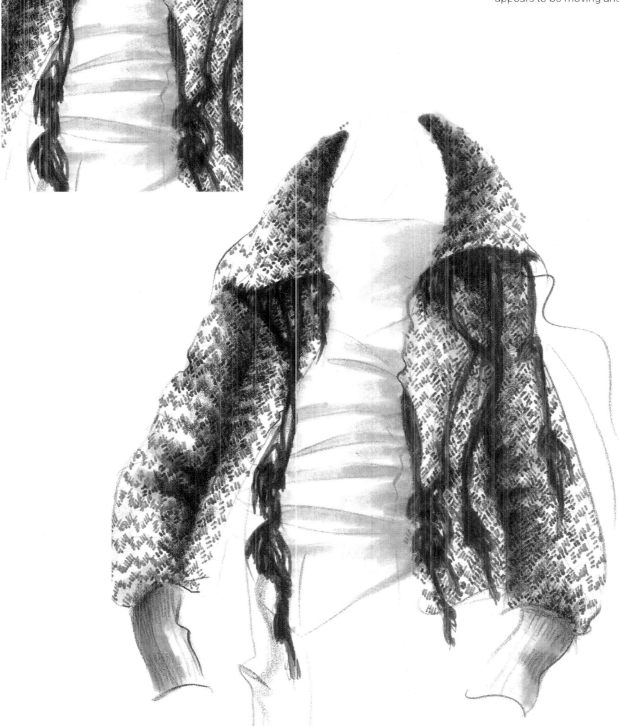

plain fabrics

DESIGN: BATTISTONI

Sleek tailored wool suit, shirt, tie.

The three-quarter pose reveals a different set of details from the frontal view.

As there is some foreshortening in the three-quarter figure it is easiest to begin the drawing with a well-planned-out croquis, showing the proportions of the figure and where the central axis falls.

Draw the silhouette of the jacket and fill in with pink marker. Shadows are drawn in using the side of a brown colored pencil. The shirt is light blue marker. Hair is drawn with simple shapes and filled in with brown pencil. The face is drawn using brown and black colored pencils.

Skin tone is the same color as the suit, a light pink, applied from the reverse side of the paper. The tie is drawn using the fine points of the blue and pink markers.

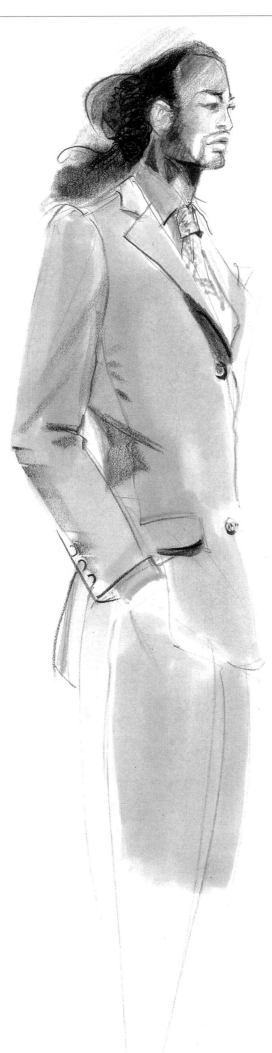

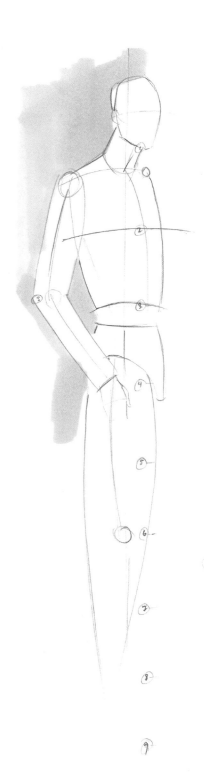

patterned/embroidered fabrics

Tailored suit with velvet collar, shirt, tie.

When drawing tailored garments made of dark fabric, it is useful to include a separate ink drawing so the details of the tailoring can be clearly seen. The drawing can be duplicated and used as the basis for the finished drawing.

Note that the weight of the figure is on the front leg and the fabric drapes towards the left.

The suit is filled in with a cool brown marker from both sides of the paper and colored pencil is used to draw in the shadows under the pockets and in the drape of the jacket and pants. The spicer pattern is drawn in with black pencil. The tie is filled in with magenta marker and the collar with a black marker. The facial features are drawn in with a grey colored pencil. Note that the cuffs of the shirt are elongated and extend beyond the cuffs of the jacket.

Skin tone is an application of walnut colored marker made from the reverse side of the page

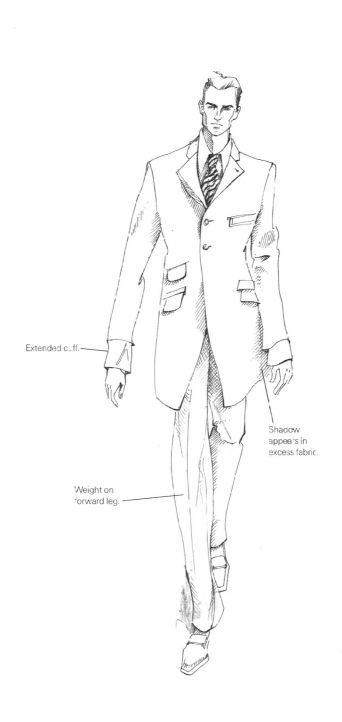

Extended cuff.

Shadow appears in excess fabric.

Weight on forward leg.

denim/patterned fabrics

DESIGN: ALBERT NG

Patterned, multi-striped t-shirt, blocked, striped generated-print overshirt, denim knee-length shorts, novelty stockings, flip-flops, wrist-band, striped beanie.

Draw the silhouette of the clothes with a light colored pencil, paying attention to the drape in the hat, the outer shirt and the denim pants.

The shirt is a combination of complex patterns which could look garish and sloppy if not well balanced. Here, however, patterns of different scales are subtly combined to result in a strikingly successful design. The drape of the shirt is shaded with a light-blue colored pencil and the horizontal stripes drawn in, breaking the line of the stripes at the fold to indicate the reflection of light at the highest point. The other stripes are drawn in—the order does not matter as they are all of the same level of saturation—with blended magenta, pink, green and yellow markers.

The sleeve and the interior of the shirt have different patterns but are drawn in the same manner. The collar of the shirt is blended magenta and the t-shirt is filled in with turquoise and red marker. The denim pants are filled in with blue marker with white pencil used on the surface of the folds to show the texture and color of the pants. Note that the lining of the denim is shown where the fabric is reversed at the waist. This is drawn by first applying a light layer of blended blue, and creating the white texture of the reversed denim by drawing a cross hatch pattern with a white pencil. The stocking is drawn with blended magenta and the pattern of the stocking is drawn with magenta pencil. Take care to draw the pattern design of the stocking as a curve around the calf of the leg. The hair is drawn using blended grey, blended blue and blended magenta applied in successive layers to create a luminous effect.

The fabric at the wrist is filled in with turquoise and magenta markers and the shadows are defined with turquoise and magenta colored pencils. The flip-flops are filled in with turquoise and black markers.

Skin tone is beige marker with a second layer of beige marker mixed with pink applied to show the shadows. The stubble of the beard is indicated using grey or brown pencil. The hat is drawn with blended blue marker applied from the reverse side; the shadows of the folds are defined with blue colored pencil and blended light-blue marker.

A cast shadow is finally applied under the body with blended black, magenta, yellow and green marker, with white pencil highlights. This shadow further enhances the textural richness of this drawing.

DESIGN: AKADEMICS

denim/soft fabrics

Sweatshirt, denim pants.

Relaxed drape, relaxed guy. A typical laid-back, street-smart young man with laid-back street-smart styling.

Draw the silhouette with a light grey pencil, indicating copious amounts of drape. Fill in the mid-section of the sweatshirt, the stripe along the sleeves and the collar with a blue marker. The letter A and the text on the shirt are drawn with the fine point of the same blue marker. Define the shadows of the drape in these blue sections using a second layer of the same color. Deepen the shadows with a black pencil and show the remaining shadows of the sweatshirt and the pants with a blended yellow marker, deepening these shadows with a blue-green blended colored pencil. Add texture to the denim pants using the side of a blue colored pencil, indicating top-stitching with the same pencil. Enhance the shadows in the pants with black pencil.

Skin tone is applied with a walnut colored marker, leaving a white area in the middle section of the face along the nose, lips, chin and neck. Blended pink is used on the forehead and the features of the face are defined with black pencil.

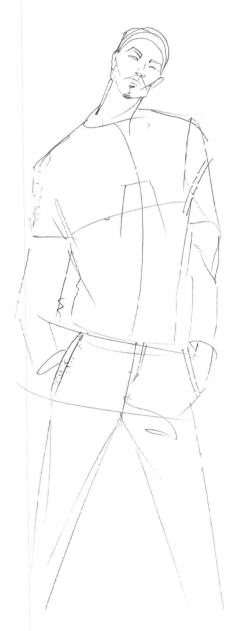

denim

Shirt, denim pants, satchel.

This drawing shows multi-layering and detailing in men's clothing; color here is of secondary importance.

This drawing has been left partly unfinished to show how it is possible, particularly when beginning to draw with markers, to break a drawing down into distinct segments of the same color that can then each be filled in separately. This technique avoids difficulties that can be encountered where garments of different colors overlap or, as in this case, cross over bare skin, and where the underlying layer of color would show through to the top layer.

Note the structure of the collar, the placement of the buttons, the position of the zipper and belt loops, the seam at the armhole and drape of the sleeve and pants.

The drawing also serves as an example of the use of skin tone color to accent the garment—the juxtaposition of the near-black skin tone and white shirt displays the strongest of value contrasts.

DESIGN: UNKNOWN

leather

White sweater, knee-length leather breeches with gathered hem, leather shoes.

The emphasis in this drawing is on the shiny, high-fashion breeches; the other garments are of lesser importance.

Draw the silhouette of the pants and top with a very light line. Subtly define the edge of the sweater with blended grey. Fill in the pants with a light blended green applied from the reverse side of the paper. Add shadows to the drape with a blended magenta, adding a second layer of blended green, a third layer of blended pink and a final layer of blended yellow. The highlights on the tops of the folds in the pants are drawn with white pencil; the drape of the pants that pulls towards the knee is drawn with dark grey pencil as well as the toggle and cord tie at the bottom of the pants. The face and hair are drawn with dark grey pencil.

Skin tone and the background to the face are blended layers of pink, magenta and blue. The same colors are used as a cast shadow under the figure. Black marker is used for the shoes, with white pencil for the accents.

cashmere

Three-quarter length cashmere coat, scarf.

Cashmere is a thick, softly draping fabric with a distinctive sheen.

Draw the silhouette with a light brown pencil noting that the fabric has wide, rounded folds at the elbow. Fill in with a warm brown marker and apply a second layer from the reverse side of the paper. Shadows are enhanced using the side of a black pencil. The sheen of the cashmere is indicated by applying white with the side of a pencil to the areas next to the deepest shadows. A thin line is drawn at the corners of the collar with the point of a white pencil to show highlights.

The face is drawn with blended grey, and the hair, skin and scarf are all drawn with blended magenta, green and beige as accents to the coat.

wool/layered fabrics

DESIGN: LEFT, DOLCE & GABBANA; RIGHT: JACKET, JOHN VAVATOS, PANTS, TIMBERLAND.

Left, thick vest, two t-shirts, wool pants, gloves, boots, wool knit cap, portfolio; right sweater, pea coat, pants, hat, gloves, boots, cap.

For outdoor activities in cold weather garments are often layered. When layered garments are drawn, the upper garments should be partly open so the garments underneath can be seen.

All of these fabrics are soft and thick, and require mutliple layers of marker. Note the overlapping arms help to unify the composition.

Draw croquis for both figures and the silhouettes of the garments on top. Take great care to show the layers of each garment and how it follows the contours of the body. Fill in each separate garment with a base color—on the left, taupe for the t-shirt, olive green for the vest, beige for the pants; on the right, warm-grey for jacket, sweater and pants, cool-grey for the gloves. Because these fabrics are textured, a second and third layer of a slightly darker value color are added, and a final application of pencil used in all garments to indicate texture. The figure on the right has been left unfinished on the right side so the way in which the layers of marker are built up can be clearly seen.

White pencil is used to bring out highlights on buttons, the hand, the white t-shirt and the edges of the lapel. The gloves and hats are drawn in the same manner.

Skin tone is taken from the base color of the pants for each of the figures, helping to unify the composition of each figure.

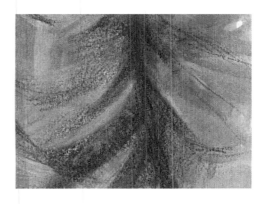

DESIGN: (FROM LEFT) BODYGLOVE, O'NEILL, HOTLINE, O'NEILL

rubber/latex

Wetsuits.

These wetsuits hug the body so tightly that there is virtually no drape in the fabric.

The croquis are drawn and the contours of the suits drawn on top making sure that the the bottom of the sleeves, collar and bottom of the legs bend around the figures. The wetsuits are slightly wider than the torsos of the croquis.

The geometric sections of the suits are drawn in with light grey pencil and the various areas then filled in with flat applications of colored markers. Shadows and highlights are applied using black and white pencil.

printed fabrics

Left, sweater, brooch, printed pants; right, printed vest, printed coat with hood, loosely-draped pants, shirt and shoes.

DESIGN: NR AND DOMENIC MONTELONGO

printed fabrics

Left, jacket, pants, sneakers; right, hooded top, shirt, boxer shorts, pants, shoes.

do not do's of men's fashion drawing

DESIGN: NR

DO NOT DO's: sweater, jacket and pants.

There are a number of DO NOT DO's in this drawing: the silhouette of the garments do not reflect how they would fit on a male figure—the cap of the right sleeve is too wide, the sweater is too short and the pants are shaped at the hip more for a female shape. Shading and light is inaccurate, does not follow the drape and is randomly placed: the patch of light on the right sleeve bears no relation to anything. The head is too small for the body, and, not surprisingly, the figure looks rather anemic.

DO NOT DOs OF MEN'S FASHION DRAWING

Many mistakes can be made when drawing men, especially when they are drawn by women: for women, men are both difficult to understand and difficult to draw! In general, women tend to draw men in the same way they draw themselves— that is, as women— giving them too many curves and overly feminine faces.

The following are among the most common mistakes made when drawing men's fashion. These are definite DO NOT DO's.

1. DO NOT place shirt collars too low on the neck. They should reach almost to the jaw-line.

2. DO NOT add too much fullness to the sleeve at the shoulder seam or it will resemble a woman's sleeve.

3. DO NOT draw closures from left to right— for men they fasten right to left (in the drawing the closure is in fact one of the few things that are correct).

4. DO NOT draw hips too wide.

5. DO NOT draw the waist too high—it should be at 3¼ heads (a woman's is at 3)

6. DO NOT draw eyebrows arched like a woman's; they are more horizontal.

7. DO NOT make the face soft and curved—it should be angular.

8. DO NOT draw the chin and jaw too small—men's are larger and squarer.

9. DO NOT make the forehead too slim

10. DO NOT make the hair too full and rounded

11. DO NOT make eyes too rounded and too large.

12. DO NOT make hands and feet too small.

practice and exercises

1. Using a croquis from the Appendix draw the silhouette of a shirt and pants. Fill in the shirt with a floral print and the shirt with geometric print.

2. Draw a croquis in an active pose. Add the silhouette of a t-shirt and shorts to the figure and add stripes.

3. Draw three figures wearing jeans (i) with two zippers, (ii) with four pockets, (iii) with frayed bottoms.

4. Using a croquis from the Appendix, draw a shirt and pants for the following activities: (i) watching TV with friends, (ii) attending a birthday party, (iii) walking in the park.

5. Design two outfits to accompany accessories chosen from those included at the end of this chapter.

6. Copy the drawing on the opposite page and change the colors of the fabrics.

7. Copy an image of a man in a tailored wool coat. Use the image in this chapter or one from a magazine.

8. Copy a photograph of a man in denim jeans. Copy a photograph of a man in a leather jacket.

practice and exercises

9. Using images from this chapter as references draw (i) an outfit with an "edgy" street look, (ii) a young businessman's outfit, (iii) an outfit for an athlete .

10. (i) Draw a man's two-piece business suit. (ii) Take the jacket from the suit and match it with a different pair of pants to create a 'more hip" look.

11. Draw a croquis wearing a sleeveless t-shirt and pants and add a graphic image onto the t-shirt.

12. Draw a croquis in an active pose and dress with top and pants using (i) three zippers (ii) ten snaps, (iii) toggles and/or velcro.

13. Draw a shirt and casual pants on a croquis and include prints showing ethnic influences.

14. Draw any garment or accessory using shiny fabric.

15. Draw a shirt, necktie, jacket, pants and coat in plain fabric on a croquis.

16. Draw an outfit for a man using all of the following fabrics: snakeskin, printed cotton, fur and leather.

17. Draw an active sportswear outfit.

18. Draw an outfit with plain fabric and then draw again using printed fabric.

CHILDREN'S FASHION

little girl/infant

DESIGN: UNKNOWN

Left, little girl with denim jacket, white t-shirt, bow; right, infant with denim pants, pink sweater, pink parka, pink bow.

When children of different age groups are drawn together they should be shown with the poses characteristic of their respective ages in order for the drawing to appear realistic. From a compositional point of view, note that the tilt of the infant's head leads the eye to the other figure.

For the little girl on the left, first draw the silhouette of the jacket, t-shirt and hair with simple shapes. Fill in the jacket with blue marker and apply shadows with a second layer of the same color. Leave a small amount of white to indicate the edge of the lapel. The hair is filled in with brown marker, with the curls at the edge indicated with a blended version of the same color. The facial features are drawn with a light-brown colored pencil.

Skin tone is applied from the reverse side of the paper, using a light brown mixed with pink. A second layer is applied from the top side of the paper to indicate shadows around the nose and cheeks.

For the infant, draw the silhouette of the clothes and the head using simple shapes. Remember that infants are three heads in proportion and have no necks. All infants' features are soft, round and pudgy, so avoid dark lines or harsh contours. Fill in the pants with blue marker, using a second layer of the same color for shadows. The sweater and parka are filled in with the same pink marker, and the soft shadows of the parka are filled in with a second layer of the same color using a circular motion. The face is drawn in with brown colored pencil. Remember the features are large and soft—babies' eyes are the same size as those of adults. Hair is drawn with a light beige marker using a tight circular motion to indicate curls.

Skin tone is applied from the reverse side of the paper using a light blended brown and blended pink is applied from the top side to indicate shadows on the face. The pink bow is drawn in with blended pink.

The croquis are 4 1/2 and 3 1/2 heads.

DESIGN: LEFT, UNKNOWN; RIGHT,
TUTTO PICCOLO

toddler/infant

Left, red, sleeveless t-shirt, red-striped cotton pants with ruffles, red belt; right, baby with knitted cap, sweater, scarf and pinafore.

Babies and small children have soft, round bodies. Their moods—and expressions—can change from near-ecstasy to utter misery in a flash. These drawings show two of the extremes.

For the toddler on the left, draw the silhouette of the clothes taking great care to show how the garments fit around the arms and tummy. Fill in the top with red marker leaving white space for the sunny design. For the stripes, first draw thin lines in with colored pencil and then the thick lines in the same red marker once the positioning is correct. The hair is filled in with black marker and the features drawn with black colored pencil using very thin lines.

Skin tone is applied from the reverse side of the paper using blended beige and pink. Note that applying the skin with a light touch makes it appear healthy and translucent.

For the baby, draw the contours of the cap, scarf, sweater and pinafore. Fill in the cap, scarf and sweater with several layers of red applied from both sides of the paper. Add shadows and details of the knitted garments using the side rather than the point of a black pencil to indicate softness in the fabric. Fill in the pinafore with several layers of ultramarine blue until the paper is saturated. With a dark blue pencil draw in the ribs of the corduroy.

A baby's face is difficult to draw because it has no flat planes; it is all based on rounded forms. Care must be taken to avoid harsh contours and strong applications of color, as children so drawn often look like old men or the elder Winston Churchill (whose portrait as a baby appears later in this chapter). Since there are no edges to features, all areas of shadows have to blend into one another; it is important to apply colors very lightly and build up shadows softly so they have no sharp edges. The cheeks here are a subtle application of blended beige and pink and the eyes a subtle application of blended light blue.

DESIGN: TRICONE

little boy, 6–8

Vest, shirt, backpack, jeans, shoes.

This little boy is made to look very grown up with his cotton vest and jeans—an outfit much favored by teenagers and the pre-teens who take their fashion cues from them—and his spiky gelled hair.

Draw the silhouette of the clothes making sure that the shirt and jeans have lots of curves to indicate the many folds. Children's clothes are always made to fit loosely and comfortably. Use a soft blended blue to indicate the shadows of the folds of the shirt, making sure the shadows are not the same size and are rather wide to show the soft drapes of the shirt, especially at the elbow.

The tailored vest has less drape than the shirt and is created by filling in with a blended beige and defining the contour with a thin, black line. The black line also gives the idea that the vest sits on top of the shirt and casts a shadow on it. Note that the zipper closure is drawn on the opposite side (from right to left) from that of a little girl's outfit. Pants and backpack are filled in with cobalt blue, and black pencil is applied to show shadows in the folds of the pant and straps of the backpack. White is applied to the surface of the folds of the pants to indicate the white thread seen in all denim.

The features of the face are drawn with the sharp point of a black pencil. Avoid using black around the nose and do not outline the mouth—little boys' lips are not as full as those of little girls. The hair and shoes are filled in with black marker.

Skin tone is a light layer of blended beige applied from the reverse side of the page. Light pink is added to the cheeks to show healthy, glowing young skin.

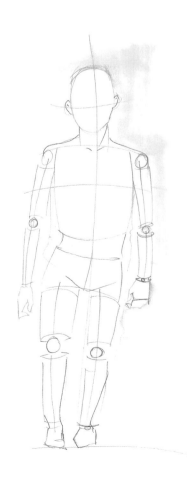

DESIGN: IOTTUM

little girl with rabbit

Sweater, striped full skirt, scarf, socks, shoes, hat, rabbit.

This little girl is delighted to be holding her pet rabbit, which is snuggling into the warmth of her wool sweater on a brisk morning.

The croquis is about 4½ heads. Draw the garments with a light pink pencil and indicate the folds of the skirt. An application of light pink blended marker is applied to all the garment areas from the reverse side of the paper. The stripes of the skirt are defined with a brown marker, bending the stripe around each fold. Shadows are applied to the folds of the skirt, sweater and scarf with a blended grey marker. The hat is filled in with several layers of cool brown and the features of the face applied with a light application of grey pencil. Hair is a blended pink.

Skin tone is blended beige applied from the reverse side of the paper. The socks are drawn with blue marker and the shoes with brown marker. The rabbit— which looks more like a guinea pig than a rabbit—should be drawn and positioned better than it is here!

little girl with rabbit

front/back/side/three-quarter view croquis

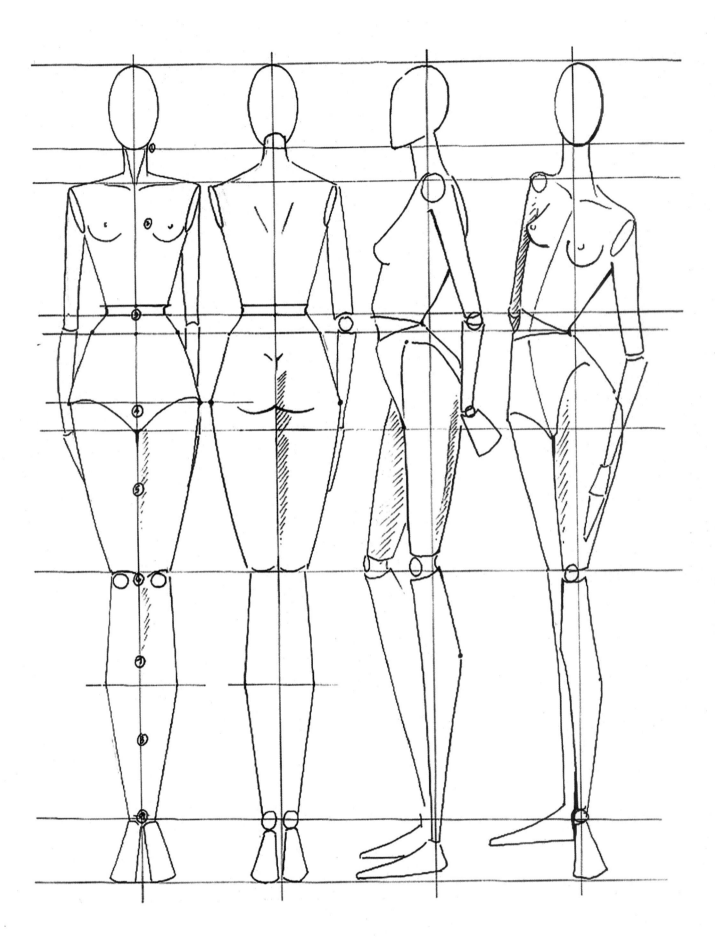

front view croquis—variations

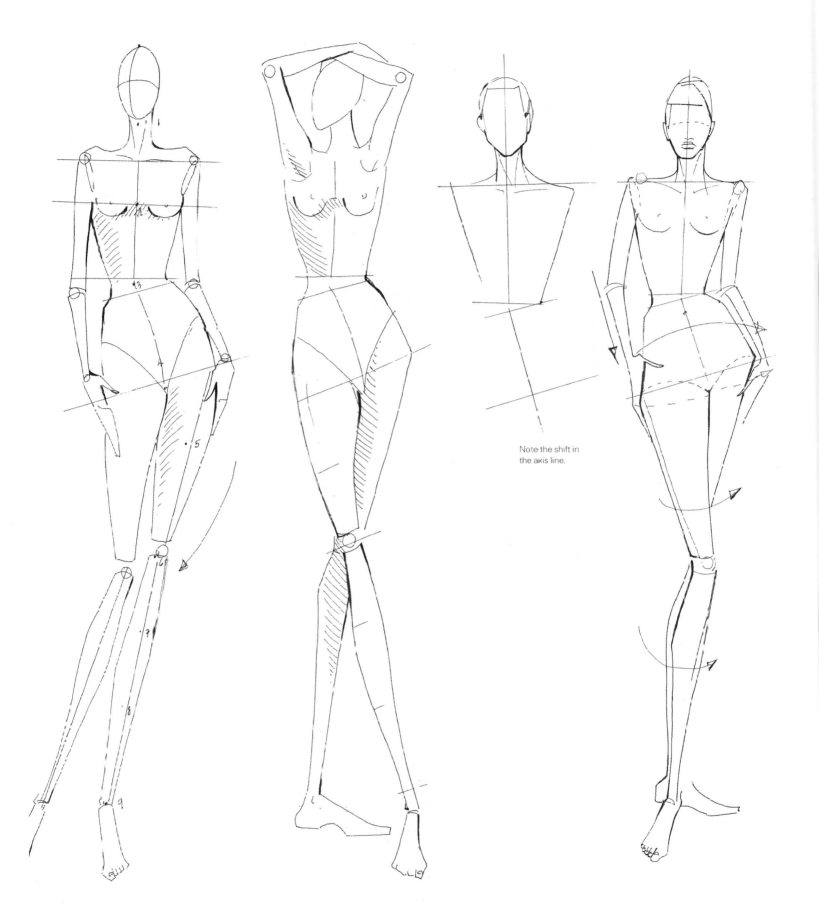

Note the shift in the axis line.

Left, front view croquis with weight on the right leg. Note the hip pivots up on the right side. Right, front view croquis with weight on the right leg, arms raised and left leg partly forward.

Front view croquis with weight on the right leg, left leg bent at the knee. Note these are three-dimensional figures, even though they are just croquis, and garments placed on the figure must bend around it, as indicated by the curve of the arrows.

men's croquis/sophisticated, fleshed-out poses

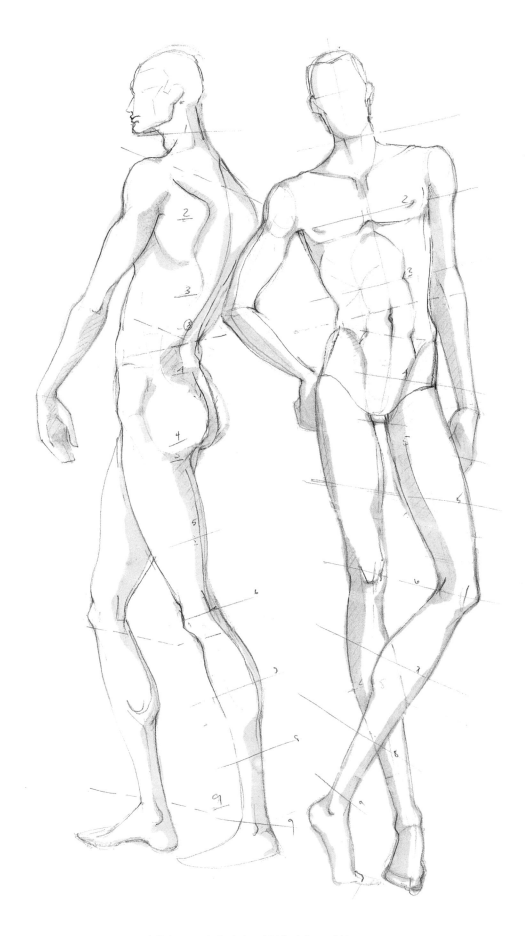

Left, three–quarter back view; right, front view, weight on left side.

men's croquis/sophisticated, fleshed-out poses

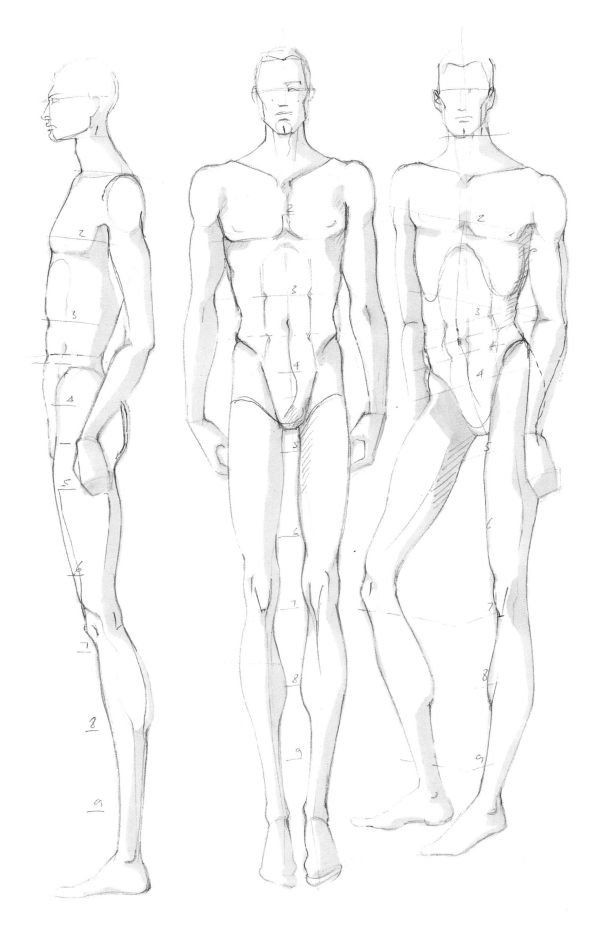

Left, side view; middle, front view; right, three-quarter view

three-quarter–side view female croquis/ with bathing suit

Three-quarter/side
figure lit from left.

Three-quarter/side
figure lit from left
with bathing suit.

croquis and silhouette/croquis

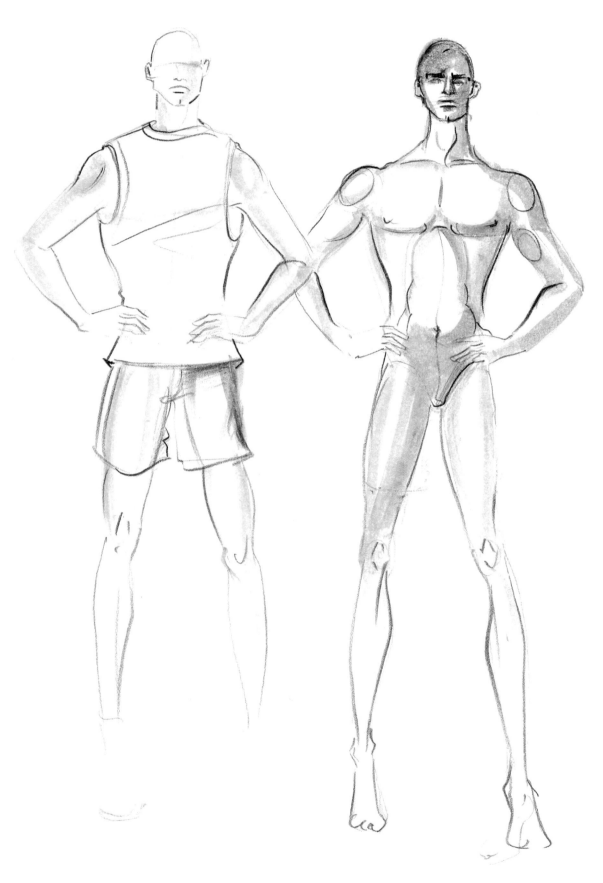

Left, man's croquis with clothing silhouettes; right, man's croquis.

front view male croquis/croquis with suit

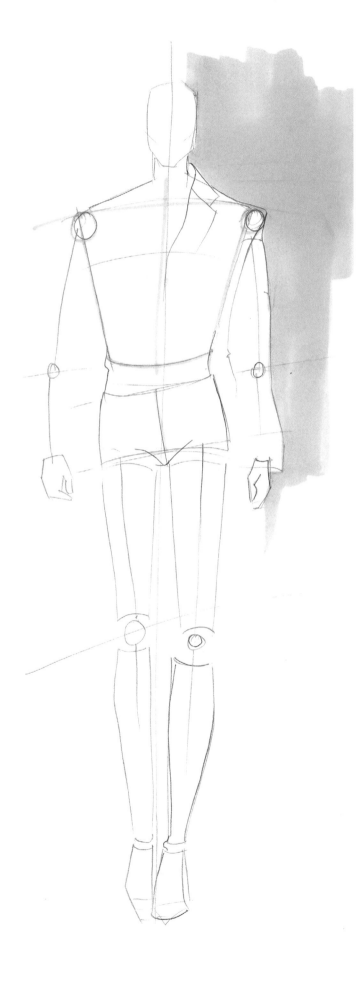

Front view croquis.

Front view figure with suit.

muscular man

Muscular man, front and back view.

back view male croquis/croquis with silhouette

Back-view man with silhouette of pants.

Back view male croquis.

front view female croquis/with garments

figure and garment templates

beachwear/lingerie

FIGURE AND GARMENT TEMPLATES

The drawings on this and the following pages provide croquis and simple garment silhouettes suitable for developing designs and changing styles.

534

figure and garment templates

trench coat/sleeveless top/pleated skirt

figure and garment templates

active sportswear/female swimmer

figure and garment templates

active sportswear/female surfer

figure and garment templates

tailored jacket/skirt/halter t-shirt/sleeveless t-shirt/man's briefs/boots/t-shirt/jeans

Left, tailored jacket,skirt; center, halter t-shirt, sleeveless t-shirt, man's briefs, boots; right asymmetrical t-shirt, jeans.

figure and garment templates

sweater/bow/buttons/flared pants/ duffle coat/t-shirt/shorts/boots/cowboy outfit

Left, sweater with puff sleeves, bow, buttons, flared pants; duffle coat with hood, t-shirt, shorts, knee-length boots; right, cowboy outfit.

glossary of terms

GLOSSARY OF TERMS

This glossary contains definitions of the technical and semi-technical terms relating to fashion drawing (abbreviated here to FD), art, and color and design theory that are most frequently used in this book. It does not contain definitions of specialized fashion terms as the large majority of those used here are explained when they first appear in the book, and in a number of cases the definitions are repeated elsewhere. For explanations of technical fashion terms not defined in the text reference should be made to a specialized dictionary of fashion, of which a number of excellent examples are available.

Abstraction/abstract shape or form
Way of communicating the essential aspects of a shape or form with a simplified visual shorthand. As more elements are removed from a drawing or part of a drawing it becomes progressively more abstract. In FD it is often used for parts of the body or face when the garments are complex.

Achromatic
Literally, without color. Achromatics are black and white and combinations of them—greys.

Additive system
The system of mixing the colors of light, as opposed to pigments. The primary colors of light when combined add together to create white light. *See also* Subtractive system.

Analogous colors
Analogous colors are adjacent to each other on the color wheel. Analogous color schemes are based on two, three or more adjacent colors.

Asymmetry/Asymmetrical
Condition where the two sides of a garment or drawing are not symmetrical: they are not exactly the same.

Asymmetrical Balance
Compositional balance achieved between objects of different visual characteristics (e.g., shape, color, size) but with similar visual weight or attraction.

Axis/axis-line
The line that divides a figure (croquis) into two. Its position shifts according to changes in poses:Iln the front view the axis line divides the figure into two symmetrical or balanced parts; in three-quarter view the figure is divided asymmetr-ically in the portions three to one; in "S curve" poses the axis line follows the curve of the body. It is often sketched in as a guideline.

Balance
State of equilibrium among the different elements in a composition.

Black graphite pencil
Standard black pencils in either wooden or mechanical form.

Blending
 In this book "blending" is the term used to refer to diluting marker color with colorless blender so less saturated, more transparent versions of the color are obtained. *See*: descriptions and illustrations of blending in Chapter One: Materials and Technique.

Cast shadow
The shadow cast by an object onto a surface, for example that cast by buttons onto a coat. The cast shadow gives a three-dimensional effect to the object being drawn.

Chiaroscuro
Drawing technique dating from the Italian Renaissance, from the Italian words meaning light and dark. It is the use of ranges of values from light to dark to approximate the appearance of shadows on real objects, indicating the three- dimensional nature of objects portrayed in two-dimensional drawings.

Chromatic
The opposite of achromatic: literally, with color. All colors that are neither black, white nor greys are chromatic colors.

Chromatic neutrals
Neutral colors formed by mixing complementary colors as opposed to neutrals formed from achromatics.

Color
Light of a particular wavelength that creates a sensation of "color" in the brain when perceived by the eye.

Color accents
Small amounts of a single color applied as contrasts to the dominant color in a composition or outfit.

Color contrast
The various ways in which colors differ from and contrast with each other. These include (according to Johannes Itten):
 Contrast of hue
 Light-dark contrast
 Cold-warm contrast
 Complementary contrast
 Simultaneous contrast
 Contrast of saturation
 Contrast of extension

Color chord
Groups of colors from non adjacent parts of the color wheel that combine in a harmonious fashion, similar to the combination of notes in a harmonious musical chord.

Color discord
Color discord occurs when two or more colors clash rather than harmonize with each other. *See also* Color harmony

Color dyad
Color chords formed of two complementary colors.

Color harmony
Pleasing color relationships or schemes based on groups of colors with formal relations within the color wheel (*See* analogous colors, color triads, color tetrads)

Color schemes
Systems for combining colors harmoniously. Color schemes are either formal, based on relations within the color wheel, or informal, based on looser principles.

Color temperature
The color wheel is roughly divided into warm and cool colors, with the warm centered around red and the cool around blue. Colors also have warm or cool aspects— warm or cool whites or neutrals are used extensively in fashion drawing.

Color triad
Three equidistant colors on the color wheel. When connected they form an equilateral triangle. Triads can be formed of primary, secondary or tertiary color combinations.

Color weight
The theory that different colors have different "weights" in relation to other colors. For example, pink is light, brown is heavy.

Color wheel
An ordering of the colors, (or "hues") of the spectrum of white light (with the addition of purple by Sir Isaac Newton) into a wheel, or circle, simplifying the study of relations among the different colors. Color wheels have also been created relating to the pigment (or "subtractive" colors). *See* Chapter Two: Color and Design.

Colorless blender
The solvent that the pigment of markers is suspended in, but with no color pigment— hence "colorless". Colorless blender is available in tubes like markers and is an essential tool for mixing colors and creating a range of subtle effects with gradation of color.

Cold/cool colors
Colors on the blue side of the color wheel.

Complementary colors
Colors directly opposite each other on the color wheel. The primary complementaries are blue and orange, red and green, and violet and yellow. Opposing secondary colors and secondary/tertiary colors are also complementary colors. Complementary colors neutralize each other when mixed together in pigment form.

Content
In composition, the "content" is the subject matter of a drawing (in FD, the garments or accessories being drawn) as opposed to the form of the composition— the way the subject matter is presented.

Core-light
A long highlight that forms on shiny fabric along the length of the leg or arm or other cylindrical form in close-fitting garments or similarly in transparent or semi-transparent fabric where the body underneath is perceived.

Croquis
The French word for "sketch" refers to the nine-head figure (an elongated figure whose length is equivalent to nine heads as opposed to approximately eight heads in reality). The croquis is basic to all modern fashion drawing.

Cross-hatching
A technique for representing shading/value in drawings usually with ink or pencil by layering series of parallel lines.

Design
Any ordered arrangement of visual components.

Design Elements/Elements of Design
The basic visual elements used in creating art and design: line, shape, form space, value, texture, scale and color.

Design Principles/Principles of Design.
The principles underlying "good" compositional design. They are harmony/unity, focal point/emphasis, balance, scale and proportion.

Details/constructional details
The smaller constructional parts of a garment that are visible, for example, top-stitching, buttons, hems, seams, cuffs, collars, trim. Often details are shown that appear constructional but are purely decorative and are included for stylistic reasons.

Drape
In general, the way a fabric made into a garment hangs on the human figure. The "drape" of a fabric or garment is the part of the fabric on the figure that hangs loosely and does not touch the figure. Different fabrics drape differently on the figure and often have a characteristic "drape."

Elements of Design
See Design elements.

Equilibrium
Balance achieved among different design elements in a composition.

Flat application of color
An application of a single color. When drawing fabric or skin tone, a single application of one color gives a flat, two-dimensional look. Three-dimensional effects require the application of more than one color in order to realistically represent the lighter and darker parts of the surface.

Focal point
Part of a composition emphasized so that the eye is drawn to it and then to the other parts.

Foreshortening
The way parts of objects appear to shorten the further they are from the viewpoint they are observed from, and the way this is accurately represented in drawing on a two-dimensional surface. A simple "flat" pose such as the standard front view croquis

Subtractive System
Objects are perceived to be of a particular color because their surfaces have absorbed, or "subtracted" all the constituent elements of white light except those of the color that is perceived. The subtractive system also refers to the way pigments, as opposed to rays of light, mix. Pigments filter out, or "subtract" certain frequencies of light waves corresponding to different colors. As more pigments are mixed together more and more colors are subtracted, resulting finally in black or near-black.

Symmetry
A quality of a composition where the elements on either side of a central axis are identical.

Tertiary colors
The colors that result from combining a primary color and an adjacent secondary on the color wheel. Each primary color can combine with two secondaries to give a total of six tertiaries.

Tetrad
A color scheme of four hues based on a square or rectangle defined by the position of the hues in the color wheel.

Texture
The surface quality of an object when felt. Although the feel or "hand" of a fabric cannot be directly represented in a drawing, fabrics of different textures can have markedly different appearances. If a fabric is drawn realistically and accurately a viewer who is familiar with fabrics will be able to intuitively sense how the fabric feels to the touch as well as how it appears.

Tint
The result of mixing white or a lighter grey to a hue.

Tonality
If a composition is dominated by a single hue or color, even though other colors are present, it is described as exhibiting a "tonality" of that color.

Tone
The result of mixing a color with grey, black or white, i.e., a tint or shade. Accurate depiction of colors in realistic light conditions involves reproducing subtle, continuous gradation of tones as the surface moves towards and away from the light source.
See also Gradation of tone.

Translucent
Translucent materials allow the passage of a certain amount of light but not sufficient to allow the forms of objects beyond the surface to be clearly distinguished.

Transparent
Transparent materials or surfaces allow the uninterrupted passage of light. In drawing, transparency is indicated when two materials or surfaces overlap but both are clearly visible.

Triad
A color scheme based on three colors from the color wheel, that are spaced at equal distances from each other and that form an equilateral triangle if connected. A triad is often regarded as the most balanced color scheme because the colors always stand in the same relation to each other on the color wheel as the relations among the three primary colors.

Unity
One of the basic principles of design stating that the different parts of a composition should be related to each other in unified whole.

Value
The degree of lightness or darkness of chromatic or achromatic colors.

Value emphasis
Creating emphasis or a focal point in a composition through use of a dramatic contrast in values.

Value contrast
The light and dark contrast existing between colors, both chromatic and achromatic.

Vibrating colors
Colors that create a vibrating or flickering effect where they touch. Usually seen with colors of contrasting hues and similar values.

Warm colors
Colors from the "warm" side of the color wheel, those closest to red/yellow.

Warm–cold contrast
The contrast between "warm" and "cold" (or cool) colors.

index

ACKNOWLEDGEMENTS

This book was from the outset a hugely ambitious project that would require, for the drawings alone, a considerable amount of highly skilled help merely to come to fruition. I was fortunate enough to be able to count on such help from a small group of talented and dedicated assistants who worked with me through most of the more-than-three years the book took to complete: Euri Huang, Soyoung Kim, Karolina Maszkiewicz and Jisook Paik are wonderful illustrators whose collaborations with me are the reason why so many good drawings have been completed for the book. I cannot thank them enough, and if the book is successful in achieving its goals it will be in large part due to their excellent work. A special thank you also to my friend and professional colleague Michael Perlman for his superb contributions.

Simon Johnston provided invaluable input and guidance in the process of developing a design and layout for the book that would prove suitable for showcasing a large amount of strong visual material and in designing the cover. I am very grateful to him for all his help.

Stefani Greenwood was responsible for the long and challenging task of pulling all the drawings and text together and helping to shape the book into its present form. Her flair for design and layout and understanding of the concepts to be illustrated in the chapter on Color and Design amounted to a big contribution, and I am most grateful for all her help.

Scott Council displayed professionalism, flair, patience, and generosity with his time when shooting the photographs included in the chapter on Materials and Technique. I am extremely grateful to him and also to Ginger Cho, who modeled for the shoots.

I was delighted to be able to reproduce drawings by Ruben Alterio, Christian Lacroix, Vik Muniz and Demetrios Psillos in the book and thank them all for giving their permission to do so. They are all among the greatest artists of modern fashion and the inclusion of their work adds greatly to the book as well as providing inspiration to all who see them. Thanks also to their representatives who helped make their participation possible: Sylvie Flaure of At Large in Paris, Bérangère Broman at Christian Lacroix in Paris and Erika Benincasa in New York.

Iris Huang, Shannon Figgins, Jisoook Paik (with her other hat on), Albert Ng and Dominic Montelongo contributed designs and drawings that have made greatly added to the rich diversity of garments and drawing.

The highly professional librarians at the Fashion Institute of Design and Merchandising (FIDM) in Los Angeles provided invaluable assistance in locating images and examples of the huge variety of garments shown in the book. I would particularly like to thank Cynthia Aaron, Rosario Benavides, Carol Buckles, Jeff Castillo, Peter Davis, Delois Delapena, Robin Dodge, Monika Earle, Rosanna Garcia, Norris Hambrick, Molly Jones, Sophie Lalazarian, Francisco Platt Murillo, Sandra Panameno, Guillermo Petra, Glenda Ronduen, Jennifer Ruden and Karen Schultz for all their help and also Jim Glenny for his work in creating one of the best fashion libraries in the US.

Thank you to Renée Weiss Chase at Drexel University for reviewing the book and her critical comments and suggestions in all areas, and to Dr. Kenneth Fehrman at San Francisco State University for his helpful criticism and suggestions for corrections and improvements in the chapter on Color and Design. Thank you also to Ofelia Montejano, James Clay and Wendy Suni at FIDM for their advice on technical fashion issues, Mary Stephens at FIDM for her support, and Vern Anthony at Prentice Hall for his support and help.

Willis Popenoe was most gracious and generous in taking time out of his busy schedule to review the final manuscript. It is always a challenge for someone whose communication skills are more developed on the visual side to match the text to the standards of the drawings; Willis' assistance in achieving clarity and balance was invaluable.

Thank you to Barbara McGuire at MacPherson Art for her support and the literally hundreds of colored markers and blenders used in making the drawings, and to Mike Travers and the staff at Letraset UK.

Finally, I would like to thank my partner David Eno who provided help and guidance at every stage of the project and without whom the publication of this book would not have been possible.